D0948589

Ancestor Worship and Korean Society

Ancestor Worship and Korean Society

ROGER L. JANELLI
DAWNHEE YIM JANELLI

Stanford University Press, Stanford, California   1982

Stanford University Press
Stanford, California
©1982 by the Board of Trustees of the
Leland Stanford Junior University
Printed in the United States of America
ISBN 0-8047-1135-6
LC 81-51757

To Yim Suk-jay

Preface

Students of Korean society have certainly not ignored its ancestor cult. Demographers have viewed a commitment to ancestor worship both as an index of traditional values and as an obstacle to family planning. Western missionaries have long been concerned with beliefs and rituals involving ancestors, for the Christian prohibition of these traditions has cost their churches many converts. Korean folklorists have investigated ancestor seances performed by shamans. Sociologists and historians have recently attempted to relate changes in ancestor-ritual procedures to major social and ideological developments in Korean society during the fifteenth through eighteenth centuries. And modern ethnographers have given their attention to ancestor worship simply because of its continued importance in contemporary Korea.

This abundant interest in the Korean ancestor cult has yielded fine descriptions of ritual procedures, but the analysis of these religious traditions has advanced very little. Lack of progress has been made all the more obvious by the impressive results of research on similar religious ideas and rites in China, Japan, and sub-Saharan Africa. Borrowing freely from this earlier research, we have looked primarily to social relations rather than Confucian ideology for an interpretation of our Korean data.

We also use the work of predecessors to identify Korean parallels to ancestor cults in other societies as well as to identify what is uniquely Korean. Our purpose here is to contribute to the comparative study of these religious traditions by establishing causal relationships—or at least correlations—that appear in more than one society. The potential contribution of Korean ethnographic data to this comparative enterprise has already been surmised by some outside of Korean studies (Freedman 1958: 137; Newell 1976: xii). Indeed, their calls for an investigation of Korean ancestor worship turn out to have been extraordinarily perspicacious. Korean beliefs and practices offer significantly variant manifestations of principles that have emerged from the study of ancestor worship elsewhere in the world. As a result, Korea provides a unique vantage point from which to test, refine, or reformulate earlier hypotheses.

For those interested primarily in Korean ancestor worship itself, we have tried to provide an intensive study of how its rites and ideas relate to their social and cultural contexts; thus we hope to show how the ancestor cult of one rural kin group is interconnected with that group's social organization, its ideology, and the social experiences of its members. In addition, we have utilized historical and ethnographic literature on Korea in order to assess the applicability of our interpretations beyond our sample community.

We have prepared this book not only for those with a special interest in the comparative study of ancestor worship or in traditional Korean society; we have also kept in mind folklorists and anthropologists concerned with folk religion in other societies. Our analysis of the Korean ancestor cult deals with two important issues in this field: interpersonal variation and mutual incongruity of diverse religious beliefs. Our data show how such variation and incongruity arise from and are sustained by the heterogeneity of social experiences encountered even by members of the same family or village.

Our fieldwork in Korea began in September 1973. Except for occasional visits to Seoul, we spent nearly all of the following ten months in Twisŏngdwi, a rural Korean village, gathering data on the ancestor rituals offered there. Our goal in this initial fieldwork was to identify what a villager needs to know in order to perform an ancestor ritual. The results of that research, a detailed description of ritual procedures, can be found in Roger Janelli's Ph.D. dissertation (1975).

In December 1977, we returned to Korea with a different objective: a comparative social analysis of the Korean ancestor cult in the light of similar studies from China, Japan, and sub-Saharan Africa. For the next eight months, we compiled data on social relations, who worships whom, and who believes what concerning ancestral affliction in Twisŏngdwi.

Many people helped us during our several years of research, though we alone must answer for any omissions or errors. By their generous cooperation, the villagers of Twisŏngdwi greatly eased our data gathering and analysis. They were exceptionally kind hosts as well. We are indebted to all of them, but particularly to Kwŏn Kŭn-sik for taking a special interest in our personal comfort as well as in the progress of our research. To him and his brother, Kwŏn O-sik, we are indebted for extremely perceptive insights into Korean culture and society. As the following pages show, we benefited immeasurably from their ideas. We also profited in no small way from the help of several Korean folklorists, anthropologists, and sociologists. Han Sang-Bok, Kang Shin-Pyo, and Moon Seung Gyu provided invaluable comments on the applicability of Freudian theory to the Korean ancestor cult. Choi Jai-seuk, Im Tong-gwŏn, Kim Taik-Kyoo, Lee Du-Hyun, and Lee Kwang-Kyu shared with us unreservedly their mastery of Korean social organization and folk culture. We wish to thank Song Sun-hee for useful and helpful discussions on Korean clans. To Yim Suk-jay, Dawnhee Yim Janelli's father and doyen of Korean folklorists, we are especially grateful. His life-long study of Korean folklore and encyclopedic knowledge of Korean history and culture were our constant reference sources. He also helped us translate the ritual text that appears in Chapter 4. To him we gratefully dedicate this book.

We are also indebted to several Western colleagues who share our interest in Korean ancestor worship and with whom we have been freely exchanging ideas during the past few years. Martina Deuchler taught us to appreciate the enormity of Korea's social and cultural changes during the early Yi dynasty. Paul Dredge and Griffin Dix generously shared the results of their own field-work and provided very helpful suggestions as our interpretations gradually took shape. Laurel Kendall first impressed upon us the differences between men's and women's religion in rural Korea. Jim Palais and Martina Deuchler read our entire manuscript and offered many perceptive comments. And Clark Sorensen directed our attention to Kim Jae-ŭn's important analysis of Korean parent-child relationships.

Intersocietal comparison is a dangerous scientific venture, and we would not have undertaken the task without the kind encouragement and generous assistance of several specialists in other areas of the world. Meyer Fortes, Ivan Karp, and Igor Kopytoff taught us a great deal not only about African social organization and ancestor worship, but also about the issues involved in their analysis. Arthur P. Wolf, Chen Min-hwei, Stevan Harrell, David Plath, Robert J. Smith, Suzuki Mitsuo, and Ch'oe Kil-sŏng did the same for China and Japan, and also helped us to identify how these social and cultural traditions vary throughout East Asia. Ivan Karp, Robert Smith, and Arthur Wolf took on the added task of reading our manuscript and offered several helpful comments.

To the editors at Stanford University Press we wish to express our appreciation not only for unfailing patience but for sound advice as well. J. G. Bell inspired us to write our final chapter; John S. Feneron guided the transformation of our manuscript into this published volume with discernment and meticulous care; and Andrew Alden contributed greatly to the readability of our prose with his skillful editing.

Funds for our fieldwork during 1977–78 were provided by a Fulbright-Hays award and by an Indiana University Summer Faculty Fellowship.

R. L. J.
D. Y. J.

Contents

Figures and Tables

Figures

Tables

Ancestor Worship and Korean Society

Introduction

The study of ancestor worship has an eminent pedigree in two disciplines: social anthropology and folklore (Goody 1962: 14–25; Newell 1976; Fortes 1976; Takeda 1976). Despite obvious differences in geographical specialization and intellectual orientation, researchers in both fields have shared a common approach to this subject: both have tried to relate the ancestor cult of a given society to its family and kin-group organization. Such a method is to be expected of social anthropologists, given the nature of their discipline; but even the Japanese folklorist Yanagita Kunio, whose approach to folk culture stems from historical and nationalist concerns, began his work on ancestors with a discussion of Japan's descent system and family structure (Yanagita 1946). Indeed, connections between ancestor cults and social relations are obvious. As we pursue this line of analysis, we shall see that rural Koreans themselves are quite sophisticated about such matters.

Many studies of ancestor cults employ a combination of social and psychological approaches to explain the personality traits attributed to the dead by their living kin. Particular attention has long been given to explaining the hostile or punitive character of the deceased in many societies (Freud 1950; Opler 1936; Gough 1958; Fortes 1965). Only recently, however, has the popularity of such beliefs been recognized in China, Korea, and Japan (Ahern 1973; A. Wolf 1974b; Kendall 1977; 1979; Yoshida 1967; Kerner 1976; Lebra 1976). The earliest and most influential studies of ancestor cults in East Asia, produced by native scholars (Hozumi 1913; Yanagita 1946; Hsu 1948), overemphasize the benign and protective qualities of ancestors. Some regional variations notwithstanding, this earlier bias appears to reflect a general East Asian reluctance to acknowledge instances of ancestral affliction. Such reticence is not found in all societies with ancestor cults, however; nor, in Korea, China, and Japan, is it equally prevalent among men and women. Therefore, we seek not only to identify the social experiences that give rise to beliefs in ancestral hostility, but to explain the concomitant reluctance to acknowledge these beliefs and its varying intensity throughout East Asia.

In view of the limited amount of ethnographic data available from Korea, we have not attempted a comprehensive assessment of the ancestor cult in Korean society; instead we have kept our focus on a single kin group. We have drawn on data from other communities, however, in order to separate what is apparently true of Korea in general from what may be peculiar to communities like Twisŏngdwi, a village of about three hundred persons that was the site of our fieldwork.[1] In this task, we benefited substantially from three excellent studies of Korean ancestor worship and lineage organization (Lee Kwang-Kyu 1977a; Choi Jaiseuk 1966a; Kim Taik-Kyoo 1964) and from two recent accounts of Korean folk religion and ideology (Dix 1977; Kendall 1979). Yet we are still a long way from a comprehensive understanding of how Korean beliefs and practices have changed over time, correlate with different levels of class status, or are affected by regional variations in Korean culture and social organization.[2]

Because we want to provide a monograph accessible to a rather diverse readership, we avoid using Korean words and disciplinary terminology whenever possible. Where a Korean term is particularly important, we give it in parentheses immediately after its English translation. Korean-alphabet orthographies for these words appear in the Character List, with Chinese-character equivalents for terms of Chinese derivation.

As for disciplinary terminology, we have adopted only the anthropological term "lineage," which is of central importance to our study. We use "lineage" to denote an organized group of persons linked through exclusively male ties (agnatically) to an ancestor who lived at least four generations ago. (A married woman could be said to have an informal membership in her hus-

---

[1] Twisŏngdwi is the folk name of the village. Its official names are Kagong-ni Hubuk and Kagong-ni 4-ri.

[2] Relatively isolated villages on the peninsula and communities located on islands, for example, have ancestor cults that differ significantly from what appear to be the main traditions of rural Korea (Han Sang-Bok 1977: 82; Lee Kwang-Kyu 1977a: 15–16).

band's lineage until her death.) Thus, the term "Twisŏngdwi lineage" designates the agnatic kin group located in the village of Twisŏngdwi. This term does not refer to a line of ancestry. Smaller lineages may collectively constitute a larger lineage; for example, the descendants of two brothers may form two lineages but also ritually observe their common descent from an earlier agnatic forebear.

We follow in this book a few practices that prevail in the field of Korean studies. Korean terms are romanized according to the McCune-Reischauer system, except where Korean authors have established different romanizations for their names. We also cite full Korean names in references, giving surnames before personal names.

A few folkloristic conventions have been followed as well: we provide comparative annotations for texts of oral literature and give particular attention to the identities of informants. The latter is really more than a convention, for it stems from a theoretical concern with individual variation even within a relatively homogeneous community (Dégh 1977: 391–99; 1979: 3–8). To be sure, we have not identified persons where they might be embarrassed by being identified; but such instances are few. The members of the Twisŏngdwi lineage have good reason to be proud of themselves and their efforts to adhere to the best values of traditional Korean society.

We begin, in Chapter 1, with a brief overview of the Twisŏngdwi lineage's history and social organization. Chapter 2 is devoted to the organization and developmental cycle of Twisŏngdwi families. As we shall see, these data are especially important to the analysis of ancestor cults.

Chapters 3, 4, and 5 focus on the rituals that informants associate with formal ancestor worship and Confucianism. Here our goal is not to provide a complete and detailed description of ritual procedures—such descriptions are available elsewhere—but to show how these rites articulate with family and lineage organization in rural Korea.

Chapter 6 deals with parts of the ancestor cult that informants do not usually associate with ancestor worship or Confucianism: ancestor seances, folk eschatology, and ancestral hostility. Through these beliefs and ritual practices, occupants of different social positions reveal their respective views of particular deceased persons as well as their perceptions of their own and others' social relationships. We will try to show why women's views are generally different from men's.

In Chapter 7, we review our findings in the light of comparative evidence from China and Japan and in turn view the ancestor cults of these countries from the vantage point of the Korean example. As we shall see, old facts take on new meaning when viewed from a different perspective.

❦ 1 ❦

The Twisŏngdwi Lineage

The Twisŏngdwi lineage is a branch of a much larger kin group, the Andong Kwŏn, which traces its origins to the tenth century A.D. The founder of this large kin group, Kwŏn Haeng, was a local official in the Andong region who supported the nascent Koryŏ dynasty (918–1392) in its struggle for hegemony over the Korean peninsula. In return for his services, the new dynasty awarded him the title of Merit Subject and the Kwŏn surname (Yu Hong-nyŏl 1974: 208–9). Today, his agnatic descendants number in the hundreds of thousands and are spread throughout the length and breadth of Korea. They publish a monthly newspaper, update their genealogy at irregular intervals, own an ancestral hall in Andong (see map on p. 8), offer rites for their founding ancestor four times a year, own farmland that provides rental income to meet the expenses of these rituals, and engage in a variety of other corporate activities.[1]

The seventeenth generation of Andong Kwŏn included at least a hundred men (*Andong Kwŏn-ssi sebo* 1961). One of them, named Kwŏn Po, left Kaesŏng and settled south of Suwŏn. The transfer of the Korean capital from Kaesŏng to Seoul, shortly after the Koryŏ dynasty fell to the Yi (1392–1910), apparently prompted Kwŏn Po's move.[2]

Kwŏn Po had good connections. His father was a second cousin (six *ch'on* genealogical distance) of Kwŏn Kŭn, a neo-Confucian ideologist and one of the most famous politicians of the early Yi

---

[1] Descriptions of such large kin groups and their activities can be found in Lee Kwang-Kyu (1975: 144–53) and Biernatzki (1967: 354–425, 499–506).

[2] Various bits of evidence suggest this interpretation. The Andong Kwŏn genealogy (*Andong Kwŏn-ssi sebo* 1961, vol. 1) and the *Mansŏng taedongbo* (1972, vol. 2: 107) show that Kwŏn Po's father, Kwŏn Chu, held office during the Koryŏ dynasty; and Twisŏngdwi informants say that Kwŏn Chu is buried at Kaesŏng, the Koryŏ capital. In addition, the genealogy (1961, vol. 2: 71) shows that one of Kwŏn Po's great-grandsons was born in 1490, so Kwŏn Po himself was probably born about 1400, during the period when the Korean capital was being moved.

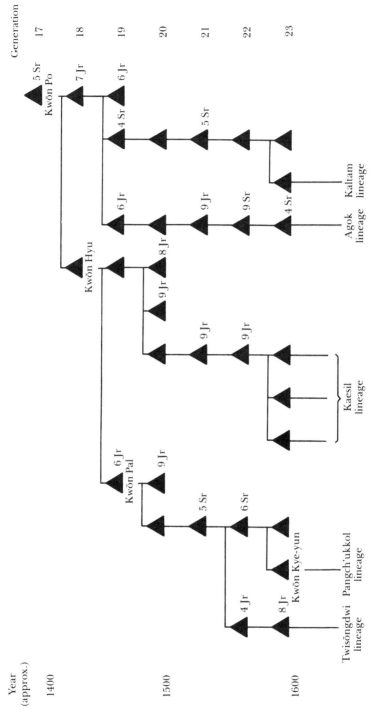

Fig. 1. Kwŏn Po's early descendants. Civil-service ranks range from 1 (highest) to 9, and each has a senior and junior level.

dynasty. Kwŏn Po himself eventually rose to the position of Third Censor (*hŏnnap*), a fifth-level senior post in the Office of the Censor General (*Mansŏng Taedongbo* 1972, vol. 2: 107; *Andong Kwŏn-ssi sebo* 1961, vol. 2: 66). As Figure 1 shows, several of Kwŏn Po's immediate descendants also held middle- or low-level positions in the central government's bureaucracy.[3] Kwŏn Po's descendants eventually formed the five local lineages identified at the bottom of Figure 1. Ancestral grave locations suggest that the Kaltam group or one of its ancestors moved to their present site, fifteen kilometers northwest of the other four lineages, a few generations after Kwŏn Po's original settlement. Kwŏn Po himself is buried next to Agok village, and both of his sons are buried about halfway between Twisŏngdwi and Pangch'ukkol.

Informants say that Kwŏn Po's younger son, Kwŏn Hyu, migrated to Kaesil village, where one branch of his descendants now constitutes the Kaesil lineage. Kwŏn Hyu's own younger son, Kwŏn Pal, settled a few hundred meters west of Kaesil. Kwŏn Pal's descendants later formed the Twisŏngdwi lineage and village.

The process of local lineage formation continued with the creation of the Pangch'ukkol lineage, located a few kilometers east of Twisŏngdwi and Kaesil. This lineage, the newest of the five, was formed gradually, by several generations of emigrants from Twisŏngdwi. Since its twenty-third-generation ancestor, Kwŏn Kye-yun, is the seniormost forebear buried in Pangch'ukkol, informants assume that he was the first ancestor to settle there. If their assumption is correct, this initial settlement occurred about 1600.[4] The last immigrant arrived almost three hundred years later: one member of the Pangch'ukkol lineage, now in his seventies, says that his father migrated from Twisŏngdwi to Pangch'ukkol at the age of four.

[3] The positions shown in Figures 1 and 2, taken from the Andong Kwŏn genealogy (*Andong Kwŏn-ssi sebo* 1961, vol. 2: 66–104), represent each ancestor's highest office. We have omitted posthumously awarded ranks, purchased titles (*t'ongjŏng*) (see Shin 1974: 35), and four *ch'ambong* (9 Jr) positions attributed to lineage members born between 1880 and 1894. Except for Kwŏn Po's *hŏnnap*, moreover, we have not been able to verify the offices of these ancestors in other sources.

[4] The younger brother of Kwŏn Kye-yun's father was born in 1552 (*Andong Kwŏn-ssi sebo* 1961, vol. 2: 72). Kwŏn Kye-yun himself, therefore, was probably born during the latter half of the sixteenth century.

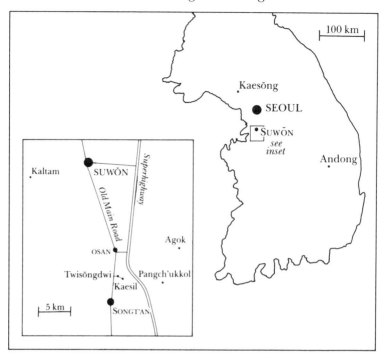

While the descendants of Kwŏn Po were forming their five local lineages, the Korean kingdom was undergoing major cultural
and social transformations. Whereas Buddhism had been the
prevalent religion of the Koryŏ era, the new Yi dynasty adopted
neo-Confucianism as its state creed and launched a vigorous at-
tack against Buddhist ideas, institutions, and practices. Kwŏn
Kŭn, the second cousin of Kwŏn Po's father, and Chŏng To-jŏn,
the ancestor of a nearby Chŏng lineage, were the most prominent
leaders of the early Yi anti-Buddhist campaign (Kalton n.d.).
The earliest monarchs of the Yi dynasty, who ruled Korea until
the mid-fifteenth century, were eager to reduce the vast land
holdings and numbers of clergy that the Buddhist monasteries
and temples controlled. They were less enthusiastic about sup-
pressing Buddhist beliefs and rites (Deuchler 1980a: 78–79). By
the latter half of the fifteenth century, however, the court's attitude had changed. One of the first edicts of King Sejo (1455–68),

for example, prohibited Buddhist monks from attending or praying at funerals (Weems 1962: 315). As a result of such economic and ritual prohibitions, Buddhism never regained its former popularity.

Major changes in Korea's central government accompanied its ideological transformation. In brief, political power shifted away from a hereditary nobility toward a class of scholar-officials (Han Woo-keun 1971: 203–7) whose access to political power was based heavily on their mastery of Confucian writings as demonstrated by success in a Chinese-style civil-service examination (Wagner 1974).[5]

Such evidence as we have points clearly to an increased emphasis on patrilineal descent and primogeniture during the seventeenth and eighteenth centuries. Whereas property had once been inherited almost equally by all children, the rights of daughters were gradually eliminated and eldest sons were granted much larger shares than their younger siblings (Choi Jai-seuk 1972; 1976: 26–29; Lee Kwang-Kyu 1977b: 360–89).[6] Adoption practices also became more rigidly agnatic (Peterson 1977) in that sonless families began to adopt as heirs only persons related through purely male ties. Husbands no longer went to reside at their wives' homes at marriage (Deuchler 1977: 15–17). And most important, Korean lineages either were formed for the first time or emerged out of kin groups that had been quite differently organized (Deuchler 1980a; 1980b). Individuals always had agnatic kin, of course, and brothers and close cousins must have cooperated in some activity or other since antiquity. But

[5] The civil-service examination system had been instituted in Korea much earlier, but its importance as a means of political advancement was greatly enhanced during the Yi dynasty (Kang 1974; Wagner 1974; Henthorn 1971: 67). For a brief discussion of changes in political structure during the early Yi dynasty, see Han Woo-keun (1971: 203–7). A recent review of the historiography of this period is found in Kawashima (1978).

[6] Ultimogeniture is common among coastal villages where gathering sea plants provides a major source of income (Lee Kwang-Kyu 1975: 77–78; Han Sang-Bok 1977: 55). Among some mountain villages where shifting cultivation is practiced, youngest sons inherit the houses of their parents, and on Cheju Island, sons divide their parents' property equally (Lee Kwang-Kyu 1975: 77–78). For a discussion of kinship among Korean shamans, who belonged to the lowest of Korea's major social classes, see Ch'oe Kil-sŏng (1978: 53–121, 134–48). Ancestor worship among these groups appears to differ in many ways from the prevalent Korean pattern (Lee Kwang-Kyu 1977a: 15–16; Han Sang-Bok 1977: 81–82).

more distant agnates do not appear to have organized themselves into groups with corporate functions until after the Koryŏ dynasty.

Precisely when and why Korean lineages emerged are still unresolved issues (Deuchler 1980b; Choi Jai-seuk 1976: 29; Ch'oe Yŏng-ho 1974: 626). A few large, eminent, and dispersed kin groups like the Andong Kwŏn began compiling genealogies as early as the fifteenth and sixteenth centuries, but in that period there were no more than a score of such publications (Ch'oe Yŏng-ho 1974: 625–26). Production of genealogies began to flourish in Korea after 1600 (Wagner 1972: 143).

The earliest genealogies evidently preceded the formation of lineages. They were the fruits of historical research undertaken by a few scholarly men. Only after 1600, when the updating of a genealogy depended primarily on new names from each of the group's constituent units (Wagner 1972: 143), did compiling genealogies become a corporate activity and thus imply the existence of lineage organizations.

A variety of other evidence suggests that Korean lineages emerged after 1600. Though the formation of lineages is often attributed to the influence of neo-Confucian ideology during the early Yi dynasty, Korean neo-Confucianists of the period do not mention lineages in their very voluminous writings (Ch'oe Yŏng-ho 1974: 626). Chinese neo-Confucianists, too, had said very little about organizing groups of agnates but instead devoted their attention to the family and kinship in general (Freedman 1974a: 73).

William Henthorn (1971: 191, 208) has suggested that political factionalism and competition for government positions fostered the development of politically prominent lineages in Korea. In the first two centuries of the Yi dynasty, passing the higher civil-service examination practically assured one some kind of bureaucratic appointment (Ch'oe Yŏng-ho 1974: 611–12). After the Japanese invasions of 1592–1598, however, the number of successful candidates in both the civil and the military examinations increased dramatically (Wagner 1974: 3–4; Quinones 1980: 692–93), too much for all to be accommodated with government positions. In the fierce competition that resulted, lineage membership often provided the backing and contacts needed for appointment to office (Kawashima 1977: 8–10). Later, political factions, which began to dominate court politics in the last quarter of the sixteenth century, came to recruit entire lineages and not merely individuals. So important were these political coalitions that many kin groups refused to intermarry with lineages belonging to rival political factions (Henderson 1968: 448; Cho Oakla 1979: 122).

There was certainly some connection between political power and early lineage organization. The Andong Kwŏn and the Munhwa Yu, the first groups to compile comprehensive genealogies in the fifteenth century, were among the most politically successful lineages of the early Yi dynasty (Ch'oe Yŏng-ho 1974: 625–27; Kawashima 1977: 11). Even by the end of the dynasty, the number of those passing the higher civil-service examinations from the Andong Kwŏn was exceeded only by those from the Chŏnju Yi, the royal lineage (Wagner 1972: 151).

Localized lineages like the Twisŏngdwi kin group, which were typically segments of the politically powerful agnatic organizations, also seem to have emerged after 1600. The available evidence, though not conclusive, indicates that the oldest local lineages are descended from ancestors who first settled in their respective villages during the fourteenth, fifteenth, and sixteenth centuries (Kim Tu-hŏn 1949: 136; Kim Taik-Kyoo 1964: 140–45; Biernatzki 1967: 50, 211–12, 262, 323; Pak Ki-hyuk 1975: 77–78, 117–18, 144–45; Wagner 1972: 143). Like Kwŏn Po's immediate descendants, these founding ancestors often came from nearby and sent out sons who spawned additional kin groups in neighboring communities. Only after the Japanese invasions, however, do we find evidence of at least a handful of agnates living in a single community and presumably constituting a local lineage. In the village studied by Kim Taik-Kyoo, for example, the founding ancestor is said to have arrived in 1355, but current lineage members are all descended from two brothers who lived in the late sixteenth century. Several related lineages, founded by collateral agnates a few generations above or below the two brothers, inhabit nearby communities (Kim Taik-Kyoo 1964: 140–45). Among many other Korean local lineages, the first settler did not arrive until the seventeenth century or later (e.g., Brandt 1971: 120; McBrian 1979: 111–12).

Along with the ideological and social transformations of the Yi dynasty came changes in ancestor worship. The *Book of Family*

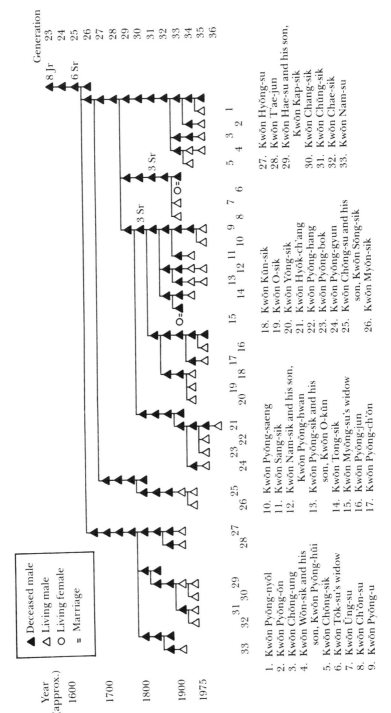

Fig. 2. Genealogy of Twisŏngdwi-lineage household heads.

1. Kwŏn Pyŏng-nyŏl
2. Kwŏn Pyŏng-ŏn
3. Kwŏn Chŏng-ung
4. Kwŏn Wŏn-sik and his son, Kwŏn Pyŏng-hŭi
5. Kwŏn Chŏng-sik
6. Kwŏn Tŏk-su's widow
7. Kwŏn Ŭng-su
8. Kwŏn Ch'ŏn-su
9. Kwŏn Pyŏng-u

10. Kwŏn Pyŏng-saeng
11. Kwŏn Sang-sik
12. Kwŏn Nam-sik and his son, Kwŏn Pyŏng-hwan
13. Kwŏn Pyŏng-sik and his son, Kwŏn O-kŭn
14. Kwŏn Tong-sik
15. Kwŏn Myŏng-su's widow
16. Kwŏn Pyŏng-jun
17. Kwŏn Pyŏng-ch'ŏn

18. Kwŏn Kŭn-sik
19. Kwŏn O-sik
20. Kwŏn Yŏng-sik
21. Kwŏn Hyŏk-ch'ang
22. Kwŏn Pyŏng-hang
23. Kwŏn Pyŏng-bok
24. Kwŏn Pyŏng-gyun
25. Kwŏn Chŏng-su and his son, Kwŏn Sŏng-sik
26. Kwŏn Myŏn-sik

27. Kwŏn Hyŏng-su
28. Kwŏn T'ae-jun
29. Kwŏn Hae-su and his son, Kwŏn Kap-sik
30. Kwŏn Chang-sik
31. Kwŏn Chŭng-sik
32. Kwŏn Chae-sik
33. Kwŏn Nam-su

Ritual (Chinese *Chu-tzu chia-li;* Korean *Chuja karye*), by the neo-Confucian Chu Hsi, became the basic text for regulating ritual procedures (Moon Seung Gyu 1974: 73; Deuchler 1977: 5; Yi Hae-yong and Han Woo-keun 1976: 166–67). Its influence is still evident in the numerous etiquette manuals that are popular in Korea today. In addition, ritual responsibilities were altered to the pattern now followed in Twisŏngdwi. Commemorating ancestors became almost entirely the obligation of eldest sons, women were excluded from officiating at the rites, and ritual responsibility could no longer be assumed by a wife or a daughter's son in the absence of an agnatically related male heir (Lee Kwang-Kyu 1977a: 13–16; Deuchler 1977: 29; 1980b: 652).

Exactly how all these changes were related is an intriguing question. Although the prevailing view has attributed the changes in descent, inheritance, and ritual procedures to neo-Confucian influence, the considerable time lag between the adoption of neo-Confucianism and its alleged effects argue that other factors may well have been at work (Choi Jai-seuk 1976: 26–29; Yi Hae-yong and Han Woo-keun 1976: 166–67, 175).[7] Moreover, recent research by Martina Deuchler (1977: 15–17; 1980a; 1980b: 651–52) indicates that neo-Confucianism itself was reformulated during the first two centuries of the Yi dynasty as it accommodated to prevailing Korean customs. We shall return to this issue in Chapter 7.

The Twisŏngdwi lineage underwent its own transformation during the Yi dynasty. Whereas its early Yi ancestors had been relatively successful at obtaining government positions, the eighteenth, nineteenth, and early twentieth centuries were a period of social and economic decline. Office holding was rare among the lineage's twenty-sixth and subsequent generations (see Figure 2). By the time Japan annexed Korea (1910–45), few of the lineage's households owned enough land to support themselves. Most earned at least part of their subsistence by working as tenant farmers, as did four-fifths of the rest of Korea (Choi Hochin 1971: 265; Lee Hoon K. 1936: 157). Beginning in the eighteenth century, numerous new descent lines arose, as the genealogy of current household heads shows (Figure 2).

---

[7] The years following the Japanese invasions also witnessed the introduction of several new crops and the widespread adoption of more intensive agricultural methods (Michell 1979–80: 82; Kim Yong-sŏp 1975; Shin 1978). Major demographic changes may also have occurred (see Michell 1979–80).

Although the Twisŏngdwi lineage was no longer at its economic peak by the time of the Japanese annexation, the kin group apparently retained some of its former prestige in its immediate area. At least three lineage members served as township head (*myŏnjang*) during the annexation years. It would have been uncharacteristic of the Japanese to appoint anyone to this position unless he had some social standing in his local society. One of these township heads also served as a staff member (*chigwŏn*) at a local Confucian school (*hyanggyo*). In addition, the lineage produced at least one graduate of the prestigious Keijo Imperial University (later known as Seoul National University). Thus the lineage was able to uphold its gentry (*yangban*) status, initially acquired by patrilineal descent from its office-holding ancestors.[8] As late as 1965, its members would not carry funeral biers, for such labor was traditionally thought to be demeaning and unworthy of gentry. Said Kwŏn Kŭn-sik, the lineage's treasurer and its most influential member, "We weren't great gentry, but nobody looked down on us either."

Recent Prosperity

Prosperity returned to Twisŏngdwi only during the last few decades. Informants say their economic condition improved substantially thanks to the Korean land reform of the early 1950's, when they obtained ownership of land that they had been cultivating as tenants. In fact, a comparison of lineage households with other Korean farm households suggests that they enjoy at least an average farm income. Though Twisŏngdwi is too far

[8] During the Yi dynasty, *yangban* enjoyed not only high prestige and local political power but also such legal privileges as access to civil-service examinations and exemption from military service or its equivalent tax. Their social position is popularly thought to have been a supposedly hereditary status acquired by many through purchase or illicit means (and lost to others for failing to live up to the ideals of gentry behavior). However, historians have been unable to determine the extent of social mobility and the actual criteria for entitlement to *yangban* status during the Yi dynasty; whatever the criteria were at its outset, they may well have changed subsequently; and even during the Yi, these criteria were perhaps as much contested as they are today (see Chapter 5; Goldberg 1973–74; Wagner 1974; Ch'oe Yŏng-ho 1974; Shin 1978). Persons now labelled with this term are, as in the Yi dynasty, supposedly agnatic descendants of former *yangban*, though many contemporary Koreans cynically observe that "nowadays, anyone with money is a *yangban*." Today's *yangban* no longer enjoy any special legal privileges, and both their prestige and their local power have been eroded considerably during the past few decades.

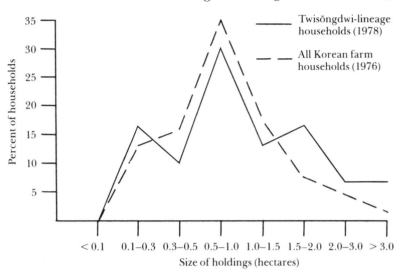

Fig. 3. Land cultivated by Twisŏngdwi-lineage and all Korean farm households (latter statistics are from Ministry of Agriculture and Fisheries 1977: 26–27).

north to permit much double cropping, average land holdings per household are somewhat larger, and their productivity better, than national averages (see Figure 3). Four-fifths of the land cultivated by the lineage consists of paddy, which is more productive than dry fields; and yields from Twisŏngdwi paddy are particularly high (Table 1). Moreover, rice from the Twisŏngdwi area is prized for its taste and commands the highest market prices.

Land reform was not the only cause of the lineage's recent prosperity. From 1963 to 1978, the Republic of Korea's real gross national product grew at an average rate of better than 10 percent a year (National Bureau of Statistics 1978: 447–51). A disproportionate share of that growth was centered on Seoul, and many young adults of the lineage and other rural Koreans emigrated there.[9] Twisŏngdwi's location, however, enabled even those lineage members who stayed behind to benefit from their

[9] For discussions of urban migration in Korea, see Lee Man-Gap and Barringer (1978) and Kwon Tai Hwan et al. (1975: 62–78).

TABLE 1
Twisŏngdwi-Lineage and National Farm Economy

Measure	Twisŏngdwi lineage	Korea
Land utilization rate (1976)[a]	110%	138%
Cultivated ares per farm household (1974)[b]	116	94
Composition of cultivatable land[c]		
Paddy	79%	56%
Dry field	21%	44%
Paddy yields (kilograms per are)[d]		
1972	35.2	33.1
1976	48.7	43.3

[a] The Korea figure is from Ministry of Agriculture and Fisheries (1977: 32). The figure given for Twisŏngdwi is the average for Kyŏnggi Province.
   [b] The Korea figure is from Ministry of Agriculture and Fisheries (1977: 23).
   [c] The Korea figures are from Ministry of Agriculture and Fisheries (1977: 33).
   [d] The Korea figures are from Ministry of Agriculture and Fisheries (1973: 134–35; 1977: 302–3). The figures given for Twisŏngdwi are the averages for P'yŏngt'aek County, the Kyŏnggi Province subdivision in which the village is located.

nation's economic growth more than the residents of most other farming villages. Twisŏngdwi is located only 50 kilometers south of downtown Seoul, and less than a kilometer from a highway that served as the main link between Seoul and the rest of the country until a new superhighway opened in the early 1970's. (See map on p. 8.) A bus trip to the center of Seoul takes only about an hour and a half, and buses leave every ten minutes. The road also links Twisŏngdwi with the nearby towns Songt'an and Osan, which lie four kilometers south and north of the village, respectively. Songt'an, whose population in 1978 was about 60,000, grew up around an American air base built around the time of the Korean War. A few villagers go to Songt'an to sell their surplus vegetables and eggs. Osan, with a 1978 population of some 35,000, is an older town with a railroad station. In addition to its regular shops, it has a traditional market that meets every five days.

Several lineage families have taken advantage of Twisŏngdwi's easy access to the outside world to supplement their farm income. In 1973–74, the period of our first fieldwork among the lineage, two family heads commuted daily to jobs in Seoul. A few others earned most of their income by working as semiskilled laborers at nearby construction sites, and another was a real-estate broker. A few unmarried women traveled to jobs in small factories not far from the village. Rice dealers from Osan sent their trucks right up to the door of the village grain mill, giving lineage members a convenient outlet for their surplus rice. And the grain mill itself provided another lineage member with the major part of his income.

Because so many lineage families were pursuing nonfarming sources of income, and because several young adults of the lineage had emigrated from the village, a shortage of agricultural labor developed in Twisŏngdwi. As a result, daily wages for farm labor, 600 *wŏn* (US $1.50) in 1973, were significantly higher than those in many other villages.[10] These attractive wages induced several non-Kwŏn people to move to Twisŏngdwi and hire out as farmhands.

According to informants, the first nonlineage family settled in Twisŏngdwi in 1930, when a hired laborer brought his wife to live in the village. (Although such families may have belonged to lineages in their home villages, we call them "nonlineage" to distinguish them from Kwŏn families.) During the 1940's and 1950's, a few more nonlineage households were established in the village. Most were headed by sons-in-law, men who had married lineage daughters and settled in Twisŏngdwi. Not until the late 1960's, however, did large numbers of nonlineage persons move into the village. By 1973 there were three workers who lived and ate in the home of their lineage employer, seven sons-in-law and their families, and sixteen unrelated households.[11] Most of the householders in this last category were landless and earned their livelihood as farmhands for lineage members (see Table 2).

Since most of the nonlineage families were poor and worked for lineage households, they constituted their own social class in Twisŏngdwi. Shortly after we arrived in the community, the village chief (*ijang*) told us that the inhabitants could be roughly divided into two categories, the Kwŏn people and the "coming-and-going people" (*watta katta hanŭn saram*). This view was shared

[10] Daily wages were even 200 *wŏn* higher if the employer did not provide meals. By contrast, Griffin Dix (1977: 560) reported a daily wage of only 500 *wŏn* during the following year in a village near Taejŏn.

[11] Except for the one lineage household that included three hired workers, no Twisŏngdwi family habitually shared a common dwelling and food supply with non–family members. Only when providing statistical data, therefore, do we distinguish between families and households.

TABLE 2

Lineage Affiliation and Land Ownership

	Number of households	
Affiliation of household head	Total	Land-owning
Twisŏngdwi lineage member	33	32
Son-in-law	7	4
Unrelated	16	2

by many others, though another lineage member refined it somewhat: nonlineage households, he said, could be subdivided into unrelated households and those of sons-in-law, "half-sons" as a third lineage member jokingly called them. Although sons-in-law were generally thought to occupy a position somewhat below lineage members, a few of the older sons-in-law now head some of the wealthiest households in the village and wield considerable influence.

The relative statuses of the lineage and unrelated households in Twisŏngdwi followed a traditional Korean pattern for farming communities inhabited primarily by a single local lineage and its non-kin hired workers, but the degree of discrimination was not as great as in villages where the two groups had coexisted for several generations.[12] For example, no one in the lineage objected openly when one of its younger members married the niece of an unrelated household head in 1974, though marriage partnerships are one of the most conservative indicators of social class in rural Korea. Some informants were even willing to admit that the bride's uncle had probably been of gentry origins. (His behavior was as genteel as that of most lineage members.)

Continued growth of the Korean economy, an increase in rice yields of 40 percent, and a doubling of the value of rice in real purchasing power all contributed to the growing prosperity of the Twisŏngdwi lineage during the mid-1970's. When we returned to the village in 1977, signs of prosperity were visible everywhere. Nearly every house had a television, most had electric fans, some had running water and refrigerators, and one had a telephone. Three lineage members had built new, mod-

---

[12] For a classic study of such a village, see Kim Taik-Kyoo (1964). His work includes a 52-page English summary. English-language material about this village can also be found in Kim Taik-Kyoo (1968) and Park Sang-Yŏl (1967).

ern houses. Several others had enlarged existing rooms, though much of the added floor space was taken up by new television consoles.

Equally important to the lineage's prosperity were the opening of Korea's new superhighway system in the early 1970's and a government policy of locating new industries outside of Seoul. The new superhighway's exit on the southern edge of Osan, a few hundred meters from the old main road, made the southern side of this town an attractive location for industries wanting easy access to the capital. Between 1960 and 1973, the population of Osan township grew at an average rate of 3 percent a year, only slightly above the national growth rate, but between 1973 and 1977 its average annual growth rate was 9 percent.[13] Dozens of new factories mushroomed along the four-kilometer stretch of road linking Twisŏngdwi with Osan. By the summer of 1978, two factories and a chicken farm had been built within a few hundred meters of Twisŏngdwi, and two more factories were under construction. Shortly after noon and 5 P.M. of every working day, when the factories let out, small crowds of workers could be seen walking to their homes in the village. Several lineage members had added, or were adding, new rooms to their homes to rent to newly arrived construction and factory workers. Since 1973 the number of unrelated households had nearly doubled.

Local industrialization also increased the demand for land on which to build new factories. As a result, the price of dry fields skyrocketed to more than three times that of paddy. Plots of dry field measuring four square meters (one *p'yŏng*), which had typically sold for 500 *wŏn* (US $1.25) in 1973, sold for 18,000 *wŏn* ($36) in mid-1978.[14] One lineage member sold his orchard and moved about fifteen kilometers south, where he used the proceeds to acquire another orchard three times as large.

The industrialization of Twisŏngdwi was not an unmixed blessing for the lineage. Although the factories provided jobs for many members of lineage households and attracted newcomers

---

[13] The 1960 Korean census found a population of 17,449 in Osan township (Economic Planning Board 1963a: 35). A figure of 25,000, given to us in 1974 by clerks at the township office, was probably a late-1973 estimate. Four years later, the clerks informed us that the township's population was 35,360 as of October 1, 1977.

[14] In 1974, the Korean government altered the monetary exchange rate from 398 to 484 *wŏn* per U.S. dollar (National Bureau of Statistics 1978: 336). The rate remained there until 1980.

who needed housing in the village, they also provided alternative employment to those who had originally come to Twisŏngdwi to fill the agricultural labor shortage. As a result, farm labor became more scarce. Nonlineage members told us they had more requests for day labor than they could fill. One side effect of this development was a noticeable rise in the social status of hired farm workers. At the village picnic in 1978, some of these men were seated with the lineage elders, a seating arrangement we had not seen four years earlier. The class division of Twisŏngdwi into lineage members and hired workers, which had really begun only in the 1960's, was rapidly disintegrating in the 1970's.

Social Organization of the Twisŏngdwi Lineage and Village

Although the immigration of nonlineage families, coupled with the emigration of lineage families, has now reduced lineage households to a minority in Twisŏngdwi, the lineage still controls village government. Lineage members continue to regard Twisŏngdwi as "their" village, and though this attitude weakened noticeably during the 1970's, the lineage's domination of village politics is still plainly evident. At the annual village meeting (*tae tonghoe*) held in December, when most important village matters are formally decided, about three-fourths of the participants are lineage members.

In addition to dominating the village politically, lineage members feel a greater responsibility for its welfare. A list of contributions to the village treasury in 1977 showed that about 78 percent of the funds came from lineage households in Twisŏngdwi. A wealthy lineage member who had emigrated to Seoul decades ago (the graduate of Keijo Imperial University) donated another 9 percent, and sons-in-law the remaining 13 percent. Unrelated households had contributed nothing.

Nonlineage householders tend not to participate in village government for a variety of reasons. In 1973, one told us frankly that he resented the lineage members' attitude of superiority as well as their political domination. Though he spoke out freely at village meetings, he felt he had no real influence or prestige in Twisŏngdwi. He also stayed away from all major social events, and he eventually left the village. But few other nonlineage persons are openly dissatisfied; rather, they stay uninvolved because they are not yet established citizens of the community. Most are relative newcomers, and many do not own their homes, pay taxes to the village, or contribute their labor to village improvement projects. The five or six nonlineage household heads who do play a more active part in village affairs have all lived in Twisŏngdwi for at least a few decades and own their own houses and farmland.

Rather than discourage the involvement of nonlineage persons in village government, lineage members have been taking increasingly positive steps to further their participation. For example, even by the early 1970's only one of the three hamletchiefs (*panjang*) was a lineage member; the others were a son-inlaw and the head of an unrelated household. These positions are neither powerful nor prestigious, but they do carry some responsibility. As assistants to the village chief, the three hamlet chiefs collect small ad hoc taxes and contributions for village projects, as well as census data, from the households of their hamlets. If nothing else, these positions mark their incumbents as solid citizens of the Twisŏngdwi community.

By the mid-1970's, the lineage had made a greater political concession to their nonagnates. For the first time, the lineage surrendered the position of village chief; it went to a son-in-law, one of the largest landowners in the village.

In addition to lineage affiliation, a number of other social divisions can be found in Twisŏngdwi. Age, sex, residence, and membership in voluntary associations cut across lineage membership and thus divide the lineage as well as the village. (The lineage itself is also internally segmented along genealogical lines, a mode of division we discuss in Chapters 4 and 5.) Wealth, although it affects a household's prestige, the influence of its members in village affairs, and the selection of one's closest friends, is not a basis for major social divisions.

Age ranks with lineage affiliation in its importance to social divisions in Twisŏngdwi. Villagers speak of "elders" (*noin*) usually meaning men over about 55, and "young people" (*chŏlmŭn saram*), usually meaning men up to 50 or 55 but often restricted to men under 40.

Age classifications entail more than linguistic conventions; they are the most important basis for political factionalism in Twisŏngdwi. Age-based factions operate openly in two separate domains, village government and lineage government. The village government is supposed to be more egalitarian, a form of "democracy" (*minju-juŭi*), as one informant put it. At village meetings, younger men assert themselves rather freely before their elders, and vote on an equal footing with them.[15] In 1976, they overcame the elders' opposition and had a 35-year-old lineage member elected village chief, taking the position away from the 49-year-old son-in-law to whom the lineage had surrendered it a year or two earlier. The son-in-law, though no lackey of the lineage elders, was not a political activist, and some of the "young people" had grown impatient with his conservatism. A year later, they returned the position of village chief to the son-in-law. The young people, some of whom worked outside the village, admitted that managing the village interfered too greatly with their economic pursuits. Perhaps they also realized that the village chief is not all that powerful and can be effective only if the village is united behind him. Indeed, the position has traditionally been viewed as rather onerous, though election to it is an honor.

In the domain of lineage government, the young people have had even less success. Because age and generational rank, as well as propriety, must be observed scrupulously at lineage meetings, young men cannot assert themselves in front of their elders. An elder, moreover, usually remains active in lineage affairs long after he has surrendered to his eldest son the voice of the household in village government. Throughout the 1970's, the young people's efforts to simplify lineage-sponsored ancestor rituals were effectively thwarted by the elders.

The division of Twisŏngdwi according to age and lineage affiliation applies primarily to the social life of men. Women do not organize themselves into such large and visible groups, but instead form a sort of hierarchy based on age and wealth. Their major divisions need not be congruent with men's, because social activities of the two sexes outside the home are separate. Women have no formal political role and do not even attend the annual meetings of the lineage or village. Typically, men and women form segregated groups when working in the fields. Even if a

---

[15] In his ethnography of a Korean village, Vincent Brandt (1971) shows that village social structure is primarily egalitarian whereas lineage structure is hierarchical. Our informants were well aware of this difference. Each age group sought to exploit one or the other of the structural principles to its own advantage.

husband and wife attend the same social event, such as a wedding, funeral, or sixtieth-birthday celebration, each sits with others of the same sex. And groups of men and women travel separately when they go on a shopping trip or social outing to Osan on traditional market days.

The age and sex divisions of Twisŏngdwi were neatly illustrated when we took souvenir photographs of a village picnic. The women, who had been busy preparing the food, all stood together in the cooking area for their photograph. The men, on the other hand, formed three groups: the elders, a middle-aged group in their forties and fifties, and a group of young men in their late twenties and thirties. The three groups joined for another photograph, taken to decorate the village meeting hall.

Twisŏngdwi is also divided territorially into hamlets. Strung out along the southern slope of a ridge that gradually rises to the east, they are called from west to east, the lower, middle, and upper hamlet (arem-maŭl, chunggan-maŭl, wim-maŭl). Each contains a tight nuclear cluster of houses, though the lower and upper hamlets also include a few houses separated from the main settlements by a few hundred meters. The middle and upper hamlets adjoin one another, and the lower hamlet is only about 50 meters from the middle hamlet. Since the hamlets as well as the houses are so close to each other, almost any house in the village is a short walk from any other. Located in the middle hamlet, where they can easily serve the entire village, are the village meeting house, an old village well, the grain mill, and two shops. Both shops sell wine and a wide variety of food and other household needs.

Informants of all three settlements agree that the residents of the lower hamlet are the most kindhearted and those of the upper hamlet the least so, but this sentiment was the only expression of hamlet solidarity we found. In Twisŏngdwi, unlike some other Korean villages (Dix 1977: 487–89, 547–48; Brandt 1971: 45–49), hamlet affiliation per se matters little in daily life. The hamlets have no corporate functions or activities; the hamlet chief's tasks are only administrative. Since individual households participate directly in village government, a hamlet chief does not represent his hamlet politically, as a village chief represents his village before township officials.

Proximity of residence, by contrast, is important in day-to-day

The upper hamlet of Twisŏngdwi in 1974.

activities. Neighbors are near at hand whenever a need arises. Each time we moved in or out of Twisŏngdwi, our closest neighbors helped load and unload our belongings. "A nearby neighbor is better than a distant cousin" (*mŏn sach'on poda kakkaun iusi natta*) is a well-known proverb whose variants are found throughout East Asia (Yi Ki-mun 1962: 1, 192–93; Fried 1953: 181; Buchanan 1965: 109). In Twisŏngdwi, close kin are often neighbors as well (see Chapter 4), but intimate ties form between neighbors regardless of kinship. Both men and women tend to form their closest friendships with the nearest neighbors of similar age and wealth, and young children most often play with others who live nearby so they can be within earshot of their houses.

Voluntary associations are yet another form of social grouping in Twisŏngdwi. The Mutual Assistance Society (*yŏnbang-gye*) provides help at funerals, weddings, and sixtieth-birthday celebrations in members' households. The Wives' Society (*punyŏ-hoe*) raised the capital necessary to establish the first shop in the village

TABLE 3

Lineage Affiliation and Membership in Voluntary Associations

Association	Number of households		
	Lineage	Sons-in-law	Unrelated
Mutual Assistance Society	22	4	5
Green Pine Society	22	4	5
Wives' Society[a]	26	5	8

[a] Members are registered in their husbands' names.

in 1974. And the Green Pine Society (*ch'ŏngsong-hoe*), organized by the younger men of Twisŏngdwi, collects money for various village projects.

Although membership in the last two of these voluntary associations reflects sex and age divisions in Twisŏngdwi, the benefits of all three extend beyond their own members to the entire community. For example, in 1978, the Mutual Assistance and Green Pine Societies provided funds for the annual village picnic and souvenir towels commemorating the event. The towels were distributed not only to every household, but to all people living in rented rooms, including us. And the shop financed by the Wives' Society is a convenience available to anyone.

In theory, voluntary associations have nothing to do with kinship, yet the lineage's overwhelming presence in these organizations is clearly reflected in their memberships (see Table 3). Moreover, the major officers of the Mutual Assistance and Green Pine Societies are all lineage members. Leadership of the Wives' Society is divided between women who are married to lineage men and lineage daughters who are married to resident sons-in-law.

Ties to the Outside World

The Twisŏngdwi lineage has never been an isolated group. At its inception, the kin group's ancestors served in the Korean government's bureaucracy. Very likely these early ancestors joined with those of four other branches to commemorate Kwŏn Po, just as their descendants do today. Later, during the Japanese period, not only were some lineage members appointed to local township offices, but a few others traveled to Japan, and one even went to Oceania with the Japanese army. Today, nearly all young men of the lineage serve in the Korean army for two or three years.

The lineage has also been linked to other local villages in a variety of ways. Almost all men of the lineage completed primary school, which children of several local villages still attend together. Some went on to middle school, high school, and even college, and thereby became part of even wider social networks. A few also studied at a traditional Korean school (*sŏdang*) in a neighboring village, where they learned Chinese characters and were introduced to major Chinese classical texts.[16] Because marriage between known agnates is prohibited (and has been since at least the early years of the Yi dynasty), wives came from and daughters married into other villages. Lineage members also regularly attended the traditional market in the town of Osan, as did residents of other nearby villages. Finally, the lineage has had special ties to the two closest villages, located within a few hundred meters of Twisŏngdwi. The nearest shaman (*mudang*) lives in one of these communities, and some of their residents were formerly hired to carry the bier at lineage funerals. Occasionally, lineage members hire men from these villages as farmhands or even exchange labor with them.

Despite these extra-village contacts, Twisŏngdwi retained its rural character and strong sense of community in the early 1970's. At that time, lineage households still produced nearly all their own food. They referred to themselves as "country people" (*sigol saram*), a term that contrasts with "Seoul people" (*Seoul saram*). At major social events in the village, the great majority of the guests were always Twisŏngdwi lineage members. At lunar New Year and the Harvest Moon Festival (Ch'usŏk), the major holidays of the year, many emigrant kinsmen and their families would return to the village for the festivities and ancestor rituals. Although labor was occasionally exchanged with people of other villages, most exchanges were among the residents of Twisŏngdwi. Finally, members of lineage families took great pride in their community: several told us that it contained not one "bad person" (*nappŭn saram*).

By the late 1970's, Twisŏngdwi's sense of community and rural character had clearly weakened. Purchases of food and other goods at the village shops and in the local towns had risen. The

---

[16] For a discussion of these rural schools and their curriculum, see Dix (1977: 15–73) and Rutt (1960: 23–42).

influx of construction and factory workers had made it difficult for all residents to know each other on a face-to-face basis. One lineage member who had always made it his business to know every villager confessed that he could no longer recognize all those who were village residents. One lineage family had begun going to Seoul on holidays because the eldest son had established his own family there. And television had given villagers access to an outside world that was unimaginable only a few years earlier. When we went to visit the lineage treasurer one evening, we found him watching a weekly episode of "The Six Million Dollar Man," dubbed with a Korean sound track.

2

Families of the
Twisŏngdwi Lineage

Twisŏngdwi lineage households are fairly representative of Korean farm households in size and composition. In 1973 they averaged 5.9 persons, just below that year's national average for farm households of 6.0 (Ministry of Agriculture and Fisheries 1977: 22–23). The proportion of Twisŏngdwi lineage families with a stem or extended form (45 percent) is somewhat larger than the average for Korean *rural* families, but is apparently in line with that of *farm* families in other villages.[1]

These statistical averages can be misleading, however. Hidden behind them are wide variations in the sizes and structures of different households; moreover, these variations reflect not so much different types of domestic groups but rather different phases in a normal family's development and growth (Choi Jai-seuk 1976: 19; Fortes 1958: 3). The evolution of a normal family reveals Korean descent and residence principles in operation. It

---

[1] Since 1973 the average size of Korean farm households has declined noticeably (Ministry of Agriculture and Fisheries 1977: 22–23). By 1978 it had dropped to 5.1 persons (National Bureau of Statistics 1979: 95). In Twisŏngdwi, however, household size has remained constant since 1973. Local industrialization has allowed many Twisŏngdwi lineage members to work at factory or construction jobs while living in the village.

As for family structure, comparable averages for all Korean farm families are not available. Two population surveys reported respectively that 36 percent (Choi Jai-seuk 1966b: 157–61; 1976: 18–19) and 28 percent (Moon Hyun-Sang et al. 1973: 46) of all *rural* Korean families were nonnuclear (stem or extended). Another (Kwon Tai Hwan et al. 1975: 58) reported 36 percent and 32 percent in 1966 and 1970, respectively. These figures are significantly lower than the 45 percent we found in Twisŏngdwi, but a large part of the discrepancy is probably due to the inclusion of town dwellers and nonfarming families in the "rural" category used in these published sources. In a study of another Korean lineage village, where farming was the major occupation, Kim Taik-Kyoo (1964: 90) found that 54 percent of the lineage families and 45 percent of all families in the village were nonnuclear.

also explains a good deal about inheritance and interpersonal relations within the family. As we shall see, all of these structural and affective aspects of family life are reflected in relations with ancestors.

Structural Development of the Family

Ideally, every Korean family exists forever. With each succeeding generation, its headship passes from the father to his eldest son. In more technical terms, the ideal Korean family is a patrilineal stem family that is perpetuated through primogeniture. When an eldest son marries, his bride joins the household and remains there with her husband and his parents.

A younger son's bride also enters her husband's natal household upon marriage, but only temporarily. The new couple's length of residence varies with the region and the particular circumstances of each family (Lee Kwang-Kyu 1976: 17), but it seldom lasts more than a few years. In Twisŏngdwi, a younger son and his wife establish their own household before the birth of their second child. Typically, they build or move into a house in the hamlet of the husband's natal family.

A daughter, unlike a son, leaves her natal household at marriage. Usually she joins her husband's family in another village, but even if her husband comes to live in Twisŏngdwi, the new couple establishes a separate household. One lineage member and his son-in-law lived in the same building for several years, but their residence arrangement did not obscure the autonomy of their respective households. Besides living in separate parts of the house, each family was listed as a separate household in the township office, each registered its land in the name of its own household head, and each held its own memberships in the village's cooperative societies.

When the usual residence norms are followed, a Korean family proceeds through a regular sequence of structures. Figure 4 depicts this sequence starting with a family newly established by a younger son, the usual form of new households.

Figure 4a shows a husband and wife and their unmarried children of both sexes. As these children mature they marry in turn. Normally, the eldest son marries first and brings his wife into the household, as shown in Figure 4b. After the eldest son's marriage, two developments usually occur simultaneously: he and his

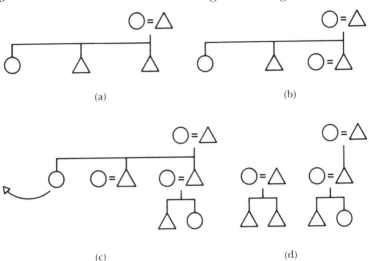

Fig. 4. Typical growth and structure of a Korean family. (*a*) A new family. (*b*) The family after the eldest son's marriage. (*c*) The extended family. (*d*) Formation of two families from the extended family.

wife produce their own offspring and his younger siblings marry. The resulting structure, sometimes called a "joint" or "extended" family, is depicted in Figure 4*c*. It is normally short lived, for younger sons and their wives move out after a few years and establish their own households, which take the initial form shown in Figure 4*a* and in the left side of 4*d*. Upon the death of the elderly parents in the original extended household, shown in the right of Figure 4*d*, it too assumes that structure.[2]

The above sequence portrays an ideal developmental process, one that represents a set of expectations, shared by Twisŏngdwi villagers and social scientists alike (e.g., Choi Jai-seuk 1976: 15–17; Lee Kwang-Kyu 1976: 15–17), from which a particular family's deviation can be explained and its compromises negotiated. Of course, not everyone lives to old age; some couples have

[2] Families of more than three generations are rare in Korea; even among farm families in rural villages, less than 3 percent have four or more generations at any point in time (Economic Planning Board 1963b: 78–79; Choi Jai-seuk 1966b: 133–35; Kwon Tai Hwan et al. 1975: 56). During the period spanned by our fieldwork in Twisŏngdwi, only one lineage family exceeded three generations, and only for a few years in the mid-1970's.

no children; and a few people desert their spouses. In the following pages, we will show how Twisŏngdwi families traditionally dealt with these and other contingencies.

In recent decades, urban industrialization and rural emigration have posed a significant threat to the ideal development of farm households. Many sons leave their natal families, some even before marriage, to find work in Seoul. The effects of their migration are a continual reduction in average family size and a steady increase in the ratio of nuclear to nonnuclear families (Kwon Tai Hwan et al. 1975: 55–59). Even in Twisŏngdwi, where local industries have offset these trends in recent years, the eldest sons of eight lineage households had emigrated from the village. Their parents, left alone or with younger offspring, were reluctant to leave the comfort and security of their familiar community, but many had made plans to move in eventually with their eldest sons. None seemed bitter, however; instead, they were glad that their children enjoyed the economic opportunities available in urban centers.

Parents and Children

During their first two years, Twisŏngdwi children receive a great deal of affection, indulgence, and nurturance from both parents. Infants and toddlers are seldom separated from their mothers and never left unattended. No crib or cradle deprives the child of physical contact with its mother, with whom it sleeps and on whose back it travels, held in place by a blanket wrapped around both mother and child. Children of this age are frequently held and fondled, often at their own request. Crying quickly brings attention and soothing efforts, and very often a mother's breast as well. Koreans are always shocked when they learn that American parents let infants and young children sleep alone in separate rooms.

During these early years, children are hardly punished at all: to control her child's behavior, a mother usually uses a pleading tone and seldom a harsh voice. Nor are infants expected to follow any strict routines. They are fed on demand, allowed to stay up with parents, and toilet trained by the gentlest of procedures. Generally, Korean children are not expected to complete their toilet training until the second half of their third year (Moon Seung Gyu 1971: 21). Even if an infant endangers its own safety, parents try to distract it or bribe it with food rather than scolding or forcibly separating it from a dangerous object. The Korean funeral chant presented in the next chapter reminds offspring of the affection and indulgence so generously given by parents in these early years.

Children do not receive such indulgent treatment after their second year. Breast-feeding usually ends during the third or fourth year, but occasionally continues to the age of five or six (Moon Seung Gyu 1971: 19; Osgood 1951: 95). Mothers prefer to wean their children gradually, but the birth of another child sometimes requires a more abrupt termination.

Children over two are often left in the care of older siblings or occasionally older cousins; as a result, play groups in Twisŏngdwi usually include children of various ages. Or a grandmother may care for a small child as one of her major tasks. As with breast-feeding, however, the change from infantile treatment is gradual. It is not uncommon to see a boy of four carried about on his mother's back.

Though children receive less parental attention as they grow older, they are seldom excluded from grown-up activities or separated from parents against their will. As Vincent Brandt (1971: 173) has noted, adults seldom mind the presence of children at any activity in the village. If youngsters create a disturbance or interfere with the task at hand, they are told to be quiet or get out of the way. Rarely are they ordered to leave; usually they are simply ignored. For example, several children gathered at the lineage rituals in 1973, not only for a close look at us but also to receive some fruit or candy after each ritual was completed. Only when their noisy shouting drowned out the recitation of the formal address to the dead, and when they were using an ancestor's grave mound for a slide, were they reprimanded.

Children are subjected to increasing demands as they grow older. In their fifth and sixth years, children begin to help with farm and household chores, acquire the rudiments of table manners, and observe the basics of linguistic etiquette.[3] In their seventh and eighth years, children begin school. They are also asked to perform heavier farm chores and more serious tasks, such as watching the house when no one else is at home. As they ap-

---

[3] Accounts of honorific forms in Korean can be found in Wang Hahn-Sok (1979), Dredge (1976), and Martin (1964).

proach adolescence, children, especially boys, become increasingly formal with their fathers. More frequent and serious insistence that he submit to parental authority transforms a boy's warm and spontaneous association with his father to a stiff and awkward relationship.

Scolding and even physical punishment may well begin as early as a child's third or fourth year and gradually become more intensive. We rarely saw adults hit children, but corporal punishment is probably more common in private (Madrigal 1979: 83). The disciplining of the three-year-old girl of a nonlineage family, since it was public and commented on by several villagers, provides some indication of attitudes toward physical punishment.

The little girl went one day with her grandmother to an engagement celebration in the village.[4] Eyeing an elaborate food arrangement prepared for the new couple and their close kin, she kept asking for some of the food. As soon as one of the village women helping with the preparations gave her some, the girl was scolded by her grandmother—"Beggar!" she said.

The grandmother's epithet was apt. The girl had followed a beggar's strategy by making a nuisance of herself until her demand was met. Korean children commonly employ this technique, especially with their mothers. Wandering ghosts, too, use the same method in order to extort food offerings from their victims.

Shortly after being scolded, the young girl was physically punished. The newly engaged couple were sitting in a room by themselves, and the girl had been warned not to enter. Overcome by curiosity, she opened the door and peeked inside. For this, her grandmother hit her. It was not a forceful blow—the grandmother could easily have struck her much harder—but it brought the girl to tears anyway.

This act met with immediate approval from other village women, but for reasons we had not anticipated. These women, most of whom were wives and mothers of lineage members, noted that the girl had not tried to run as her grandmother walked threateningly toward her. A child who shows such stubbornness should be hit, one woman observed. Others readily assented. In fact, children of all ages often run away in time to escape punishment

---

[4] This type of celebration, which entails an exchange of gifts between the bride and the groom, began recently in Twisŏngdwi.

(e.g., Brandt 1971: 172). Their misbehavior is probably forgotten by the time they return, for a parent's or grandparent's anger seldom lasts very long. Defiance is a more serious offense.

Our impression is that in general, Korean childrearing practices lie between those of China and Japan in their degree of harshness. We never saw or heard of Korean children of any age subjected to the kind of physical abuse reported from Taiwan (M. Wolf 1972: 65–79; Ahern 1973: 214–15). Yet Korean parents are not as patient and nurturant as their Japanese counterparts (cf. Befu 1971: 151–70). A systematic survey of childrearing techniques in 186 societies coincides with our impressions. Korean practices were found to be less permissive than Japanese and more permissive than Chinese during both the early years of childhood (ages four to seven) and the later years (ages seven to twelve) (Barry et al. 1977: 203).

Although offspring gain more responsibility during adolescence and adulthood, they remain young children forever in the eyes of their parents. Perhaps this is true in most societies, but in Korea the prolongation of young childhood and dependence on parents is especially pronounced. Koreans themselves are well aware of this reluctance to acknowledge that children have matured: a well-known stereotype is the 80-year-old father who warns his 60-year-old son to be careful crossing the road.

Korean parents see no point in encouraging their children to be independent or self-reliant but instead place greater emphasis on dependence, obedience, and cooperation (Brandt 1971: 173). Most of our Korean friends were amused to learn that American parents give their children a periodic allowance and expect them to manage their own finances. Korean children demand and receive money from their parents as the need arises. Wealth belongs to the entire household, and though parents manage it they do not own it to the exclusion of their children. Another example of inculcating dependence can be seen in the Korean practice of controlling children by threatening them with ghosts, Americans, or other imaginary monsters rather than parental punishment. One of Korea's most popular folktales tells of a mother who tries to stop her child's crying by telling him that he will be eaten by a tiger (Choi In-hak 1979: 21–22). Kwŏn Myŏn-sik's wife once tried to get her three-year-old son to stop crying by telling him that Roger Janelli would give him an injection. By offering protection or siding with children against these external dangers, parents strengthen their offspring's emotional dependency (Hahn Dongse 1972: 186; Dix 1977: 84).

Among the most obvious examples of intergenerational dependency are the expenditures made by parents to educate their children and, more recently, to back their business ventures. One lineage family was reduced to near-poverty after it financed the eldest son's college education and his wife's yard-goods store in Seoul.

Heavy outlays for children's education and business ventures are based not only on parental affection but also on the expectation of reciprocity. Children are initially dependent on their parents, and in return parents are ultimately dependent on their children. Parents need care and support during old age as well as ritual sacrifices in the afterlife. An expenditure made for the sake of a child's future, therefore, is not lost to the parents. The economic and ritual interests of successive generations are identified rather than opposed in the minds of rural Korean villagers (Hahm Pyong-Choon 1975: 340; Dix 1977: 204; Yoon Hong-key 1976: 158–60).

In Twisŏngdwi, the corporate form of each household also inhibits independence and fosters mutual identification of successive generations. A number of legal and economic institutions maintain the unity of household members. Only one person per household votes at village meetings; taxes and corvée labor are assessed on a per-household basis; working children contribute all their earnings to the household before receiving in return a small portion for their own use; each household contributes one gift at weddings and funerals; population data at the township office are recorded according to household membership; and memberships in the village's cooperative societies are also on a household basis. In the one case where a father and his eldest son were both members of a cooperative society, informants regarded the case as anomalous and volunteered an explanation: when the society was founded, the son and his wife had temporarily moved out of his father's house because of family conflict.

In his analysis of intergenerational relations in Korea, educational psychologist Kim Jae-ŭn (1974: 43–58) labels the parent-child relationship "nondualistic." He argues that Korean children maintain a strong sense of dependence on parents throughout adolescence and later life. Unlike children in most Western societies, Korean children never develop a strong sense of independence or personal identity; instead, says Kim, they view themselves primarily as extensions of their parents. Similar observations have been advanced by several others (e.g., Hahn Dongse 1972; Lee Kwang-Kyu 1975: 63; Harvey and Chung 1980: 148; Brandt 1971: 173).

Although this view represents a consensus among writers on Korea, it fails to differentiate sons and daughters. Watching parents play with and fondle an infant, one senses little sexual discrimination; but actually differential treatment of children may begin at birth. Half-hearted attempts at female infanticide, though rare, were not unknown. One lineage woman, in the presence of her seven- or eight-year-old maternal granddaughter, told us how she had placed the girl on a cold floor immediately after birth, hoping she would die. "But look how well she grew up!" mused the grandmother. Unwanted female babies might be abandoned at the gate of a stranger's house (e.g., Harvey 1979: 63). One childless couple in Twisŏngdwi gained a baby daughter this way. Very likely someone in the village had secretly acted as intermediary, for the baby would not have been left by coincidence at the home of the couple most likely to welcome her. Our suspicions were aroused when one village woman subtly inquired about our own willingness to receive a child in the same way.

Korean women who have described childrearing practices (Harvey 1979: 260–69; Han 1949: 69–73) have paid more attention than most other ethnographers (e.g., Moon Seung Gyu 1971; Osgood 1951: 47, 49, 93–96; Brandt 1971: 171–74) to the differential treatment of sons and daughters. Harvey (1979: 263) maintains that Korean girls are expected to be cognizant of their inferiority by their third or fourth birthday. We have no way of knowing whether a child's awareness of sexual discrimination begins that early, but a girl of six could hardly be oblivious to her inferior status. Even casual observation and listening to village talk quickly teaches that boys are more highly valued than girls. The anxiety of a sonless mother is unmistakable. She may visit a local Buddhist temple, consult a fortune-teller, or try various other supernatural remedies (Cha Jae-ho et al. 1977: 115–23). Other villagers will readily comment about her misfortune. One lineage woman was obviously embarrassed when the spirit of her deceased mother-in-law spoke at a seance and chided her for producing only daughters. Another village woman who finally gave birth to a son after bearing several daughters said, "At last I can feel at ease." Such embarrassment and anxiety do not arise in women who have given birth only to sons. One of the female shamans who visited Twisŏngdwi to perform a ritual impressed on us the importance of having sons: "Daughters," she said, "are useless."

A girl who grows up in Twisŏngdwi not only sees and hears of sexual discrimination; she experiences it as well. Her parents will not make great sacrifices for her education. If she has a younger brother, she will probably be told to look after him, but boys are rarely asked to care for their younger sisters. A girl is not likely to have a major shamanistic ritual performed for her if she is ill, though the practice is not uncommon for a boy. And at her parents' sixtieth-birthday celebrations, her brothers will bow to their parents ahead of her, regardless of their respective ages.

The inferior treatment systematically meted out to daughters results from structural rather than affective causes. As Kwŏn Sang-sik's sister once observed, "A son doesn't care about you as much as a daughter does." But daughters are regarded as less precious than sons because they eventually marry out, become strangers, and contribute to another family's welfare. The cost of raising sons is an investment from which future benefits are realized; the cost of rearing daughters is a loss. This theme finds explicit expression in Korean folklore. A family that married off three daughters can sleep soundly without locking its gate, according to a popular Korean proverb (*ttari sesimyŏn munŭl yŏrŏ nok'o chanda*) (Yi Ki-mun 1962: 167); they would be too poor to tempt a thief.

Korean women are not merely separated physically from their natal households at marriage; in popular opinion, they shed their loyalties and affective ties as well. One Korean folktale tells of a married woman who cheats her natal family out of the auspicious grave site intended for her father so her father-in-law can occupy the site (Choi In-hak 1979: 146–47; Yoon Hong-key 1975: 28). A well-known Korean proverb says that "a female offspring is a thief" (*ttal chasigŭn todungnyŏnida*): first she takes a dowry out of the house at marriage, then if she returns for a visit, she is always looking for things to bring back to her husband's home (Yi Ki-mun 1962: 167). In fact, women who marry into Twisŏngdwi do not enjoy frequent contacts with their natal kin. None of their natal villages are within easy walking distance. Most return visits by married women are institutionalized and occur on specific occasions. A married woman returns to her natal village to give birth to her first child; to attend weddings, funerals, and sixtieth-birthday celebrations of her close natal kin; to participate in funerals and major mourning-period rites for her parents; and to make an annual visit shortly before the lunar New Year. According to a common Korean belief, a woman stops longing for her natal family after ten years of married life (Brandt 1971: 132; Harvey 1979: 269). In Twisŏngdwi, many older women have not been to their natal villages in years. The few who manage to retain some ties have a representative of their natal kin group at their funerals.

Because girls receive less supportive treatment, and are raised in anticipation of their becoming strangers to their natal households, it is unlikely that they depend on or identify with their parents to the same degree as their brothers. Some writers have suggested that this personality difference results from similar family structures and discriminatory treatment in China and Japan (M. Wolf 1972; Beardsley et al. 1959: 299). Women in these societies are also likely to be more self-reliant and individualistic than men. We shall pursue this comparison in Chapter 7.

Entering a Husband's Family

Because marriage transfers a bride to the groom's family, her adjustment to married life is far more difficult than his. As a new-comer to an already established household, she is expected to master its routines and recipes. Her husband and his family, by contrast, have little desire to alter their way of life for her. Everyone says that a bride's early years of marriage are especially difficult.

Despite their recognition of the bride's plight, a husband's family extends little sympathy to her. One young woman looked particularly forlorn on the third day of her wedding ceremony, when she was brought to bow before the ancestor tablets commemorated by her husband's segment of the lineage. Ignored by everyone until the last few ritual preparations were completed, she spent most of her time staring at the floor. Her act of obeisance required several arduous bows, and two young women of her husband's family were supposed to assist her. They often became engrossed in conversations with their natal kin, however, and left the bride to her own resources.

Nowadays, when love matches are more common, perhaps a bride's transition is eased by some support from her husband. But no man displays much affection for his wife in front of his parents or other people. Moreover, a new bride traditionally entered Twisŏngdwi as a stranger to her husband. Informants over 40 chuckled as they told us of seeing their spouse's face for the first time on their wedding day.

When marriages were arranged by parents, most brides came from families and lineages of comparable social standing. Most Koreans agree that a woman should not marry too far beneath her. Not only will her personal adjustment to humbler circumstances be more difficult, but her new family is likely to resent her former social standing. Neither should a woman marry far above her natal family: a potential groom's family and lineage would be reluctant to accept a woman of much lower social standing, since marrying down would adversely affect their own social status and the privileges, discussed in Chapter 5, that attend it.

Because the Twisŏngdwi lineage enjoyed more prestige than most of its near neighbors, it did not take wives from adjacent villages. Instead, lineage members found suitable partners in villages within ten to twenty kilometers. Had they been more illustrious, they would have had to search even farther afield (Deuchler 1977: 10).

Persons who married into the village commonly acted as go-betweens and helped arrange further marriages between their natal kin and the Twisŏngdwi lineage. As a result, several pairs of lineage members are related agnatically and through other genealogical ties as well. The maternal grandfather of Kwŏn Tŏk-su's children, for example, was the younger brother of Kwŏn Pyŏng-nyŏl's paternal grandmother. And the wife of Kwŏn Ŭng-su's son is the sister's daughter of Kim Pyŏng-ik, a son-in-law of Kwŏn Nam-sik.

Although some women had relatives already living in Twisŏngdwi when they married into the village, these relatives offered little assistance. They were rarely of the same hamlet, age, and sex—all of which would have been necessary for the bride to form a close alliance. Her husband's kin, moreover, would have resented such an alliance for it would have undermined their authority. Both in-laws and outhouses should be far away from the main house, according to a well-known Korean proverb (*sadon chip kwa twikkanŭn mŏlsurok chot'a*) (Yi Ki-mun 1962: 162, 266). Ties with natal kin are thought to make a bride's adjustment to her new home all the more difficult (Lee Kwang-Kyu 1975: 64).

A new daughter-in-law works under the constant supervision of her husband's mother, from whom she is expected to learn the family's traditions. Ideally, a bride should respect and obey her mother-in-law as she would her own mother, but no one is surprised if the two women cannot enjoy a completely amicable relationship. Conflict between them is as common in Korea as it is in China and Japan, where similar residence patterns prevail. Their mutual animosity is a recurrent theme in Korean oral literature. One humorous proverb, for example, describes a mother-in-law's reluctance to sponsor the shamanistic rite that she desires, because her first son's wife would be able to enjoy herself along with the other women (*kut hago sip'ŏdo manmyŏnŭri ch'um ch'unŭn kkol pogi silt'a*) (Yi Ki-mun 1962: 56).

Instances of mother-in-law and daughter-in-law conflict are not hard to find in Twisŏngdwi. One widowed mother moved out of her eldest son's house and went to live with her second son because she could not get along with her first son's wife. Some villagers attributed the suicide of another woman to the harsh treatment her daughter-in-law had given her. An elderly widow, whose children had all emigrated from Twisŏngdwi, went to live with her third son in a nearby community because her first son's wife made her feel unwelcome at their home in Seoul. In still another household, an eldest son and his wife temporarily moved out of his natal home. Informants said that the wife and the parents could not agree on the family budget, and also that the wife had a bad relationship with her mother-in-law.

Conflict between a young wife and her husband's mother is exacerbated by their rivalry over the affections of the young husband. A mother may view the wife as a threat to the warm relationship she had enjoyed with her son. One elderly widow, noted for her ribald humor and an especially difficult relationship with her daughter-in-law, put the matter quite bluntly: "Men forget about the hole they came out of and just think of the hole they enter."

As she struggles with her mother-in-law, a new wife is not likely to get much support from her husband's family. In a dispute, her husband's sisters usually side with their mother rather than with the newcomer. With her husband's father and elder brothers, she is supposed to have a formal relationship bordering on avoidance. When a wandering ghost caught one villager and made him ill, his younger brother's wife visited a shaman and obtained instructions for a cure. Her neighbors later criticized her for performing such a personal service on behalf of her husband's elder brother. Only with her husband's younger brothers can a woman enjoy an informal and often intimate relationship. After her own child died, one lineage woman wet-nursed her husband's infant brother. Such literal mothering is rare because of demographic circumstances, but not because of social norms.

Although a woman may not establish strong rapport with most of her husband's natal kin, she commonly enjoys warm relationships with her husband's brothers' wives. Kwŏn Pyŏng-ŏn's mother fondly remembered living with Kwŏn Pyŏng-nyŏl's mother during the early years of her marriage. One elderly widow, who married into the village at the age of thirteen, confessed that she disliked her husband during the first years of their marriage. To avoid his sexual advances, she often slept with her husband's elder brother's wife.

Even after establishing separate households, many women maintain their closest friendship with one of their husband's brothers' wives. Kwŏn O-sik's and Kwŏn Yŏng-sik's wives are next-door neighbors and are usually seen in each other's company. Kwŏn Ŭng-su's wife is the closest friend of Kwŏn Tŏk-su's widow. Such close relationships are possible because brothers usually live in the same hamlet and often have wives of similar ages. Moreover, as Lee Kwang-Kyu (1975: 95) has observed, the relationship between brothers' wives tends to follow that of their husbands. Compared to Chinese brothers, who are enmeshed in a competitive struggle over division of family property (Freedman 1958: 21–27, 134; Cohen 1976), Korean brothers enjoy a far more harmonious relationship (Lee Kwang-Kyu 1976: 14–16). We will explore the relation between property division and fraternal relations more fully in later chapters.

A woman's ties to her husband's kin, however, are always tenuous. As in Japan (Embree 1939: 213–14), her marriage may not even be legally registered for a few years (Knez 1959: 70). The lapse occasionally causes awkward problems. One lineage member died and left a small heir before his marriage had been recorded at the township office. Rather than being registered as an illegitimate offspring, the child was recorded as the adopted son of his father's younger brother. The lineage's genealogy and everyone in Twisŏngdwi naturally ignored this legal fiction.

A bride's social transition from her natal household and kin group to her husband's is really a lifelong process. Throughout her married life, a woman is a marginal member of both sets of kin. At marriage, she does not assume her husband's surname but keeps her own. To her natal family, as we have seen, her marriage had made her an outsider (*ch'ulga oein*).

As elsewhere in East Asia, a young wife strengthens her ties to her husband's family and enhances her own status when she gives birth to her first child. At the least, she demonstrates her ability to produce offspring. If the child is a son, the event is of greater importance. A male child is a more welcome contribution to her husband's household and descent line because he helps to ensure their continuity for another generation.

Even the birth of a son, however, does not guarantee that a woman will be remembered forever as her husband's spouse. If her husband dies young—and sometimes even if he does not—a wife may leave his household and village, remarry, and end her ties to his kin. Normally she leaves her children with his family, for they are unlikely to surrender these offspring, especially if they are boys. Her new husband, moreover, would not welcome them. Remarriage for women is still considered unchaste in rural Korea and receives frequent condemnation in Korean oral literature (Kim Jae-On 1977). Children by a former husband would be a public advertisement of a wife's sullied past.

Only by dying as a member of her husband's family can a woman ensure her marital status and thus be certain that her death-day will be recorded in the lineage's genealogy and observed annually by her descendants. As Lee Kwang-Kyu (1975:

62–63) has pointed out, it is a woman's death that makes her a full-fledged member of her husband's kin group. Evidently this is why part of her marriage document (Dredge n.d.: 9), or pieces of red and blue-green cloth symbolizing marriage, are buried with her.

Because a married woman joins her husband's family later than he does and holds only conditional membership in his household, it is unlikely that she depends on or identifies with his parents as strongly as he does with them, or they with him. He is their precious child from birth. In short, husbands and wives have very different relationships with the senior members of the household. This point may be obvious, but it is extremely important for understanding the psychological dynamics of ancestor worship. The husband's parents become the primary ancestors with whom the couple must deal, and husbands and wives deal with these ancestors in very different ways.

Parents and Their Adult Sons

A younger son becomes a household head (*hoju*) and receives his inheritance within a few years of marriage. Property division occurs whenever a younger son moves out and establishes his own household. Though he is always allotted less than his eldest brother, the respective shares vary greatly, depending on the needs and other circumstances of their families (Lee Kwang-Kyu 1975: 74–79; Pak Ki-hyuk 1975: 100–101). Typically, their father determines the allotments. Usually he still controls his household when his younger sons move out; occasionally, however, a father has already surrendered effective headship or died before division. In such cases, the eldest son determines how much each son receives; in this small minority of instances fraternal conflict over property division is more likely to arise.

Unlike his younger brothers, the eldest son is formally denied household headship and ownership of household property until the death of his father. Even after an 82-year-old lineage member had become senile, his 66-year-old eldest son insisted that his father was still head of their household. The Korean legal code likewise upholds the ownership rights of a household head over his household's property until his death (Bae Kyung Sook 1973: 67, 147).

Formal titles and legal statutes, however, are often incongruent with other social facts. In southwestern Korea, fathers apparently retain authority throughout their lives, but in other regions, as in Twisŏngdwi, they do not (Lee Kwang-Kyu 1975: 79–81). After reaching the age of 60, both men and women are expected to begin passing on the responsibilities of farm and household management to the succeeding generation. According to the traditional system of time reckoning prevalent throughout East Asia, 60 years is the length of one complete cycle.[5] Thus, a parent's sixtieth birthday is marked by a major celebration, traditionally held to denote the completion of an active life (Song Yo-in 1976). The opinions of the aged are supposed to be respected, and younger people find it difficult to do anything that their parents strongly oppose; but it is also thought that elders should not interfere too greatly in day-to-day decision making. In advanced old age, parents become entirely dependent on their children, especially their eldest son and his wife, for their care and support. A 65-year-old widow who rented out a room in her home faithfully handed over the rent money each month to her son and daughter-in-law, though she sometimes complained that they did not give her enough spending money. She was shocked when we suggested she keep the rent money for herself.

The discrepancy between legal codes and village traditions was clearly illustrated in the 1978 village census. During the initial tally, Kwŏn Kap-sik was listed as the head of his household, though he was an eldest son and his 72-year-old father was still living in his household. (The father died a few months later.) When the census data were collated and transferred to the township office's records, however, the listing was rearranged to show the father as household head. This was necessary because the township records follow the civil code in designating a father as the legal head of household until his death.

De facto transfer of household headship is marked by a shift of residence within the home (Lee Kwang-Kyu 1975: 81–82). The couple who effectively manage the household occupy the "inner room" (*an-bang*), members of the succeeding generation occupy the "opposite room" (*kŏnnŏp-pang*), and surviving mem-

---

[5] For a description of this system of time reckoning, see D. Y. Janelli (1977: 43–45).

bers of the previous generation live in an outer room (*sarang-bang*) (see Figure 5). As Kwŏn Yŏng-sik noted, a couple's life history is marked by a series of changes in residence: they move from the opposite room to the inner room when they assume headship of their household, and they retire to the outer room when they surrender it to the succeeding generation.

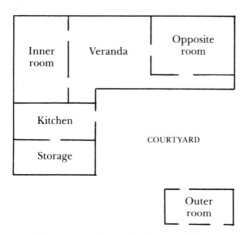

Fig. 5. Floor plan of a typical Twisŏngdwi house.

Although the sixtieth-birthday celebration and shift in residence both signal the surrender of household authority by the senior generation, neither event marks a sudden transfer of authority, and rarely do the two events coincide. The transfer occurs gradually as the balance of power shifts from one generation to the next. During their joint tenure, fathers and sons are really partners in their household estate, their powers waning and waxing respectively as the years pass.

This transmission of authority does not always proceed smoothly. We have already noted the reluctance of Twisŏngdwi elders to relinquish leadership of the lineage and village to younger men. Competition over household authority is not as obvious, but it certainly exists—the eldest son and his wife who temporarily established their own household are a good example. Some informants said it came about because members of the two generations could not agree on how to allocate their house-

An eldest son and his wife bow after presenting wine to his parents at the sixtieth-birthday celebration of his father.

hold budget. In another lineage household, a father confessed that he is glad his sons were born relatively late in his life. His kinsmen even envy him, he claimed, because he will not have to surrender headship of his household until he is very old and really needs to be cared for.

Obvious conflict between sons and parents in Twisŏngdwi is rare, partly because the lineage members desire to maintain gentry standards of behavior. In another Korean village, Vincent Brandt (1971: 202) noted that overt conflict between sons and parents occurred primarily in non-gentry families. In yet another Korean village, where the dominant lineage could advance only the weakest claim to gentry status, father-son conflict sometimes erupted in violent and bloody clashes (Dix 1977: 120).

Some effort at controlling hostility toward parents is probably made throughout Korea. Psychiatrist Hahn Dongse (1972) wrote that repression of hostility toward superiors, including parents, is a major cause of emotional disturbances among Korean men. Cornelius Osgood, in his study of a non-gentry rural village, noted how sons repress hostility toward their fathers and exclaimed: "God only knows how many Korean sons must hate their fathers" (1951: 48). Yet another illustration can be seen in this excerpt from a Korean short story: "Chŏngsik wondered what would happen if father died. So many unexpected deaths were reported in the papers nowadays. He remembered that he had often wished father would die when he was whipped for poor report cards in his primary school days. Chŏngsik shuddered with shame for so thinking" (Lih Jeong-duc 1966: 29).

Even during adolescence, a son's relationship with his father is stiff and formal. In public at least, fathers remain aloof from their adolescent and grown-up sons. Sons in turn are expected to defer to their father's wishes and respect his authority. We never saw a mature son talk back to or disagree publically with his father. Thus adolescent and adult sons are rarely at ease in their father's presence. Even mature sons may not smoke in front of their fathers, and if they drink wine, they must turn away as if to make their drinking less obvious.

Though to a lesser degree, similar deference is due all senior agnates. Some men smoke in the presence of their father's cousins, but they either turn their backs or hide their cigarettes in cupped hands. We have seen that they may disagree with senior kinsmen at "democratic" village meetings but not at lineage gatherings. Occasionally, however, such restrictions impose a sort of noblesse oblige on lineage elders as well. Once we were walking with elderly Kwŏn Hae-su when he unexpectedly slowed his pace. He pointed to some young men of the lineage walking ahead of us and explained, "If I catch up with them, they'll have to stop smoking."

Fathers and their adult sons, especially their eldest sons,[6] usually avoid each other at public occasions in Twisŏngdwi. Such avoidance may well be a means of averting open conflict, as Meyer Fortes (1959; 1961) suggests in his analysis of institutionalized avoidance customs among the Tallensi of West Africa. Although Koreans lack explicit taboos on this point, it is readily apparent that mature sons are expected to keep clear of their fathers in public. One eldest son with whom we had been talking got up and departed as soon as his elderly father appeared at our door. He excused himself simply by stating that he had to leave now that his father had come. On another occasion, when the father had accompanied us to a village meeting, another lineage member politely asked him to leave so that his son could attend. Fathers and eldest sons do not attend village meetings together, apparently because only one man is needed to represent the household.

Intergenerational conflict in Korea, however, should be sharply differentiated from that reported from sub-Saharan societies. In sub-Saharan societies the conflict arises out of the opposing interests, both economic and jural, of successive generations (Fortes 1961; Goody 1962). Sons profit at their fathers' expense. Property and other important rights are vested in persons rather than households, and the welfare of parents, in this world or the next, is not seen to depend on the welfare of their offspring. In Korea, by contrast, intergenerational dependency and the mutual identification of sons and parents overwhelm any opposition of interests. Because eldest sons are obligated to care for their

---

[6] Of the 30 male lineage household heads, 17 were eldest sons because they had no elder male siblings who lived to maturity. Another had assumed the duties of eldest son upon the death of his elder brother, who had married and left a young heir. Yet another had become an eldest son by adoption. In his study of another Korean village, Kim Taik-Kyoo (1964: 93) also found three-fifths of the households headed by eldest sons.

aged parents, they must assume at least de facto control of the household and its property; otherwise, they cannot fulfill their responsibilities. Thus, fathers and sons argue over who is better able to manage their common estate. Conflict arises because the old view "young people" as incompetent children while the young regard the old as senile and old-fashioned.

The identification of a father's best interests with those of his sons was particularly evident in one informant's account of an incident in his family. It was the only time an adult spoke freely to us of "conflict" with a parent. Family quarreling, especially between a son and his parents, is so embarrassing that normally Koreans are very reluctant to discuss it with outsiders. Yet our informant volunteered his account without shame, for he used it not to illustrate intergenerational conflict but to demonstrate the difficulties that arise when caring for aged parents.

Because the father seemed very lonely after his wife died, his sons found another woman to provide him with companionship in his old age. Unfortunately the woman turned out to be a schemer with whom their father became helplessly infatuated. She soon began to persuade him to transfer all the property of his household to her name. When he finally consented, our informant moved out of the house and refused to return until his father had rid himself of the woman. The old man eventually yielded, for he knew he could not live without the help of his eldest son.

That incident was not a unique occurrence. We also know of a widower in Seoul who had planned to invite a woman into his house, but his children argued that she had sinister designs on their household's property. The man eventually yielded, recognizing that his own welfare was best promoted by protecting the property for his children. Thus, even where intergenerational conflict explicitly involves property, informants do not view the interests of successive generations as antithetical.

Because an eldest son inherits most of his natal household's property, the burden of caring for aged parents falls primarily, but not exclusively, on him. Junior sons also share this obligation. Koreans do not specify an exact proportion of responsibility to be borne by each son; instead, all are ultimately responsible for the welfare of their parents. If an eldest son fails to provide adequately for them, the contingent responsibilities of junior sons become readily apparent. One lineage widow, whose children had all emigrated from Twisŏngdwi, went to live with her third son in a nearby village because she preferred it to the home of her eldest son in Seoul. In another lineage household, the eldest son died and left the care of his mother to his younger brother. Even if an eldest son faithfully discharges all his obligations, however, younger sons are expected to contribute at least occasionally to their parents' welfare, and they commonly provide gifts of food, clothing, or money.

All sons have at least some responsibility toward their aged parents because of the reciprocal dependence of successive generations. Parents may depend on all their sons because all their sons have depended on them. As Koreans see it, each son incurs a debt in his early years, one later to be repaid. Yet offspring can never repay parents fully for the gift of life, for the affection and indulgence that parents so freely bestow during their children's earliest years, and for the many sacrifices they make on their behalf (Lim Yoon-taeck 1979). As the texts recited at some ancestor rituals put it, "An offspring's debt to his parents is as limitless as the sky."

Such is the ethic of filial piety. No other moral axiom has received greater emphasis throughout the history of Korean society. When the study of Confucianism was instituted in Korea during the seventh and eighth centuries A.D., the *Hsiao Ching* (Korean: *Hyo kyŏng*), the Chinese classic on filial piety, was among the first texts adopted (Henthorn 1971: 66–67; Yi Hŭi-dŏk 1973: 8). The proper relationship between father and son soon became the paradigm for all hierarchical relationships in a moral society, including that between subject and ruler. During the Koryŏ and Yi dynasties, the central government promoted filial piety by rewarding outstanding instances and prescribing harsh penalties for infractions (Yi Hŭi-dŏk 1973). During the early Yi dynasty, when neo-Confucianism was adopted as the state creed, the court ordered the promulgation of exemplary cases of conduct, including filial piety. These were published in classical Chinese as well as the new native Korean alphabet, with illustrations, in order to encourage such behavior among the masses (Chang Dae Hong 1962: 103–5, 301). Included were stories of sons who fed their own flesh and blood to their ailing parents.

Filial piety was a virtue not only supported by the court. Actual instances of sons feeding their own flesh and blood to parents seem to have occurred until the end of the Yi dynasty (e.g., Lim Yoon-taeck 1979). A survey undertaken in 1971 revealed that 87 percent of rural married women thought children's support of their aged parents was always necessary; only 11 percent thought that the necessity for care might depend on individual circumstances; and a scant 2 percent thought it unnecessary (Moon Hyun-Sang et al. 1973: 48).

Another indication of the importance of filial piety in Korean society can be found in oral literature. Folktales about feeding and caring for aged parents abound (Choi In-hak 1979: 163–76) and are viewed as an important means of morally educating children. When asked, "What kind of stories are instructive for children?" 47 percent of women in rural villages selected stories of filial piety in preference to stories about famous scientists or businessmen (42 percent) or "interesting fairy tales or old tales" (11 percent) (Chung Bom Mo et al. 1972: 474–75).

In Twisŏngdwi, the village code of ethics imposes a set of very high standards for the care and treatment of parents, one that few can satisfy. When conflicts arise in a household between the retired generation and their successors, villagers both young and old usually sympathize with the parents and find fault with the younger generation. Allegations of neglect and mistreatment are heard far more often than cases of exemplary filial piety. By contrast, no one ever criticizes their neighbors for rearing children harshly.

Korean children, especially eldest sons, are thus confronted by a difficult responsibility in later life. Though everyone openly acknowledges that caring for parents is onerous and demanding, offspring must accept this burden as a moral obligation. Sons do not admit openly—perhaps not even to themselves—that they would like to be rid of their parents, but the idea has certainly crossed their minds. It is found in the Koryŏjang story, one of the most popular legends of Korea. The plot is based on an alleged old custom of carrying off and disposing of parents when they became infirm. Our informants thought that the custom actually prevailed during the Koryŏ dynasty, though we know of no historical evidence that the custom ever existed at all.

In the past—well, long ago, there wasn't just one person, but several people were living then.[7] That's the way they lived. [There was a man who thought:] "My parents have lived for such a long time that I should load my mother on a pack carrier, [take her away,] and bury her in the hollow of a grave [lit., must do Koryŏjang]. She simply can't stay here any longer."

So since his mother had lived for so long, he loaded her on his pack carrier and went off to bury her. And when he went off to the mountains, the [old woman's] grandson, who was just a small boy, followed after him. When the man brought his mother there and buried her, his son picked up the pack carrier, which his father had thrown away, and began to follow him home. "Son, why are you bringing back the pack carrier?" asked the father. "Since we have buried grandmother we can get rid of that too."

"No, father. When you become old like grandmother I will bury you this way, so I really have to bring back the pack carrier."

"This is a real problem," thought the father. "I really didn't have to bury my mother." So he took the pack carrier and went back with his son to the place where he had buried his mother, to the place where he had left the food for his mother to eat until she died. He took the carrier, dug out his mother, put her once again on the pack carrier, and brought her back home.

He carried her back home and she lived for a long, long time; and then she died. Again he put her on his pack carrier and again he had to get rid of her. Since she had died, he had to get rid of her. So he loaded her up, his mother who had lived a long time, and threw her away. But after he had gotten rid of her, he didn't like to look at it [his mother's exposed corpse]. "A beast would be able to bite it, or tear off [some flesh] and eat it; and that would be awful," he thought. So he went back and got a shovel, dug the ground, and buried her. It really looked nice after that. Neither would the animals be able to get at it, nor could the crows tear at it. It was really nice.

And so, then he threw away the pack carrier. And his son said, "Yes. This is the way it should be done. I'll make a nice grave like this for you when you become old and die." That's what he said. And when [his father] died, that's what he did. When the man's life was over and he died, his son made a fine grave for him.

Everyone we asked in Twisŏngdwi knew the Koryŏjang story. The above text was given to us by Wŏn Yu-gil, Kwŏn Pyŏng-ŏn's

[7] "A long time ago, there was a person . . ." is a very common opening for Korean folktales. Kwŏn Pyŏng-ŏn's mother explicitly rejects this formulaic opening and stresses that several people (a society) existed at the time of the events to be described. Her treatment of the formulaic opening is an example of what Alan Dundes (1966) identified as "oral literary criticism."

58-year-old mother. Her version entails an elderly mother, as do many other Korean versions, but elderly fathers are more common. In some versions, moreover, the grandson is absent, and the son decides not to abandon his parent when he learns that the parent has been kindly marking the trail so that the son would not get lost on the way home. Our informant's version is unique only in its inclusion of the second episode involving death and grave construction.

The total inactivity and dependence of the elderly parent, depicted in all versions of the Koryŏjang story, is often seen in real life. The four elderly lineage men and women that we knew just before their deaths were all surviving spouses who spent most of their final months secluded in their rooms. Kwŏn Hae-su told us in the summer of 1978 that his death was not far off. The recent loss of Kwŏn Nam-sik had made him the oldest man of the lineage, so he knew his own funeral would be the next. Since he was one of our nearest neighbors and an especially kind informant, we could not avoid noticing how he kept to his room and was seldom seen about the village during the last weeks of our fieldwork. He died a few months after we left Twisŏngdwi.

The correspondence between the story and social reality evidently explains its distribution in East Asia. Its immense popularity in Japan as well as Korea (Dorson 1962: 222–23; Seki 1963: 183–84; Ikeda 1971: 218–19; Choi In-hak 1979: 292) evidently reflects the close similarity between the powerless parent depicted in the story and a fully retired parent in real life (Nakane 1967: 18–21). In China, where fathers are less likely to surrender authority during their lifetimes, the story has not been widely reported (Ting 1978: 157; Eberhard 1937: 115–17, 256–57). From Taiwan, for example, comes an altogether different tale of what "used to" happen when men became old: their children would attempt to murder them and eat their flesh (Ahern 1973: 205–6).

Adoption

Though Twisŏngdwi villagers sympathize with elderly parents who must depend on their offspring, they know that parents without male issue are far worse off. Not only will they suffer in their old age, but their ancestor rituals will also be neglected. If the couple is wealthy and has a daughter, they may use some of their property to induce a son-in-law to move into their village so their daughter can care for them. But even those parents are still left with their ritual problem unresolved. That is why, say informants, sonless parents have to adopt a male heir. The adoption may occur while one or both parents are still living, or a son may be adopted to them after both have died. The adoptive heir inherits their property, cares for them in their final years if necessary, and officiates at their funerals and ancestor rituals.

The Twisŏngdwi lineage's portion of the latest Andong Kwŏn genealogy (*Andong Kwŏn-ssi sebo* 1961, vol. 2: 97–104) includes fifteen cases of adoption, all within the past 200 years. To the thirteen cases for which full data are provided we can add another adoption that occurred in the mid 1970's, more than a decade after the genealogy was published.[8]

These fourteen cases show that heirs were always agnates of the adopting parents. This has apparently been true of adoptive heirs throughout Korea in the last few centuries (Peterson 1974; 1977), but in earlier years Korean adoption was not so rigidly agnatic. Sisters' sons, daughters' sons, wives' natal kin, and even non-kin were appointed heirs (Peterson 1977; Lee Kwang-Kyu 1977b: 328). This strict adherence to agnatic principles found in Korea during the past few hundred years is unparalleled elsewhere in East Asia (Wolf and Huang 1980; Befu 1962).

Adoptions in Twisŏngdwi also show that the lineage strictly followed three other rules, all of which are prevalent throughout Korea. Adoptive sons were always taken from the generation to which a natural heir would have belonged; parents never gave up their only son for adoption; and a brother's son was selected as heir whenever available (ten cases). When the adopting father had no brothers (three cases), or when none of his brothers had more than one son (one case), heirs were adopted from first cousins or more distant agnates.

When adoption involves the transfer of a son between households headed by brothers, the relative seniority of the brothers

[8] Unfortunately, we examined only Kwŏn Po's portion of the Andong Kwŏn genealogy (*Andong Kwŏn-ssi sebo* 1961, vol. 2: 66–104). The two incomplete cases may have involved exchanges with households outside of Kwŏn Po's branch. In one case, the genealogy shows a son was adopted from his father's descent line, but we were unable to find the descent line to which he was adopted. In the other case, we were unable to find the descent line of the natural father of an adopted son. Genealogical falsification is possible in the latter case, but not likely. As in the other cases of adoption, the name of the adopted son's natural father is included along with the usual biographical details.

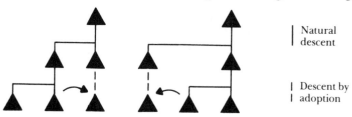

Fig. 6. Usual patterns of adoption.

usually determines whether an eldest or junior son is selected as the adoptee. As illustrated in Figure 6, younger brothers give their eldest sons to eldest brothers (four cases), but eldest brothers give one of their younger sons to younger brothers (four cases). This rule, which is common throughout Korea (Peterson 1974: 29; Lee Kwang-Kyu 1977a: 14–15) was violated only twice. In both cases, eldest brothers were given younger sons.

The nonreciprocal transfer of eldest sons to eldest brothers reflects the special status accorded a primogeniture descendant (*chongson*: eldest son, eldest son's eldest son, etc.) by those who belong to junior descent lines. Just as an elder brother has a higher status than his younger siblings, so his own eldest son retains some of that status over the younger brothers' sons. Giving eldest sons to senior descent lines, therefore, preserves the relative statuses of siblings based on birthright. One who had enjoyed superior status as an eldest brother before adoption enjoys it as a primogeniture descendant after adoption. Occasional violations of this adoption rule wreak havoc on the relative seniority of descent lines (Shima 1979: 106–9).

Violations occur because Korean adoption practices also attempt to preserve the respective property rights of descendants. Since an eldest brother inherits more property, he is usually wealthier than his younger siblings. If he dies without descendants, his younger brother would inherit his larger share of property from their parents and in turn pass it on to his own eldest son. That eldest son, by becoming the adoptive heir of the elder brother, therefore inherits essentially the same property he would have without the adoption.

These considerations appear to have motivated the two exceptional cases in which younger brothers gave younger sons to their eldest brothers. In both instances, the two younger brothers were wealthier than their eldest brothers. One was a government official during the Yi dynasty; the other had accumulated one of the largest land holdings in the village during the Japanese era. In both cases, their eldest sons would evidently have lost substantial property by becoming the adoptive heirs of senior but poorer descent lines.

Korean adoption rules minimize the disruptive effects of an adoption on descent and inheritance; in addition, the preference for an adoptive heir from a brother's rather than a more distant household minimizes the genealogical rearrangements caused by the adoption. As a result, the adoption also disrupts as little as possible affective ties between kin.

Although adoption is the accepted means for remedying the absence of a natural heir, informants stated openly that adopting a son is not nearly as desirable as producing a son of one's own. This attitude is not without some factual basis. Though adopted sons usually fulfill their ritual obligations to the letter, the care and support they provide their aged adoptive parents usually invites more criticism than that provided by natural sons. One adopted son, for example, migrated to Seoul and took his widowed adoptive mother with him, but she found life in Seoul intolerable and returned to Twisŏngdwi. She lived there for many years, sadly neglected by her adopted son. When she died, some villagers expressed concern that the adopted son might not even return for her funeral. Until the son arrived, the old woman's nephew (her husband's brother's son) had to assume temporarily the role of chief mourner.

The fragility of adoptive ties is also evident in the way lineage members trace genealogical links between each other. Though their printed genealogy is organized according to adoptive rather than blood ties, lineage members use only blood ties to identify the genealogical positions of an adoptee and his first few generations of descendants vis-à-vis their closest kin. Cases of adoption between distant households, because they entail greater genealogical changes, reveal even more clearly the greater importance attached to blood ties. When Kwŏn Kap-sik's mother died, for example, Kwŏn Sŏng-sik wore a mourning hat, just like Kwŏn Kap-sik's other close kinsmen. The lineage's genealogy (see Figure 2) shows, however, that they are ninth cousins (eighteen *ch'on* genealogical distance), distant relatives even by Korean standards. Though their paternal grandfathers had been brothers by birth, Kwŏn Sŏng-sik's grandfather had been adopted into another branch of the lineage. When we asked Kwŏn Sŏng-sik why he wore the mourning hat, he replied simply that he was Kwŏn Kap-sik's second cousin (six *ch'on*) and thereby ignored his own grandfather's adoption. Similarly, when observing the domestic ancestor rites and other duties of kinship, Kwŏn Sŏng-sik and the other descendants of his adopted grandfather act as if they were still members of Kwŏn Kap-sik's segment of the lineage.

The inability of adoption to bring about its intended consequences is also reflected in the folklore of Twisŏngdwi. At one seance in the village, a sonless ancestress complained pitifully about her fate and lamented that her adopted son was useless (*yangjaga ssŭlte ŏpsŏ*). The following legend, recounted to us by U Chong-sang, Kwŏn Tŏk-su's 59-year-old widow, expresses the same sentiments.[9]

There are many adopted sons. One adopted son was doing an ancestor ritual for his adoptive father. He put out two bowls of rice [for the adoptive father and mother]. But someone else saw what was happening. The adoptive father was pushed aside and the natural father came and ate the food—yes, the natural father. So adopted sons are useless; that's what people say these days.

If one digs up the root of a *chilgyŏngi* [*Plantago asiatica*], . . . [inaudible] . . . three parts, and looks through it, he can see spirits. That's what the old people said.

The natural father came and sat at the [food-offering] table, and the adoptive father sat under the table trying to eat.

And so ancestors certainly exist. Their spirits are absolutely real.

Beginning with the following chapter, we will explore in detail the relationships between the Twisŏngdwi lineage and their "absolutely real" ancestors.

[9] See Chapter 7 for a Chinese version of this narrative.

❦ 3 ❦

Becoming an Ancestor

The death of a parent initiates a series of rituals and evokes a set of beliefs that transform rather than sever relations between successive generations. In the Korean ancestor cult, deceased parents retain their dependency on offspring; filial obligations are perpetuated through ritual services; and ancestors continue to influence the lives of their descendants. As we present the salient features and the diverse traditions of this cult, beginning with the rites and ideas surrounding death and mourning, we give particular attention to its articulation with family and lineage organization.

Funeral Rites

Almost immediately after death, the deceased's body is laid out on its back. The thumbs are tied together with string, as are the two big toes. These are practical measures, say informants, taken to ensure that the corpse will later be in the proper position for shrouding and coffining. Ritual manuals and etiquette books (e.g., Ross 1879: 320–52) make no mention of tying thumbs and toes; however, the procedure is found at Buddhist funerals elsewhere in Asia (Spiro 1970: 250; Tambiah 1970: 190). Evidently it has remained from the era when Buddhism dominated the cult of the dead in Korea.[1]

Other funeral practices and related beliefs also suggest Buddhist influences. After positioning the corpse, the next step of a Korean funeral is to set out three bowls of rice (*saja-bap*) just outside the main gate of the deceased's house. The rice is for three

[1] Buddhism itself was transformed over several centuries and during its travels from India to Japan. From the time of its introduction to Korea, in the late fourth and early fifth centuries A.D., until the end of the Koryŏ dynasty, Buddhism appears to have been especially concerned with beliefs about the afterlife and rituals for the dead (see Wright 1959; Ch'en 1964; 1973; R. Smith 1974b: 16–20; Deuchler 1980b: 644–45).

messengers sent by King Yama (*Yŏmna taewang*), the Buddhist ruler of the underworld, to fetch the soul of the newly dead. Informants envision these messengers as very nasty creatures. Armed with chains and clubs, they push and pull their reluctant charge on a difficult and painful journey to the land of the dead. The hands and face of the corpse are covered with cloth to protect them from brambles encountered along the way. After completing their journey, the dead are judged and assigned new social identities in the otherworld (*chŏsŭng*). The righteous and charitable receive high positions and easy work; the wicked are given low positions of constant toil. Suicides, polluted by their act of self-destruction, must wait three years before they are sufficiently purified to enter the otherworld. Women who die in childbirth are similarly polluted, but no time limit is set for their purification.

Few Twisŏngdwi informants commit themselves wholeheartedly to these beliefs. Kwŏn O-sik and Kwŏn Sang-sik, both noted for their expertise on ritual matters, doubt that a person's soul is really taken away by the messengers. They claim that the soul remains in its mourning shrine (*sangch'ŏng*) until the shrine is dismantled at the end of the mourning period, and then the soul goes to the grave of the deceased.

Other Twisŏngdwi informants offered the explanation that each person has three souls, only one of which is taken to the otherworld. This belief was flatly denied by the ritual experts, however, and even those who offered it lacked both conviction and consensus about the location of each soul. Kwŏn Pyŏng-nyŏl's mother said that perhaps one soul went to the grave, another received the ancestor rituals offered by descendants, and the third remained in the house. But Kwŏn Pyŏng-ŏn, her nephew, noted that some families opened the gates of their houses before performing an ancestor ritual. To him, this act implied that the soul in the grave came to the house to receive its ritual offerings.[2] Perhaps one of the souls was carried away by the messengers, as some people said, he speculated. Kwŏn Chang-sik said, however, that the messengers carry away the deceased himself (or herself), and not one of the three souls: they are located in the grave, house, and air, respectively. Finally, Kwŏn Chŭng-sik's mother said that the soul in the house receives ancestor rituals, another stays at the grave, and the third is rein-

[2] For expressions of this belief, see the folktales in Chapter 4.

carnated, usually in the form of an animal, typically a bird. A few weeks after a death occurs, she said, the deceased's family visits a shaman who performs a special ritual (*chari-gŏji*) to divine the reincarnated form of their relative. Persons with red marks on their faces, she added, are twice-born human beings.

These various opinions about the fate of the soul demonstrate the uncertainty and diversity of beliefs about the afterlife found among the Twisŏngdwi lineage. Unlike the shaman in a neighboring village, who claims to have visited the otherworld, Twisŏngdwi informants do not provide vivid details or speak with confidence about life after death. We exasperated Kwŏn Tŏk-su's widow by pressing her for a description of the afterlife. "I'll have to die before I can find out," she finally protested. A Korean proverb expresses the same idea: "One has to die in order to know the otherworld [*chugŏ poaya chŏsŭng alji*]" (Yi Ki-mun 1962: 452).

It is difficult to explain the lineage's diverse views and individuals' lack of certainty in terms of variation in regional culture or religious commitment or cultural change. The women cited above, though they are not natives of Twisŏngdwi, all came from villages within twenty kilometers, and each had married into Twisŏngdwi about 50 years ago. Like almost everyone else in Twisŏngdwi, none follows the teachings of any organized religion.[3] Indeed, they do not even regard King Yama, the messengers, and reincarnation as Buddhist concepts; nor is any hint of these ideas found in the ritual manuals and etiquette books that prescribe funeral procedures. Finally, the folkloric nature of the soul's multiple locations, and the lack of consensus about such matters, appear in similar reports from elsewhere in Korea (Gifford 1892: 169–73; Clark 1932: 113; Biernatzki 1967: 139–40; Ŏm Mun-ho 1972: 214; Dix 1977: 257) as well as from Japan (R. Smith 1974b: 63–68) and China (Potter 1970a: 149; Harrell 1979: 521–23).

Diversity and doubt in personal religious opinion do not prevent Twisŏngdwi residents from acting in concerted fashion whenever a death occurs. Kin and neighbors begin arriving at the house very shortly after the death to assist with the many tasks

---

[3] Two lineage households included professed Christians. We have excluded their beliefs and practices from our study. Among the rest of the lineage, we found an almost total lack of participation in Buddhist rituals. Even touristic visits to temples were uncommon.

of the funeral. Two lineage men go to Osan to buy materials for mourning and burial clothes. Several women sew the mourning garments while others prepare food for the many visitors who come to help and to pay their respects. (Some villagers said they were reluctant to eat food prepared at a funeral lest some ghost follow them home or other misfortune befall them; but a large number of people are fed nevertheless.) Many men take turns holding a vigil through the night in the room where the corpse is laid out, shielded from view by a folding screen. Other men gather wood for cooking fires, carry the funeral bier, and dig the grave on the day of burial. A funeral in Twisŏngdwi is a village affair. The house in mourning becomes for a few days the center of social life in the community.

Funerals are expected to last "three days": the day of death, the following day, and the day of burial. This time span may be changed, however, depending on the wealth and prestige of the deceased's family. As Paul Dredge (1978: 8–9) has noted, a longer funeral allows time to notify a wider circle of people who can then come and pay their respects. This is especially useful if the deceased or the survivors are well known outside the village. It also permits a greater display of status and affluence by feasting more people over a longer time.

Participating in a funeral serves primarily to cement social ties with the survivors; most visitors are less concerned with the deceased. This typical ordering of priorities is expressed in a humorous (and somewhat cynical) Korean proverb: "There are many funeral participants when a high official's dog dies, but nobody comes when the official dies" (Harvey 1979: 169; Yi Ki-mun 1962: 137).

Cosmological reasons are sometimes cited to justify the lengthening or shortening of a funeral (Dix 1980: 50) but do not appear to be regarded seriously. Our limited evidence indicates that cosmology is rarely advanced unless it justifies decisions already prompted by other considerations. When the elderly mother of a poor and unrelated household died, her funeral lasted only two days. Informants pointed out that she had died on the penultimate day of the month, and thus a normal funeral of three days would have lasted "two months" (the month of death and the month of burial). It was better to shorten the funeral to two days, they maintained, since an even number of months would have been inauspicious. Besides, they quickly added, there were not many friends and relatives outside the village who needed to be notified. When a well-to-do lineage member died, on the other hand, his funeral took four days. The extra day was necessary, said informants, because the almanac had stated that one of the first three days was inauspicious for dealing with corpses. In fact, the deceased also had several sons and grandsons who had achieved some social prominence outside the village. By all accounts, his funeral was a truly splendid affair and was well attended: some people even came in private automobiles.

In a usual three-day funeral, the corpse is dressed (*yŏm*) on the second evening after death. This act is particularly important, say informants, because it transforms the deceased into an ancestor (*chosang*). Visitors who arrive before the dressing to express their condolences are supposed to bow only to the chief mourner (*sangju*), not the corpse, because the deceased has not yet attained ancestral status. Yet some people bow to both mourner and corpse anyway.

The new ancestral status of the deceased is signaled in several ways. Immediately after the corpse is dressed, it is coffined and returned to where it had lain, and the screen that had shielded it from the living is turned around. A red cloth banner, which identifies the deceased and is later buried with the corpse, is hung upon the screen. Both the reversal of the screen and the display of the banner show visitors that the dressing has been completed and that they should now bow to the new ancestor as well as to the chief mourner.

An ancestor tablet, also made at this time, is another indicator of the deceased's new status. It consists of a folded piece of paper containing the outer lining of the ancestor's jacket collar. This tablet is kept in the mourning shrine, which is erected at the home of the deceased at the end of the funeral. It serves as the main object of rites for the new ancestor until the end of the mourning period, when the mourning shrine is dismantled. The tablet is then burned or buried at the ancestor's grave.

While men of the lineage dress the corpse and make the new tablet, some of their wives prepare mourning costumes for the deceased's family and other close kin. As soon as the corpse has been coffined and the screen reversed, the mourners don these costumes and perform the first ancestor ritual (*chesa*) for the deceased.

The mourning costumes worn by close relatives of the deceased are usually made of coarse hemp cloth. The costumes worn by the sons of the deceased are the most elaborate. They include an outer coat, hat, and leggings of hemp; a straw rope about the waist and upper part of the head; and a cane to lean on.

Other close kin of the deceased wear similar, less elaborate mourning costumes. Only sons, for example, carry canes; daughters, daughters-in-law, and grandsons do not. Unmarried grandsons omit mourning hats as well. And at the outer limits of the mourning group, usually represented by second or third agnatic cousins (six *ch'on*, eight *ch'on*) and sons-in-law, men wear only a mourning hat.

Korean ritual manuals and etiquette books, modeled upon Yi-dynasty statutes and classical Chinese texts, specify in great detail which relatives should wear which items of the mourning costume and for what lengths of time. Lee Kwang-Kyu's (1975: 227–45) account of these prescriptions conveys their extraordinary complexity. In practice, however, both the costumes themselves and the range of kin who wear them vary greatly from one funeral to the next.[4] Informants say that much depends on how much the chief mourner is able or willing to spend. Throughout the variations in theory and practice, only one principle remains inviolate: the coarseness of the cloth or the number of items used must correlate with kinship distance. A second cousin should never use finer cloth, or wear fewer items, than a third cousin.

Although several persons wear similar mourning costumes, and though all adult sons of the deceased are dressed exactly the same way, the costume's appearance is usually explained with reference to the chief mourner alone. He, the eldest son of the deceased, is the quintessential mourner and is responsible for the conduct of the funeral. It is he who holds the head of the corpse while it is dressed.

[4] The mourning obligations detailed in Korean etiquette manuals have been heavily influenced by elite Chinese regulations (Freedman 1958: 41–50), but actual village practices differ widely from these elite prescriptions in both China (A. Wolf 1970) and Korea. In Twisŏngdwi, for example, male mourners wear their mourning costumes only during the funeral and subsequent mourning-period rituals. Elderly women sometimes wear their special clothing on other days of the mourning period as well.

Chief mourners carry canes to support themselves because they are greatly weakened by their abstinence from all but the coarsest food and by their extreme grief; so runs the traditional explanation. Of course, everyone knows that few sons really need the canes or even alter their eating habits so drastically during mourning, but the explanation nevertheless is an important commentary on how sons are supposed to act and feel after the death of a parent. Similarly, informants can cite legends of chief mourners who stayed by their parents' graves throughout the mourning period, though they cannot name anyone who actually went to that extreme.

The chief mourner's clothing is said to resemble the dress of a prisoner. He is guilty, say informants, of not providing better care to his parents and thereby not prolonging their lives. Thus the mourning costume is viewed as a tangible expression of guilt for inadequacies in the care and support of one's parents.

That sons should feel guilty upon the death of their parents is hardly surprising. A certain amount of such guilt is perhaps normal in nearly every society of the world. As Robert Smith (1974b: 130) asks in his study of Japanese ancestor worship, "Where shall we find the child who in his heart of hearts believes that he did everything possible for his parents while they lived?" (See also M. Yang 1945: 89; Dredge 1978: 14, 21). In Korea, however, such guilt feelings are probably intensified by early childrearing practices, the particularly demanding ethics of filial piety, and the developmental process of Korean households. As we pointed out in the preceding chapter, adult offspring are indebted to their parents for the especially generous care and warm affection they received in earlier years. Yet the care they give their aged parents is usually regarded as an inadequate repayment. Moreover, surviving children, especially eldest sons, may feel guilty for having wished to be rid of their parents to ease the burden of caring for and feeding them.

Whatever guilt feelings exist are easier to cope with when expressed in a traditional manner. Socially established custom de-individualizes this guilt and acknowledges that such feelings are common to everyone. Thus, the mourning costume performs a useful function in Korea by helping survivors deal with their feelings of guilt.

After the mourners put on their costumes and the first ancestor ritual is performed, visitors continue to arrive to express their condolences. Some of the village men stay at the house of mourning through the night, eating, drinking, and playing cards. Ritual activity, however, subsides until the following morning, when the corpse is taken to the grave site for burial.

The removal of the corpse requires several ancestor rituals. Separate rites are performed before the coffin is taken out of the house and loaded onto the bier, before it is carried out of the village, before it is lowered into the grave, and before the mourners return home. Each ritual includes a formal address to the ancestor, written and recited in classical Chinese, informing the deceased of the procedures about to be performed. The texts are given in ritual manuals and etiquette books. Only a few lineage members know enough Chinese to prepare and recite them.

In Twisŏngdwi and most other Korean villages, only men march in funeral processions as they travel from the village to the grave site (Moose 1911: 177; Biernatzki 1967: 193; Dredge 1978: 19; Rutt 1964: 195; but see Osgood 1951: 117). A few women must be at the grave site to feed the participants, but they come by another route.

The exclusion of women from Korean funeral processions has been interpreted by Paul Dredge (1978: 19) as a symbolic expression of their peripheral positions in agnatic descent groups. "Their exclusion from this activity," he says, "correlate[s] with other symbols of their marginal membership in the lineages into which they are either born or have married. A woman is always about to leave the lineage through marriage, and is hence an inferior member of it, or has come from outside the lineage in the process of marriage, and is therefore a person of divided loyalties." Dredge's perceptive analysis can be supported with comparative data from elsewhere in East Asia. Women are excluded from funeral processions in many communities of southeastern China (De Groot 1964: 195–97; Gray 1878: 302–3) and in other villages where lineages are important social institutions (e.g., M. Yang 1945: 89). In other Chinese communities (A. Wolf 1970; Gamble 1954: 390; Osgood 1963: 297–98; Ball 1912: 294–95; Cormack 1935: 119) and in Japan (R. Smith 1956: 86–87; Norbeck 1978: 191; Beardlsey et al. 1959: 341), where agnatic organizations are not as strong, women march in funeral processions. We will return to this comparison in Chapter 7.

The procession from village to grave is accompanied by singing and rhythmic bell ringing that help the pallbearers keep in step. Twisŏngdwi lineage members used to hire a man from a nearby village to lead the funeral-procession song and ring the bell. He was employed not only for his performance skills but also on account of his social status. Like carrying the bier, musical performance of any kind was regarded as behavior unworthy of gentry. The ritual manuals and etiquette books do not include texts for funeral chants, nor is any knowledge of Chinese necessary for singing them. Though printed texts are available, the primarily oral character of these songs is evident in their regional variations and in changes that occur from one performance to the next (Dix 1977: 210–11; Kim Sŏng-bae 1975).

The professional singer and bell-ringer died in the mid-1970's, and we were unable to record any of his performances. At the funeral processions we observed, a Twisŏngdwi villager rang the bell and the pallbearers chanted meaningless syllables; but a text of the singer's chant was reconstructed from memory by Kwŏn Chang-sik. This 37-year-old lineage member uses lines from the song to lead the singing that also accompanies pounding the earth above the corpse after burial (*talgong*):

> When my parents raised me
> What efforts they made.
> Parents lie in a wet place
> To lay their baby in a dry place.
> With food as well, they first taste it,
> Eating the bitter themselves
> And feeding the sweet to their baby.
> On the hot days of May and June
> They worry of mosquitoes and bedbugs [biting their baby];
> Though tired they cannot sleep.
> With both hands they hold a fan
> And chase away all kinds of worries.
> They carry me on their backs
> And spare no effort.
> [They think:] Silver baby, golden baby,
> Treasure baby from the deepest mountains,[5]

[5] The phrase "from the deepest mountains" connotes rarity, purity, and preciousness.

On the water, sun and moon baby[?],
Patriotic baby for the nation,
A baby with filial piety for his parents,
A baby affectionate toward his family and kin.
Could we buy you even with gold?
Could we buy you even with silver?
The extreme love we feel for you
How can we express?
When one thinks of one's indebtedness to one's parents,
Isn't it bigger than the greatest mountain?
Who would deny this?

Look here, listen to my words,
Listen to my words and then go.
Death claims both young and old,
The elderly and the youthful.
The elderly die first
And the youthful die later.
In this just world,
Like the flowing of a stream,
Seniors and juniors go in turn.
At Sumi Mountain's high peaks,
Like the flowing of the green mountain water,
They flow in turn.
Please let them flow into paradise.

Growing up under the protection
Of our parents' enormous love,
Married before the age of twenty,
After producing and rearing children of our own,
We feel grateful and indebted to our parents.

At most we live a hundred years;
Our rosy youth yields to white hair;
Inevitably death comes.
Black hair turns white,
Beautiful faces become wrinkled,
Easily life passes by.
The feeling of futility is endless.

Pleading in every possible way—
What messenger [of King Yama] would be sympathetic?
Oh, it's so suffocating and sad,
This pitiful feeling.
It's unbearably hard to part with life.
Wealth, prestige, and fame: floating clouds.

Carrying the funeral bier from Twisŏngdwi to a burial site.

Wild roses of Myŏngsa Simni,[6]
Don't feel sad that your flowers and leaves have withered.
Next year when spring returns
You will bloom again;
But our lives are as fleeting as the dew on the grass:
Once they go they never return.

When we enter the world of the dead (*Pungmangsan*),
We find endless mountains so rugged and steep.
We go and go without end—
It is indeed a long, long road.
Bid farewell to the old ancestor shrine;
Worship at the new ancestor shrine.
As we step outside the main gate,
While we recite sutras[?] they grab our hand
And push us on like the wind and rain.
As they drive us along helter-skelter
We quickly pass from high places to low places
And from low places to high places.

Though we have many siblings,
None will take our place.
Though we have many relatives,
None will join us.

Human beings born into this life
Arrive empty-handed.
Don't be concerned with material goods;
We lose our material concerns.
A lifetime's resolution vanishes in a moment.
The three days of grief come once in a lifetime.
All the thousands of coins we accumulate,
Using them up as we live,
We can't use them all.
If we live without concerns,
We won't find this fleeting life so difficult
And will find ourselves in paradise.
We can't use all our goods.
Ten thousand people pass away
Thinking of going without concern.
It's unbearably hard to part with life.

The funeral chant articulates a number of themes evidenced elsewhere: the sacrifices of parents and the love and care they

---

[6] A famous beach on the east coast of Korea.

shower upon their offspring; the indebtedness to parents; the soul's difficult journey to the land of the dead and its understandable reluctance to depart the world of the living; and the inevitability of aging and death. In addition, the song gives moral advice in urging the renunciation of worldly desires. Like the references to Sumi Mountain and paradise (*kŭngnak*), this moralizing gives the song a Buddhist tone that is not entirely consistent with present-day social values and beliefs in rural Korea; it is common, however, in this genre of oral literature (see Dix 1977: 210–11). Evidently some of the song's content has survived from the era when Buddhism dominated the cult of the dead. Yet informants do not associate the song with Buddhism. Kwŏn Chang-sik told us it was Confucian.

The funeral song is interrupted at several points during the procession as the pallbearers halt and chant, "Oh, it's so hard to go." Until they are given some money by the chief mourner or his immediate kin, they refuse to go on. The amounts are small, no more than a few thousand *wŏn* (about US $5), and the money is given to the Mutual Assistance Society, but the point of this activity is not merely economic. The demands for money, the mourners' pretended reluctance to pay, and the negotiation of an acceptable price are accompanied by a good deal of mirth and laughter and thus provide moments of comic relief in the funeral. They are also an open admission that the expression of grief may be somewhat artificial, given because it is demanded by custom.[7] Once when the pallbearers took a particularly long time before departing from the village, the mourners had to wail audibly for an extraordinary length of time. This obviously amused many of the spectators. Knowing that children are relieved of an onerous burden by a parent's death, villagers seem to acknowledge tacitly that offspring are not really all that sad when their parents die. Such attitudes also caught our attention when Roger Janelli's mother died. Returning to Twisŏngdwi some weeks after the funeral, he was met by a lineage widow who giggled as she asked, "Did you cry a lot?"

---

[7] Audible wailing is expected of mourners only at specified moments during the funeral and other mourning rites. For an account of a mourner who was restrained from wailing at the wrong time, see Dix (1977: 224–26).

Geomancy

Twisŏngdwi lineage members speak of "good" and "bad" grave locations (*myo chari chot'a* and *myo chari nappŭda*). These terms reflect opinions of the site's effects, past or potential, on descendants of the person buried there. Finding a good site is an important concern. We found little interpersonal variation in this matter: more than a dozen informants discussed grave sites with us, and all professed belief in the ability of the grave to affect the welfare of an ancestor's descendants. Several also told us of graves that had been relocated because of misfortunes suffered by various families.

Grave sites affect the welfare of descendants in two ways, one volitional and the other mechanistic. Volitional processes can be seen when an ancestor communicates dissatisfaction with the grave at a seance, appears in dreams, or sends misfortune to living kin. Informants say that the first three years after burial are a sort of trial period. If nothing untoward occurs during that time, one may safely assume that the ancestor is content with the site.

Occurrences of this kind, in which an ancestor willfully acts, belong to a broad domain of beliefs that also includes diverse ideas about the afterlife and ancestral affliction. As we shall show in Chapter 6, where we discuss these beliefs in detail, dissatisfaction with grave sites is only one of several reasons that motivate ancestors to harm their closest living kin.

An ancestor's grave can also affect descendants in a purely mechanistic way. In these cases, benefits or misfortunes are attributed to the earth's vital forces (*saenggi*), mystical powers that flow through the earth like underground streams or veins of metal ore. Any vital forces that impinge on a grave site flow through the ancestor's bones and eventually affect the welfare of agnatic descendants. Prosperity as well as the extinction or fecundity of agnatic descent lines are the effects most often attributed to these forces.

Known literally as "wind and water" (*p'ungsu*), but conventionally translated as "geomancy" in Western sources, this belief system has been highly elaborated by traditional Chinese and Korean scholars. In addition to the effects of wind and water on the earth's vital forces, geomantic theory also deals with the relationship of these forces to topography, the directions of the compass, the five basic elements, the alternation of yin and yang, and much else of traditional East Asian cosmology (Feuchtwang 1974b; Yoon Hong-key 1976). In China and Korea, geomancy entails both building and grave sites; it is also known in Japan, but there it deals only with building sites.

Because geomantic theory is so complex and difficult to learn, locating auspicious grave sites is a professional specialization in both Korea and China. And because the professional geomancer's knowledge comes from books and is supposedly acquired through laborious study, it earns him the respect of his clients. Shamans (*mudang*) and other religious specialists do not enjoy such esteem in either society (cf. Freedman 1966: 124). This connection between prestige and absence of volitional intervention relates to an argument that we develop more fully below. As we shall see, the conception of ancestors as dependent and passive beings is evident in prestigious and formal ancestor worship. The view of ancestors as active and potentially hostile is more closely related to the shamanistic belief system, which is socially disapproved.

Some Twisŏngdwi villagers have a rudimentary knowledge of geomantic theory. Kwŏn Hae-su, for example, knew that the accumulation of water below a site indicated its auspiciousness (Yoon Hong-key 1976: 48–51; Feuchtwang 1974b: 134); but no one in Twisŏngdwi is expert in such matters. When villagers need a geomancer, they hire one from outside the community and trust his judgment.

Villagers' accounts of geomancy differ from the professional's manuals in one respect: the villagers place greater emphasis on the misfortunes than on the benefits of geomancy. The recent prosperity of one lineage family was universally attributed to the grave of the household head's first wife, and the grave of Kwŏn Po was credited with the numerousness of his descendants; but poverty and lack of descendants were far more common in the accounts of geomancy we obtained. Apparently this is one reason why Twisŏngdwi villagers usually bury parents together. Placing them in separate graves would increase the chance of obtaining geomantic benefit, as Freedman (1966: 131) and Ahern (1973: 186) suggest, but it would also increase the risk of suffering misfortune.

Laying a corpse in a grave while mourners look on and wail.

Although Twisŏngdwi residents seem more concerned with misfortunes than benefits, and although they lack the specialist's familiarity with the intricacies of geomantic theory, their view of geomantic causality is fundamentally the same as that found in the Chinese and Korean geomantic manuals. We did not find, as did Emily Ahern (1973: 175–90) in a Taiwanese village, that the belief in ancestral discomfort and consequent intervention in the lives of descendants was a substitute for the belief in the mechanistic, impersonal effects of grave locations. In Twisŏngdwi, informants were equally comfortable with both ideas.

Like the professional geomancer, for example, Twisŏngdwi villagers know that the corpse must be laid in precisely the right spot if it is to convey geomantic benefits (Yoon Hong-key 1976: 60–62). A small difference can drastically alter, for better or worse, the consequences of a site. One lineage member explained that his grandfather did not deliberately make him ill, but that the precise location (as well as the timing) of his grandfather's reburial caused the accident that left him with a debilitating illness. Had the corpse been buried a few paces downhill, our informant noted, he would not have suffered his misfortune. The wife of another lineage member, whose descent line seems headed for extinction, told us that "fate" could keep the geomantic benefits of a site from the descendants by causing the corpse to be laid slightly off the correct spot. Her family had moved the grave of one of its ancestors several times in the hope that a new location would enable one of her married sons to produce children.

Like the professional geomancer, Twisŏngdwi lineage members also know that a grave site may not convey equal benefits to all descendants (Feuchtwang 1974b: 216; Freedman 1966: 130). Thus geomantic theory offers a theater for conflict between brothers or more distant agnates: each could try to bury an ancestor in the site most advantageous to himself, or each of several descent lines could compete to place its own exclusive ancestor in the same auspicious spot. In China, where relations between brothers or more distant agnates are often strained, such conflict over grave sites is common (Freedman 1966: 130–38; De Groot 1964: 1028–31).

Competition over auspicious grave sites is rife in Korea, but not between agnates; instead, most quarrels arise between non-kin (e.g., Yoon Hong-key 1976: 181–82, 187–88, 201–2; Dallet 1954: 140–41). In Twisŏngdwi, we learned of a man who forced a family of another lineage to remove their ancestor from an auspicious spot and then buried his own ancestor there. Conflicts between agnates (e.g., Kim Taik-Kyoo 1964: 170), by contrast, are far less common. In the one example of this we obtained from Twisŏngdwi, a lineage member's selfish attempt to benefit his own line at the expense of his close kin ultimately ended in failure. Informants even blamed the grave of Kwŏn Po, their seventeenth-generation ancestor, for the paucity of government officials in all five branches of his descendants. When his grave was relocated long ago, according to oral tradition, his descendants chose a location that promised many future descendants, but little success, over one that offered greater prosperity but fewer offspring.

In comparison with China, therefore, the practice of geomancy in Korea de-emphasizes differences between descent lines of agnatically related kin. The best graves, as Kwŏn Pyŏng-sik's wife put it, give prosperity and offspring to all descendants. Evidently this greater emphasis on agnatic unity in Korea is fostered by the greater harmony and economic cooperation between agnates. Conflict and competition do occur—Koreans are as human as anyone else—but they are less intense than those reported from China (e.g., M. Wolf 1968; Cohen 1976; Freedman 1966: 46; Potter 1968: 78; Watson 1975a).

The search for favorable grave sites reflects not only relations between agnates of collateral descent lines but also relations between different generations of the same descent line. Occasionally, the welfare of the living is treated independently of or even in opposition to that of the dead. In one Korean folktale, for example, a father asks his sons whether they would rather bury him in a grave that would make him a king in the afterlife or in one that would make them rich (Choi In-hak 1979: 142). One could even argue, as does Maurice Freedman, that in geomancy descendants manipulate their forebears' bones just for their own worldly benefit (Freedman 1967: 89–90). The possibility is acknowledged in Chinese neo-Confucian writings (Chan 1967: 231) and in Korea as well (Yoon Hong-key 1976: 160–61). Yim Suk-jay (personal communication), who often inclines toward cynical views of human behavior, loved the idea.

The far more prevalent interpretation of geomancy, however, stresses the interdependence of generations and the commonality of their interests. As Kwŏn Kŭn-sik put it, a grave that is good for descendants is also good for their ancestor. Ancestors, too, want their descendants to prosper and multiply, for that helps to ensure the quality and continuity of worship they receive (Yoon Hong-key 1976: 158–60). Many Korean folktales tell of sacrifices or efforts made to obtain auspicious sites—sometimes for one's own grave—in order that one's descendants may prosper (Zŏng In-sŏb 1952: 48–51; Yoon Hong-key 1976: 161–62, 174–75, 182–83). In other stories, a person is rewarded for an act of kindness with the location of an auspicious site, which brings benefits to his or her descendants (Yoon Hong-key 1976: 179, 180–81, 186). Conversely, the geomantic benefits of a mother's grave may not flow to her offspring, because of an evil deed she committed (Yoon Hong-key 1976: 177). On the whole, therefore, Korean views of geomancy identify rather than oppose the interests of

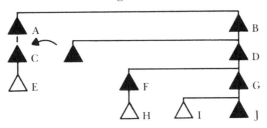

Fig. 7. Genealogical relationships between persons involved in geomantic misfortunes.

successive generations. A similar interpretation of Chinese geomancy has been advanced by at least one Chinese anthropologist (Li 1976: 334).

The following story from Twisŏngdwi is an especially rich illustration of geomantic beliefs and social relations. Because it also entails a particularly complex set of kinship relations, we have included a genealogical diagram of the relevant lineage members (Figure 7). We have also paraphrased and summarized the account, adding explanatory comments in brackets.

G was a very strong-willed person. He made all the decisions in his house even when his father [D, and grandfather, B] were still alive. When his grandfather died, G took care of all the funeral arrangements.

Since C was a natural son of B [though adopted by B's brother], he too had an interest in how B's funeral was to be conducted. He wanted to wear mourning clothes and call in a professional geomancer, but G wanted to avoid these expenses. As a result, C himself called in a geomancer. C would also have worn full mourning clothes but E, his son, opposed the idea. If the chief mourner didn't wear full mourning clothes, E reasoned, it would only cause further embarrassment to have anyone else wear them.

Now by the time C's geomancer arrived, G had already chosen a burial spot. The geomancer said the spot was a bad one, but if it had to be used, at least the corpse should be oriented in a particular direction and should not be buried on the following day. That day was designated *chungsang chungbok* [by the almanac. It was inauspicious because it implied a second death and mourning]. Nevertheless, G chose to disregard the advice of the geomancer. He buried the body the following day, in the bad location, and laid it in the wrong direction. One year later, G's father died.

G's house now had two mourning shrines on its veranda, one for B

A professional geomancer uses his compass to determine the exact direction of a grave.

and one for D. [Mourning shrines may be left standing for up to two years after death.] And when B's shrine was dismantled the following year, G himself died; so there were still two mourning shrines on the veranda.

Upon G's death, his brother F took control of G's household. [J, G's son, was in his mid-twenties at the time.]

C and F agreed to move both B's and D's graves, but each hired his own geomancer. C's geomancer found two sites, and F's geomancer found only one. The former said that the single site located by F's geo-mancer would be good for the junior descent line of the house (*chison*) [F's own line], but only temporarily, and that there would be no one left at the main house to offer ancestor rituals [that is, B, D, G, and J's de-scent line would terminate]. But F, hoping to benefit his line, insisted on using the location found by his own geomancer.

At this point, C suggested a compromise: bury D in the site located by F's geomancer [since D was F's but not C's ancestor], and bury B [the ancestor shared by everyone] in another location. But F refused even this compromise. He buried B and D together, as if they were husband and wife! [In fact, their grave mounds were a few yards apart, somewhat more distant from each other than those of spouses.]

After the reburials, F's household rapidly acquired great wealth, whereas J's household suffered several misfortunes. J's wife died before producing any male descendants, and then J himself died. Still later, F's business failed; and when F died, H inherited substantial debts.

Our informant ended his account with F's death, but we can add a few more facts to this complex tale. When D's wife died, D's bones were exhumed from the inauspicious site next to B's grave and reburied in a new location next to his wife. The new site and the direction in which the bodies were to be oriented had been determined by a geomancer. After the villagers had dug the grave, however, it was found to be slightly misaligned. This dis-covery caused one of the three genuinely heated disputes we wit-nessed among the Twisŏngdwi lineage.[8] Like the other two, the argument never came to physical blows, but both H and I were obviously enraged at the carelessness of their fellow villagers. Peace was restored only at the intervention of some lineage eld-ers. Yet no one bore any grudge after the incident. Less than an hour later, some of the men involved amiably sat down and ate a meal together, and we never heard the dispute mentioned again. Fortunately, neither H's nor I's household experienced any fur-ther disasters.

The above events illustrate several beliefs about geomancy cur-rent in Twisŏngdwi. They show, for example, that graves are more often blamed for misfortunes than credited for benefits. Moreover, the account clearly demonstrates geomancy's mechan-istic operation. It makes no mention of ancestral discomfort or ancestors' deliberate intervention in the lives of descendants. In-

[8] The other two instances entailed political conflict between elders and younger lineage members.

deed, the deaths of at least three adults, which are attributed to various grave sites, could never be attributed to ancestral volition in Twisŏngdwi. The informant who provided us with the narrative, like everyone else in Twisŏngdwi, insisted that ancestors never kill their adult offspring.

Besides illustrating beliefs about geomancy, the story provides a useful insight into kinship relations. Because it includes far more strife than we usually witnessed in Twisŏngdwi, the narrative shows what happens when agnatic ties are especially strained. Most significant of all was F's attempt to obtain geomantic benefits at the expense of his brother's descent line. As we noted earlier, such geomantic competition between close agnates is common in China but not in Korea.

Conflict over rights to jointly owned property, the major cause of fraternal conflict in China, appears to have provoked this dispute as well. After G died, as our informant noted, his household's income and expenditures came under F's control. (Other informants criticized F for later withholding from I economic benefits that rightfully belonged to him.) This new arrangement, though atypical in Korea, approaches the usual household structure that produces such fraternal strife in China: two or more families of collateral descent lines pooling their economic resources and later dividing them among themselves. Rivalry and disharmony between adult brothers, or between uncles and nephews, can be expected in the absence of a more senior parent who is a progenitor to all the families, who effectively allocates shares to each, and who ultimately divides property among his offspring. In Korea, therefore, F's economic and geomantic competition with H and I is one of the exceptions that prove the rule: the economic and religious cooperation typical of close agnates in Korea is rooted in the normal Korean system of property division and household development. We will further explore the effects of property division on agnatic relations in later chapters.

Mourning for Elders and Ancestors

When burial of the coffin is nearly finished, an advance party of lineage members returns to the home of the deceased to construct a mourning shrine (sangch'ŏng). It is normally built on the veranda, but its precise location is determined by a geomancer. The essential components of a mourning shrine are a food-offering table, an incense burner, the ancestor tablet made when the corpse was dressed, and white muslin curtains, which enclose the shrine.

The mourning shrine is the center for nearly all interactions with the new ancestor throughout the mourning period. Only a few rituals are performed at the grave. The shrine is used for an ancestor ritual as soon as the chief mourner returns from the grave, on the first and second mornings after burial, on the first and fifteenth days of each lunar month, and on the hundredth day or first and second death-days (depending on the length of the mourning period). A variety of less formal interactions with the ancestor also take place there.

In deciding when to dismantle the shrine and end the mourning period, a chief mourner has three choices. At most, a mourning period lasts until the ancestor's second death-day. This is "three years" according to Korean reckoning: the calendar year of death, the following year, and that portion of the third year up to the death-day. The mourning period may also end at 100 days after death or on the first death-day.[9]

A variety of considerations affect the duration of the mourning period. Since a longer period requires more rituals, expense, and inconvenience to the living, it offers an opportunity to demonstrate greater filial piety. Terminating the mourning period, however, entails a big feast for the village as well as a major ritual (*taesang*), and one lineage member told us he had to postpone the termination from 100 days to the first death-day in order to save up the money to pay for it. A wealthy villager, on the other hand, found a way to shorten the mourning period to 100 days and at the same time retain the midpoint feast that traditionally accompanies the ritual offered halfway through the two-year mourning period (*sosang*). By a happy coincidence, the Buddhist mourning period lasts 49 days, so he paid for a Buddhist rite and a meal for the villagers at a temple near Suwŏn. To the monks who performed the rite, it celebrated the day of the deceased's judgment and assumption of a new life, but Twisŏngdwi villagers explained

---

[9] A mother's mourning period is traditionally terminated on her first death anniversary if her husband is still alive. Also, some etiquette manuals prescribe extending the mourning period for a few months beyond the second death anniversary (Moon Seung Gyu 1974: 76). Kwŏn O-sik, one of the lineage members most familiar with elite ritual prescriptions, knew of the latter custom, but it has not been followed in Twisŏngdwi.

A mourning shrine.

to us that it marked the midpoint of the 100-day mourning period. Some also pointed to the anomaly of having the rite in a
Buddhist temple while the ancestor was back home in his mourning shrine. Lineage members said it was the first time anyone had
ever done such a thing. For a week before the event, villagers

discussed how to get to the temple, what the rite would be like, and how much money they should contribute. They seemed awkward and uncertain throughout the proceedings. As the officiating monk observed in the course of his sermon, "You people don't seem to come to Buddhist temples very often."

However long the mourning period lasts, say informants, the deceased during that time should be treated just like a living person. A burning cigarette is one of the offerings at major mourning-period rites for an ancestor who smoked. Whenever a daily meal is prepared at a house in mourning, some food is placed at the mourning shrine, as if the ancestor were still participating in family meals. Indeed, one Korean writer claimed that ancestor worship began because families missed the deceased at mealtimes (Pyun Young Tai 1926: 9–10).

Etiquette rules also show how the newly dead are treated like the living. A guest who visits a house in mourning may be led to greet (*insa*) the ancestor in the mourning shrine, just as the guest may be brought to greet an elder of the house. In Twisŏngdwi and elsewhere in Korea (Osgood 1951: 121), formal New Year's Day greetings are given to both living elders and ancestors in mourning shrines. And at the Twisŏngdwi village's picnic in the summer of 1978, packages of food were prepared for two villagers to take home to their mourning shrines. Food is sent this way to elders after autumn lineage rituals if they do not personally attend the post-ritual feasting. Finally, Kwŏn Sang-sik offered this explanation of why women participate in rites for an ancestor only during the mourning period: women bow to the living at weddings and sixtieth birthdays, he said, so they can also bow to an ancestor in a mourning shrine.

Treating ancestors and elders in the same fashion is most pronounced during the mourning period, but the similarity actually begins earlier in a parent's life and extends indefinitely beyond it. The first formal expression of this similarity can be seen in sixtieth-birthday celebrations. These occasions, which are supposed to mark the retirement of elders from active life, are not part of ancestor worship (*chosang sungbae*) in the strict sense, but in Twisŏngdwi they are colloquially known as "ancestor rituals for the living" (*san chesa*).

The resemblance of ancestor rituals and sixtieth-birthday celebrations was first brought to our attention by Kwŏn O-sik. This lineage member, regarded as having a particularly good grasp of ritual matters, surprised us one day by including sixtieth-birthday celebrations in his enumeration of ancestor rituals. When we expressed our bewilderment, he defended their inclusion by noting that ancestors are no different from elders (*mach'an'gajida*).

In calling sixtieth-birthday celebrations part of ancestor worship, Kwŏn O-sik gave us a perceptive insight into Korean thinking. As he later acknowledged, sixtieth-birthday celebrations are not really ancestor rituals, but the ceremonial forms of both are closely parallel. Objects, spatial arrangements, actions, and hierarchical relationships between the commemorators and the commemorated are very similar at both types of occasion. A table of food is set between the ancestors or elders and those who come forward to honor them (see Figure 8). About half of the foods on

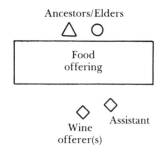

Fig. 8. Spatial arrangement used at sixtieth-birthday celebrations and ancestor rituals.

the table are eaten only on these ceremonial occasions, and all are similarly arranged according to formal rules.

The major activity at both ancestor rituals and sixtieth-birthday celebrations is offering wine to those honored. The participants come forward in turn, kneel, present a cup of wine to the commemorated ancestor or elder and his or her spouse, and bow.[10] One or more assistants pour the wine into the cup held by the offerer, then pass the cup to the elder or set it before the ancestral

[10] An ancestor is commemorated without his or her spouse at death-day rites in a few Korean communities (Martina Deuchler, personal communication; Lee Kwang-Kyu 1977a: 8). It would be interesting to know if parents are also commemorated individually at sixtieth-birthday ceremonies in these communities.

tablet. At both ceremonies, moreover, each participant offers wine and bows only to persons of greater age and higher generation status.

Similarities in the treatment of ancestors and elders continue indefinitely. Even after the mourning shrine is dismantled, descendants still provide, through ancestor rituals and maintenance of graves, the food and shelter that they owe their forebears.

As shown in Figure 9, Korean ancestor worship (*chosang sungbae*) comprises three stages of ritual interactions with the dead. During the first stage, the mourning period, ancestor rites are most numerous. During the next four generations, which span the second stage, an ancestor's veneration is reduced to only four or five domestic rituals a year (see Chapter 4). After this, in the third stage, the ancestor is commemorated only once a year with a lineage ritual (see Chapter 5). Thus obligations to forebears gradually diminish but are never extinguished entirely.

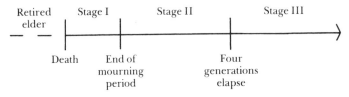

Fig. 9. Progressive ritual statuses of a Korean ancestor.

The continuation of filial obligations toward forebears even after they die is a theme expressed in Confucian writings. As Hsün Tzu puts it, one ought "to render the same service to the dead as to the living" (Fung 1952: 349). The *Hsiao Ching*, the Confucian classic on filial piety, defines this moral axiom as an obligation owed to both the living and the dead:

The service which a filial son does to his parents is as follows:—In his general conduct to them, he manifests the utmost reverence; in his nourishing of them, his endeavor is to give them the utmost pleasure; when they are ill, he feels the greatest anxiety; in mourning for them (dead), he exhibits every demonstration of grief; in sacrificing to them, he displays the utmost solemnity. When a son is complete in these five things (he may be pronounced) able to serve his parents. [Legge 1879: 480]

Rationalists that they were, most Confucian philosophers said little about the afterlife or the comforts of ancestral spirits. The purpose of ancestor rituals, in their view, was not to provide for the needs of the dead but to inculcate proper social sentiments among living kin. This motive is also accepted by Twisŏngdwi villagers. As Kwŏn O-sik told us, "When I show my children how I perform ancestor rituals, I'm telling them how they should care for me in my old age." And all villagers are aware that ancestor rituals at least express, if not reaffirm, agnatic solidarity.

Such rationalistic philosophizing, however, offers only one motive for ancestor worship in Twisŏngdwi. Korean villagers also have folk beliefs that provide quite different reasons for offering ancestor rituals and reveal a far more active image of ancestors (Dix 1979: 69–71). Informants say, for example, that an ancestor's comfort in the afterlife depends on the offerings provided by the descendants. They know that ancestors are sometimes cantankerous and cause offspring to suffer misfortune, especially when they are dissatisfied with what the descendants provide; in other words, not only are the living obligated to ancestors as they are to elders, but ancestors themselves behave like elders. These folk beliefs, most clearly articulated at shamanistic rites, are explored more fully in Chapter 6.

Neither folk beliefs nor Confucian ideology, therefore, allow death to terminate parents' interaction with their offspring. Perhaps this is why Twisŏngdwi elders face death with such composure. More than once we were struck by their matter-of-fact comments about the topic. Kwŏn Tŏk-su's widow was enumerating for us the ancestor rituals offered at Kwŏn Pyŏng-nyŏl's house when she pointed to his mother and said, "And when she dies, that will make one more." Sensing our surprise at this remark, she quickly added, "Well, she's old. It's time for her to die." Kwŏn Pyŏng-nyŏl's mother, whose death was being discussed, nodded in agreement. On another occasion, Kwŏn Pyŏng-jun pointed to the ground in the lineage's main cemetery, and said to his mother, "When you die, I think I'll put you right here."

🌿 4 🌿
Domestic Rituals

Domestic rites in Korea, presented to ancestors on their death-days and on holidays,[1] are not merely offered; they are per-formed—well or badly. Besides judging rituals on the quality and quantity of food offerings, Twisŏngdwi lineage members evalu-ate them by the participants' adherence to a set of procedural rules. Wealthier informants tend to stress the importance of food offerings, whereas those who pride themselves on their knowl-edge of ritual emphasize proper form. But all agree that neither the poor nor the ignorant can perform ancestor rituals well.

Ritual Procedures

Emphasis on the procedural aspects of domestic ancestor wor-ship is thoroughly Korean. It appears not only in the popular ritual manuals and etiquette books, which provide step-by-step instructions for these rites, but also in the several ethnographic accounts that do the same (Biernatzki 1967: 319–22; Moon Seung Gyu 1974; R. Janelli 1975: 196–219, 319–39; Dix 1979: 62–65; Lee Kwang-Kyu 1977a: 18–20). Elsewhere in East Asia, such formality is evident primarily at nondomestic rites (see Chapter 5) offered in some Chinese communities (Baker 1968: 64; see also Hsu 1948: 186–90).

[1] Domestic rites are of two major types, death-day rites (kije, or kijesa) and hol-iday rites (ch'arye). The dates of the latter vary somewhat throughout Korea. In Twisŏngdwi they are performed on (lunar) New Year's Day and on the Harvest Moon Festival (Ch'usŏk), which falls on the fifteenth day of the eighth lunar month. Elsewhere they may be performed on the solar New Year, Tano (the fifth day of the fifth lunar month), and Hansik (the 105th day after the winter solstice). Ritual offerings may be presented at graves as well as at descendants' homes on holidays, especially in Seoul. And New Year's rites may be performed immedi-ately after midnight, as in China. For accounts of these variant practices, see Kang Younghill (1931: 41–42), Kim Taik-Kyoo (1964: 163), Biernatzki (1967: 318), Pak Ki-hyuk (1975: 69–70), and Dix (1977: 118).

The great lengths to which ritual procedures are elaborated are particularly evident in the arrangement of food offerings. Printed instructions provide diagrams and rules for the placement of various dishes. Kwŏn O-sik and Kwŏn Sang-sik, two lineage members noted for their ritual expertise, gave us very detailed instructions about the proper directions to point the head and tail of a fish, the position of persimmons in relation to chestnuts, and other such esoterica.

Despite the great importance attached to the arrangement of food offerings and to other details of ritual performance in traditional and present-day rural Korea, many procedures are quite arbitrary. During the Yi dynasty, political factions contending for power in the central government are said to have adopted different food arrangements as symbols of political allegiance. When we asked Kwŏn O-sik why the red jujubes should be placed on the "east" side (the performer's right) of the table, for example, he said that this was only an established convention. Questioning it, he added, is like asking why Columbus left for the New World on the day he did and not the day before. He insisted that ritual performances must be ordered by rules, but he nevertheless acknowledged that different rules adopted by different kin groups were equally valid.

Not all Korean households place such stress on proper ritual procedures (e.g., Brandt 1971: 120; Moon Seung Gyu 1974: 80). The importance of formal rules to Kwŏn O-sik and his kinsmen derives at least in part from their use of punctilious etiquette and propriety to assert status. Those who do not advance claims to status have little need of these formalities.

The connection between social status and ancestor ritual procedures probably originated in the early Yi dynasty, when neo-Confucian ideology and etiquette were first adopted by the educated and political elite of Korean society (Yang and Henderson 1959: 264–65; Deuchler 1977: 5). Only after the elite adopted them did the masses begin using Confucian ceremonial procedures (Yi Hae-yong and Han Woo-keun 1976: 166–67). Even today, correct ritual performance is not easily attained by everyone. The ancestor tablet and formal address to the ancestors are both written in Chinese characters, and the address must be chanted with proper intonation, as one reads aloud a classical Chinese text. These skills require knowledge and training that few can (or could) obtain.

Many Koreans have questioned some of the emphasis on arbitrary rules. One of the most comprehensive etiquette books provides page after page of detailed instructions for ancestor rituals, but also cautions, "Sincerity is essential, for without it, an ancestor ritual is nothing more than an empty formality" (Ŏm Mun-ho 1972: 211).[2] Kwŏn O-sik also expressed doubt whether so much importance should be attached to formal procedures. He made his point effectively by interjecting the following story into a discussion of ritual procedures.

Some time in the past, there was a gentleman-scholar who was very learned and very courteous in his behavior. He was traveling in a mountain district and there wasn't any inn where he could stay. There was only a hut occupied by some people who cultivate mountain land. They just grew a few crops and barely eked out a living.

So according to the story there was this isolated hut, and since it was getting dark he went there to spend the night. Well, it just happened to be the day [the death-day] for the father's ritual in that house, although the scholar didn't know it. He became curious about what the people of the house were doing and the reason for their food preparation. Early in the evening he had heard them coming and going in the kitchen and preparing food. He thought that all that activity must have had some purpose. And then for a while there was no movement at all. The couple had gone out.

They had gone to the father's grave in the mountains—it wasn't far from the house—and they brought the father and mother to their house. Now these people were very ignorant. They thought that since the father had lived a long time, he was now very weak with old age. He had died after living out his natural life span and had had enough trouble making his way in daylight. How could he come in the dark of night? So they thought they should go out and bring him in. With this in mind, they went to the grave and brought back the spirits.

After waiting for a while, the scholar heard from the main gate, "Father, here is the doorway. Watch your step." That was the way they brought the spirits. Then they went up onto the veranda, and he heard, "Here is the veranda. You have to step up here." After they did that and guided them up onto the veranda to the food-offering table, the scholar heard the couple say, "Father, sit down here and make yourself comfortable." So according to the story, that's how they brought him to their house.

[2] For a translation of these ritual prescriptions, see R. Janelli (1975: 313–39).

At that point the scholar poked a small hole in the paper door [of the room where he was seated] and put his eye to it. He saw the couple, with nothing in their hands and no one between them, looking as if they were assisting someone to enter the house. He thought it was strange when he saw them seat the spirits, offer them food, and then spread their bedding in front of the food-offering table. And then the couple lay down together, and kissed, and presented a scene of lovemaking. That's the story.

So the scholar thought all this was indeed strange, but it seemed to have some resemblance to an ancestor ritual. So the scholar kept looking through the hole he had made in the door to the outer room where he was sitting and thought that what they were doing was perhaps an ancestor ritual. He thought that this way of offering an ancestor ritual was indeed strange and he began to wonder.

The couple continued for a while and then they picked up their bedding. After that they said, "Father, here is the edge of the veranda. Be careful as you step down." And the couple went beside them to the gate and said, "Here is the doorstep. Be careful as you cross it." And after a while the couple were gone and he could no longer see them. They were returning the spirits to their graves. And then, according to the story, they returned.

And so, they probably brought the food offerings to the scholar,[3] for he asked what had happened. The husband explained in detail:

"Father died of old age. How could he walk here now? So we both went and brought him. And since there was no way he could go back by himself, we accompanied him to his grave and then returned. And we had a reason for spreading the bedding in front of the [place of the] ancestor ritual. While he was alive, father said that he wanted to see me happily married and with children before he died. And so, since I married after his death, at least his spirit should see how happily we live. Therefore, in order to show him that we were living together happily, we did that."   Then the scholar thought to himself, "We educated elite rely too heavily on formal rules." Upon hearing the man's words, he compared the elite's reliance on established rules with what his hosts had done and realized how noble their treatment of the ancestors had been. Their efforts seemed so heartfelt and sincere.

And so, there are times when even a scholar can learn from ignorant people. People follow evil ways because they see evil and are infected by it. That's why there are evil men. Seeing no evil, living alone and uncorrupted in a mountain region, growing up with a pure mind—such a person has no evil. That's the story.

[3] Upon completion of an ancestor ritual, the food offerings are eaten. First the participants symbolically share a few tidbits of food, and then a large meal is eaten by all present. Thus it is customary to share the food with wives and children; and it is not inappropriate to share the offerings with neighbors or visitors.

Placing a spoon on the food offerings during a holiday rite. An ancestor tablet made of paper is attached to the folding screen behind the
table.

This is not a popular Korean folktale; only one other text of
the tale has ever been published (Choi In-hak 1979: 175). In
many ways it expresses the personality of its narrator, Kwŏn O-
sik. Though well versed in Chinese characters and traditional ritual esoterica, he can often take a detached view of his society and
question some of its most fundamental premises. Few share his
talents.

Although Twisŏngdwi lineage members emphasize correct ritual procedures and rely on etiquette books, their ancestor rituals
do not merely observe elite and written prescriptions. Many ritual practices derive from folk traditions that find no sanction in
etiquette books or other neo-Confucian texts. The books do not
say, for example, that death-day and holiday rites should be performed on the veranda, where most lineage households offer

them; instead they either say nothing about the place of performance or else prescribe that the rites be held indoors. Nor do they say anything about omitting the formal address to the ancestors when only one cup of wine is offered. These rules and practices of the Twisŏngdwi lineage apparently originated in rural villages.

In many instances, we cannot determine the derivation of a particular procedure: ritual manuals and etiquette books do not all contain the same prescriptions, all lineage members are not equally familiar with their contents, and informants have different ways of using them to justify the same ritual procedure. Both Kwŏn O-sik and Kwŏn Sang-sik, for example, said that jujubes should be placed to the far right of the offering table, with chestnuts to the left of jujubes, persimmons to the left of chestnuts, and pears to the left of persimmons (see Figure 10). This

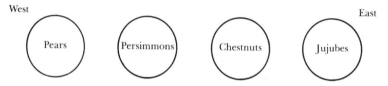

Fig. 10. Arrangement of fruits and chestnuts for a ritual offering.

was the arrangement at nearly all the ancestor rituals offered by Twisŏngdwi lineage members. According to Kwŏn O-sik, the arrangement was dictated by two rules, both commonly found in printed sources. The first, "jujubes, chestnuts, persimmons, pears" (*cho yul si i*), determines the sequence. The second, "red [i.e., jujubes] east, white [i.e., pears] west" (*hong tong, paek sŏ*), prescribes the direction. But Kwŏn Sang-sik maintained that the second rule was not used by the Twisŏngdwi lineage. If it were, he said, the persimmons would have to be placed to the right of the chestnuts because the persimmons are red and the chestnuts (which are shelled) are white.

In the absence of an organized priesthood to make authoritative rulings about such matters, folk and elite practices, individual and collective interpretations easily intermingled during the centuries following neo-Confucianism's entry into Korea. Whatever its origins, Korean ancestor worship can no longer be regarded as an external ideology superimposed on local traditions.

The supernatural and social aspects of ancestor worship are particularly independent of written sources. As we noted in the preceding chapter, neo-Confucian philosophers said little about ancestral spirits and the afterlife. Compilers of ritual manuals and etiquette books did the same. The manuals do not specify, either, the respective ritual obligations of brothers, or which kinsmen should participate in which rites. All of these matters are folk traditions. In the following pages, we will try to identify the traditions evident in domestic rituals.

The Image of Ancestors at Domestic Rites

At domestic rites, ancestors are obviously portrayed as living but dependent and inactive parents. Many ritual practices are consciously modeled on behavior appropriate toward elders (Moon Seung Gyu 1974: 80) and thereby continue the pattern begun during the mourning period. Twisŏngdwi informants say, for example, that the rituals offered on New Year's Day are just like the New Year's greetings (*sebae*) offered to living kin. On both occasions, moreover, participants scrupulously observe the social hierarchy. Within the lineage, where age and generation determine formal rank, men offer New Year's greetings only to agnates who are older than themselves and at least of equal generation status. Similarly, each lineage member participates in domestic rites only for agnates who are older and at least of the same generation as himself. No one offers formal greetings to, or participates in a rite for, a younger brother or cousin.[4]

In addition to formal ancestor rituals, other New Year's greetings are made to the dead. Ancestors in mourning shrines are supposed to be visited there, while other ancestors are greeted at their graves. These acts too are like the New Year's greetings presented to living elders, say informants. Years ago the entire lineage would assemble on New Year's Day and visit the graves of all its agnatic forebears (that is, as far back as Kwŏn Pal), they claim, but this old custom "disappeared with topknots" (the strands of hair that married men tied on top of their heads until the early decades of the Japanese annexation). Today, small

---

[1] Many ritual manuals, by contrast, prescribe participation in rites for various categories of genealogically inferior next-of-kin who have no descendants of their own. Like many of these manuals, some popular etiquette books also provide texts that can be recited to these persons at their rites. Participation in rites commemorating inferiors is common in Japan (R. Smith 1974b: 128–30) but comparatively rare in China (A. Wolf 1974b: 148).

groups of brothers and first cousins visit only the two or three most recent generations of their own ancestors. Informants say that New Year's visits to the homes of more distant agnates of the lineage have declined as well in recent years.

The treatment of ancestors as living elders is also apparent in the timing of death-day rites. Most lineage households offer these rites just before midnight of the day before the death anniversary on the grounds than an ancestor should be commemorated on the anniversary of a day when he or she had been alive (*san nal*). "After all, " Kwŏn Nam-sik argued, "the dead don't eat" (*chugŭn sarami mŏgŭlkka?*).

Those lineage households that offer death-day rites after midnight share Kwŏn Nam-sik's view that the rites are offered to "living" ancestors. Informants at these households agree that an ancestor should be commemorated on the anniversary of a time when he or she was alive, but they point out that nobody ever died precisely at midnight. Thus, the rituals can be offered shortly after 12 P.M. because the ancestor was still alive at that time. (They also maintain that a death-day ritual should be held exactly on the anniversary of death, because one of its purposes is to remind descendants of this important date.)

Still other procedures at death-day rites treat ancestors like living elders. After the food and wine are offered, for example, each commemorated ancestor is presented with a bowl of water. Kwŏn O-sik explained that this was done because the living, too, usually drink water or scorched-rice tea at the end of the meal. Moon Seung Gyu (1974: 80) has also pointed to this similarity and further argued that the number of wine offerings is derived from etiquette appropriate for the living: "Any important guests or elders would usually find themselves being treated to 'three drinks' before the meal and with tea after the meal." Moreover, the importance attached to food offerings is certainly not out of proportion to their significance among the living. We have already seen that sixtieth-birthday celebrations are essentially food offerings presented by children to their parents. By the same token, most Korean tales of filial piety hinge on sacrifices made by descendants to obtain something for their parents to eat.[5]

[5] Choi In-hak's *Type Index of Korean Folktales* (1979) has assigned Types 385–408 to stories of filial piety. Of these twenty-four types, at least half (386–89, 391, 392, 396, 397, 400, 402, 404, and 405) deal with children who provide their parents with something to eat.

In addition to modeling the treatment of ancestors upon that owed to elders, domestic ritual procedures provide other evidence of how villagers conceive of ancestors. In years past, ancestors—or at least one of their souls—resided continually in one of their descendants' homes throughout the period when they received holiday and death-day rites. Until the latter part of the nineteenth century, the lineage made a wooden tablet for each ancestor. It was kept for four generations at the home of his or her primogeniture descendant (that is, the eldest son, eldest son's eldest son, etc.). At domestic rituals, the appropriate tablets were taken out of their cabinets and presented with offerings. The care with which the tablets were handled, and the small hole bored in each to allow the spirit to enter and depart (Lee Kwang-Kyu 1977a: 11; Biernatzki 1967: 360) indicate the belief that the ancestors were present in them. After four generations, the tablet was either burned or buried at the grave of the ancestor it represented.

Only two wooden tablets remained in Twisŏngdwi during our fieldwork. They represented an office-holding ancestor and his wife of the thirtieth generation who died in 1884 and 1875, respectively. Even elderly lineage members can remember only one other pair of tablets, for twenty-eighth-generation ancestors who died in 1753 and 1755, so the custom of making wooden tablets must have ended about a hundred years ago. Today, new paper tablets are prepared for each domestic ritual and burned immediately after the ritual. This is the most common practice throughout Korea, though a few households still make wooden tablets (e.g., Lee Kwang-Kyu 1977a: 10).

Nowadays, ancestors are thought to reside somewhere else—most often their graves—and only to visit their primogeniture descendant's home for death-day and holiday rites. At those lineage households that offer domestic rites in the inner room rather than on the veranda, the door of the room is left open so the spirits can enter. Informants at other households explained that death-day rites are performed at about midnight, before the cocks begin to crow, because spirits of the dead can move about more freely at that time. Some cited the appearance of ancestors in dreams about the time of their death-days as evidence that ancestors really come and eat their food offerings. And finally,

Ancestor tablets made of wood. These tablets, the last remaining wooden tablets in Twisŏngdwi, were made for a thirtieth-generation ancestor and his wife, and were buried at the couple's joint grave in 1980.

one of the first ritual acts at a domestic rite is filling and then emptying a wine cup without placing it on the food offering table. According to informants and some etiquette books (e.g., Ŏm Mun-ho 1972: 214), the purpose of this act is to summon the ancestor's spirit (or one of them). It is unnecessary at mourning-period rituals, explained Kwŏn Tong-sik, because the ancestor is already in the mourning shrine.

Although ancestors come to receive offerings, they do nothing to initiate domestic rites. The rites are scheduled, not performed

at the demand of the ancestor, and descendants must remember
the dates, present the offerings, and invite the ancestors to eat.
Moreover, the descendants speak to ancestors on these occasions—not vice versa, as at ancestor seances.

The following address is typical of those recited at death-day
rites for a parent (see also Moon Seung Gyu 1974: 78; Dix 1979:
64). Kwŏn Hae-su recited the words from memory, though like
the rest of his kinsmen he learned the text from a printed etiquette book.

> Now is the time,
> According to the sexagenary cycle:
> The year *kap in*,[6]
> The fifth month, the month of *kyŏng o*,
> The thirteenth day, the day of *im o*.
> Your filial son, (name)
> Dares to address you openly.
>
> Honorable scholarly ancestor
> And honorable wife, our ancestress
> Of the [ancestress's natal] lineage,
> The passage of time has brought the changing of the seasons,
> And once again the ritual day has come
> When I remember, with heartfelt emotion,
> That an offspring's debt to his parents
> Is as limitless as the sky,
> And sincerely offer this pure wine and these various foods.
> May they be pleasing to you.

In sum, many ritual procedures, and informants' explanations
of these procedures, portray ancestors as living and honored, but
dependent and unassertive, elders. Ancestors do little more than
eat, receive bows, and travel back and forth between their graves
and the homes of their descendants. It is their offspring who take
the initiative, punctiliously carrying out filial obligations and re-
paying indebtedness to forebears.

However obvious this idealistic image of ancestors may appear,
it represents only one perspective. Though descendants try to
treat ancestors *as if* they are living elders, they have not lost sight
of the fact that ancestors are indeed dead. When bowing to living

---

[6] The day, month, and year of the rite are identified according to the sexa-
genary cycle used in traditional time reckoning.

elders at sixtieth birthdays and on New Year's Day, for example, Twisŏngdwi villagers, like other Koreans (Moon Seung Gyu 1974: 80), kowtow once; but to the dead they kowtow twice. Implanting a spoon in a rice bowl is one of the worst breaches of Korean table manners because this is how the rice and spoon are presented to the dead at ancestor rituals. And, as Kwŏn O-sik pointed out, the placement of jujubes, chestnuts, persimmons, and pears runs from left to right, rather than right to left, at sixtieth-birthday celebrations for living parents. These and other reversals, he speculated, symbolize the different statuses of the living and the dead.

Nor are ancestors always as passive as the formal ritual procedures indicate. Some informants, most of them women, say that failure to perform an ancestor ritual may provoke the neglected ancestor to "punish" (*pŏrŭl chunda*) his or her descendants. An even harsher image of ancestors is conveyed in the following legend, given to us by Kwŏn Tŏk-su's widow. We obtained an almost identical version from Kwŏn Pyŏng-ŏn's mother. Variants of the story are also found in other Korean villages (Gale 1898: 86–87; Choi In-hak 1979: 134–35) and in Japan (Yanagita 1970: 140–41; Yonemura 1976: 184).[7]

A long time ago there was a salt seller. He was on his way to sell his salt one day when it became dark. Now, there were two grave mounds side by side there; and since it was cold he went into the space between them and went to sleep.

While he was drowsing, he barely heard voices saying, "Eh, aren't you going?"

"I don't think I'll go. You go by yourself."

"We should go together." That's the way the story goes.

Finally, one of them went alone. It was the husband's death-day and he went by himself. When he came back his wife asked him, "How was it?"

"When I got there I found they had put a long snake into the food, and so I couldn't eat it. So I took their baby and touched it to the fire and then came back."

[Dawnhee Yim Janelli: A baby?]

Yes, a baby. The salt seller heard him say that they had prepared the food very badly. It was dirty and he couldn't eat it. So he got mad and

---

[7] We have no way of knowing whether or not this legend can be found in China. Existing indices of Chinese oral narratives (Eberhard 1937; Ting 1978) include few legends.

picked up their baby and touched it to a fire. That's what the salt seller heard while he was drowsing. Then he went down to a village. The next morning at the break of day, it became light and he entered the village.

In the village there was a house where they had performed a death-day ritual on the preceding night, the baby had been burned, and the whole house was in a turmoil.

Now he had heard [the husband's spirit say at the grave the night before] that the people of that house surely wouldn't know how to cure the baby, but that if a certain procedure[8] were followed and if the baby were given a certain medicine, it would be cured.

So the salt seller went to the house and told them exactly what to do, and the baby was cured. After the child had recovered, the people at that house were very grateful and they inquired about their guest, seated him at their home, and treated him very well before seeing him off.

And so, the healing of the baby shows that there really are human spirits. That really proves it.

[Dawnhee Yim Janelli: Why did they put a snake into the food?]

It was a hair that had gotten into the food, but they called it a snake.

So if you offer a death-day ritual, it's very difficult because you have to do it very carefully and be very clean.

This tale provides a perspective on ancestors unlike that afforded by formal ritual procedures. First, it suggests that ancestors are not as passive as the procedures would lead us to believe: deceased forebears may deliberately harm their descendants. Second, the story shows how the welfare of living parents and their children are often equated. Their identities are merged, to borrow Fortes's (1959: 36) term, so that punishment may be visited on children for the faults of their parents. Finally, the story shows how demanding and difficult to satisfy ancestors are. In their eyes, a small act of neglect is a serious offense. The final sentence, which stresses the importance of carefully preparing food offerings, was not the narrator's idiosyncratic addition to the tale; Kwŏn Pyŏng-ŏn's mother included the same coda in her telling of the tale.

Evidently, Twisŏngdwi villagers have more than one image of ancestors, even at domestic rites. At the least, these images emphasize different aspects of ancestors' personalities. Villagers' thoughts about ancestor rituals reflect their frustrations and anx-

[8] In the version of the story given to us by Kwŏn Pyŏng-ŏn's mother, the cure consisted of placing Chinese cabbage leaves on the burned skin. This cabbage is one of the most abundant vegetables in Korea.

ieties, as well as their ideals, concerning the care of elderly parents. Providing domestic rituals to often cantankerous and demanding ancestors is an onerous chore, just like the care of elderly parents. "Like the return of a death-day in a poor house" (*kananhan chip chesannal torao tŭt*) is a Korean proverbial comparison used to describe an unwelcome but recurring event (Yi Kimun 1962: 2). In Chapter 6, where we explore these views more fully, we will show that images of ancestors do not merely differ in emphasis but are somewhat incompatible to Twisŏngdwi villagers.

Ritual Obligations, Inheritance, and Fraternal Relations

Domestic ritual obligations in Korea fall parallel to the succession to household headship and the inheritance of household property. As we have seen, an eldest son normally succeeds to the headship of his natal household and inherits the largest share of its farmland. Similarly, eldest sons are normally responsible for offering the rites at their homes and bearing most of the attendant expenses. However, all male agnatic descendants are ultimately responsible for commemorating a given ancestor. First we will examine the respective obligations of eldest sons and their younger brothers, the quality of fraternal relationships, and how both are grounded in Korean inheritance practices. Later, we will pursue these same themes among wider ranges of agnatic kin.

In addition to the obligations toward his parents, an eldest son assumes any ritual responsibilities his father has had toward agnatic forebears within the three previous generations. Thus, a man commemorates a maximum of four generations of ancestors. Informants could not explain why domestic rituals should be continued for just four generations, although they recognized that some cutoff point was necessary lest domestic obligations accumulate endlessly. A four-generation rule is prescribed in Chu Hsi's *Book of Family Ritual* (De Harlez 1889: 25, 132) and in nearly all Korean ritual manuals and etiquette books. In applying this rule to actual cases, however, Twisŏngdwi families differ not only from the book but from each other.

An eldest son may inherit his father's and even his grandfather's ritual duties while they are still alive. One ritual manual

(Yi Chong-su 1962: 418–19) provides a formal text to be recited before ancestors' tablets to inform them that their seniormost descendant, though still alive, is passing on his ritual responsibilities to his son. In Korea, therefore, unlike some African societies (Fortes 1961: 171–72), a son need not wait until his father's death in order to reach full ritual maturity. During our first period of fieldwork in Twisŏngdwi, 78-year-old Kwŏn Nam-sik no longer participated in domestic rituals but had left their performance in the hands of Kwŏn Pyŏng-hwan, his 62-year-old eldest son. Four years later, when Kwŏn Nam-sik was still living, Kwŏn Pyŏng-hwan had in turn passed his ritual obligations on to Kwŏn Hyŏk-t'ae, his own 44-year-old eldest son. Since Kwŏn Hyŏk-t'ae had emigrated to Seoul, leaving his parents and grandfather in the village, Kwŏn Pyŏng-hwan had to travel to the city to participate in the rites (by that time Kwŏn Nam-sik was too weak to leave home).

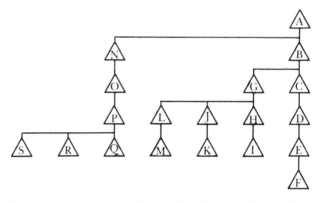

Fig. 11. Arrangement of descent lines in printed genealogies.

The distribution of domestic ritual obligations is graphically portrayed in printed genealogies, like that of the Andong Kwŏn kin group. Since the names of eldest sons are inserted directly beneath those of their fathers, each lineage member is primarily responsible for commemorating those ancestors whose names appear directly above his own. In Figure 11, the man designated by the letter "E" commemorates ancestors A through D and their wives. Those represented by letters S, R, L, J, and G have no primary ritual responsibilities; as junior sons, their obligations are secondary or contingent.[9] Some contingent responsibilities of junior sons are well defined. In Twisŏngdwi, a second son assumes all the rights and duties of the eldest son if his elder brother dies before marriage. Unless the Andong Kwŏn genealogy happened to be updated while the first-born son was alive, his name would not even be entered in it and future generations would be unaware that he ever existed. Traditionally, marriage formally transformed a child into an adult, and children are still of little structural significance. Even today, children are not given formal funerals, but are buried quietly and without ceremony by their parents and a few close neighbors or relatives.

Such was the fate of Kwŏn Sŏng-sik's elder brother. Because he died unmarried a few decades ago, his name was not added to the most recent publication of the genealogy; as a result, Kwŏn Sŏng-sik's own name appears directly beneath that of his father. Kwŏn Sŏng-sik will also inherit his father's ritual responsibilities, just as he has already assumed de facto control of his father's household.

If an eldest son dies after marriage, his younger brother's obligations depend on many circumstances but are still well defined. Normally, the obligations pass to the eldest son's heir and not to the younger brother. If the heir is a minor, however, the younger brother assumes his obligations temporarily, eventually passing them on to the heir. If a married eldest brother dies childless, an heir is usually adopted to him posthumously.

Many of these principles can be seen in the rearrangement of ritual obligations caused by Kwŏn Pyŏng-sŏp's death (see Figure 12). His younger brother Kwŏn Pyŏng-jun took over Pyŏng-sŏp's ritual responsibilities, provided for the care of their widowed mother, and gave his son Kwŏn Hyŏng-mun to Pyŏng-sŏp as his adoptive heir. Pyŏng-jun was working and living in Seoul, and Hyŏng-mun was serving in the army, but Hyŏng-mun's wife and infant son moved to Twisŏngdwi to live with Pyŏng-jun's mother. Both men later joined them. Informants say that strictly speak-

[9] On some Korean islands and remote areas of the mainland, domestic ritual responsibilities for various ancestors may be distributed among descendants of several descent lines. Lee Kwang-Kyu (1977a: 15–16) suggests that these practices may be survivals of Koryŏ and early Yi customs.

ing, Pyŏng-jun should commemorate four generations of ances-tors, just as his elder brother had done, and that as long as Pyŏng-jun is alive, Hyŏng-mun should offer rituals only for his adoptive parents, Pyŏng-sŏp and his wife. Yet no one thought anything was seriously amiss when Pyŏng-jun's absence required Hyŏng-mun to officiate at the death-day rite of his grandmother. Pyong-jun's and Hyŏng-mun's ritual obligations cannot be rigidly dif-ferentiated anyway, since a son may well assume his father's ritual role during the latter's lifetime.

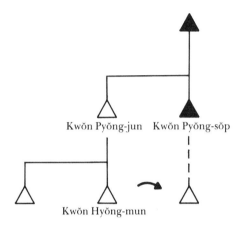

Fig. 12. An adoption in Twisŏngdwi.

The responsibilities of junior sons are less clear when their eld-est brother is alive but does not fulfill his ritual obligations. One eldest son married a Christian woman who refused to permit ancestor rituals in her house. Eventually, the rites were per-formed at the home of his next younger brother. In another lin-eage household where a similar problem arose, the eldest son's uncles (father's younger brothers) forced him to continue the rites at his home anyway.

The obligations of younger sons are similarly ill defined in the normal case, when their eldest brother accepts primary respon-sibility for offering ancestor rituals. Younger brothers and their families are usually expected to contribute some food, labor, or money, but the amount or kind of contributions depends on their wealth and the availability of labor. Women of closely related households, especially households headed by brothers, usually help prepare the ritual offerings. On the last day of 1973, for example, the daughters of Kwŏn Ŭng-su spent several hours helping Kwŏn Tŏk-su's widow, their father's brother's wife, prepare for the New Year's rites and festivities. At most death-day rites as well, the wives or daughters of close agnates usually help with kitchen chores.

The ritual obligations of sons are extensions of their filial responsibilities toward living parents. As we have seen, all sons are obligated to provide at least some care and support for their aged parents. An eldest son assumes the greatest share because it is he who remains in his parents' home and succeeds to its headship, but when a parent cannot get along with a daughter-in-law or is otherwise uncomfortable in the eldest son's house, the contingent responsibilities of junior sons come into play.

The respective obligations of eldest and younger sons toward living parents and toward ancestors also correspond to inheritance of household property. In both domains, an eldest son's rights and duties are greater than those of his younger brothers, but other than that their respective portions of privileges and obligations are settled case by case. The Korean civil code includes a precise formula for dividing an estate among heirs (Bae Kyung Sook 1973: 152–54), but no one in Twisŏngdwi ever mentioned it. Instead, the division of household property is negotiated by the parties involved. The only invariable rule is that the eldest son receives a larger share than any of his younger brothers.

The correspondence between property inheritance and obligations toward parents and ancestors is not accidental. Informants say that the extra share of land the eldest son receives compensates him for his heavier responsibilities. When an eldest son's Christian wife refused to permit ancestor rituals, we asked his father's younger brother's wife if her household would offer the rituals. "Why should we?" she answered. "We didn't get the land." The rites were eventually performed at the home of the eldest son's younger brother. In return, he received the only remaining parcel of land cultivated by his widowed mother. In the other case of the Christian wife who opposed the rites, the eldest son's uncles allegedly argued that he had to perform the rites anyway because his father, and he in turn, had received the largest share of their household's property. In fact, the father and his three brothers had openly quarreled over the division of this property.

Despite the potential for fraternal conflict that the lack of clear-cut rules entails, open conflict between brothers (or between their wives) over property rights and ritual obligations is infrequent in Korea (Brandt 1971: 139, 187, 202; Osgood 1951: 48; Lee Kwang-Kyu 1975: 95; 1976: 14–16). The wife who refused to accept ritual responsibilities because her family had received less land was a misfit in Twisŏngdwi. She detested her husband's brothers' wives and eventually left the village. Hers was the only divorce that occurred during our fieldwork. And Twisŏngdwi lineage members were scandalized by the open quarreling of the four brothers over their inheritance.

The relationship between Korean brothers is generally characterized by mutual help and cooperation, not hostility. When a younger son marries and moves out of his natal home, he usually establishes his own household in the same hamlet as his parents and brothers. This arrangement facilitates the close contact and economic cooperation enjoyed by households headed by fathers and their younger sons, and later by elder and younger brothers. Kwŏn Sŏng-sik cultivates the paddy of his younger brother, who is fully occupied with his new dairy farm. For several years, Kwŏn Yŏng-sik cultivated the land of his elder brother when he was ill. Brothers frequently lend each other farm tools and animals and jointly carry out various farm tasks; their wives often work together in dry fields as well. Throughout his life, an elder brother retains some authority over, and receives a fair amount of deference from, his younger brothers. Their families refer to each other's households as the "big house" and "little house" (*k'ŭn chip*, *chagŭn chip*) respectively. We never saw a lineage member argue openly with, gossip about, or disparage a brother. Such behavior was reserved for more distant relatives or non-kin.

Comparisons with China and Japan suggest a causal relation between land inheritance and the quality of fraternal ties in Korea. In China, where property is usually divided equally among sons, brothers are notorious for their rivalry and lack of cooperation. Conflict and competition between adult brothers and between their wives are recurrent themes in recent analyses of the Chinese family (Cohen 1976; M. Wolf 1968; Freedman 1958: 21–27). Their disharmony is said to be rooted in competition over the resources of their natal household. Though each son inherits an equal share in principle, brothers typically quibble over how the rule is applied. In Japan, eldest sons often receive an even larger share than their counterparts in Korea, yet harmony, cooperation, and mutual assistance among brothers is as common in Japan as it is in Twisŏngdwi. Japanese brothers and their families often work together, share baths, and borrow each other's farm tools (Embree 1939: 79; Beardsley et al. 1959: 259).

Thomas Smith (1959: 46) has argued that unequal property division in seventeenth-century Japan actually promoted economic cooperation between households headed by brothers. Branch households, which received less land, had more labor than they needed, whereas the main household, which kept most of the land, farm tools, and animals, had a relative surplus of these capital goods. As a result, critical resources that were abundant in one family were usually scarce in the other. With no market to mediate exchange, continuous cooperation benefited all households.

Much of Smith's argument seems applicable to rural Korea and Japan in more recent times. Though land can be bought, sold, or rented with relatively few restrictions in Twisŏngdwi, there is no market for renting farm tools, draft animals can be borrowed only in exchange for labor, and farm help is often difficult to hire on a daily basis, especially when it is needed on short notice or during peak work periods. Continuous economic cooperation between households may not be inevitable in Twisŏngdwi, but it certainly makes farm life much easier.

The timing of property division has an even greater effect on fraternal relations than the rules of division. In China, sons are expected to wait until their father's death before beginning, or at least completing, the division of their natal household's property. As a result, brothers must carry out this division among themselves and therefore view each other as rivals. In Korea, by contrast, younger sons receive their inheritance upon marriage or shortly thereafter. Their father usually determines their shares of property because normally he is alive and still in control of his household at the time of division. Fathers are probably more generous than elder brothers, but whether or not they are, Korean brothers seldom have to confront each other over property division (Lee Kwang-Kyu 1976: 14–16). Only when a father dies or retires before division occurs are brothers likely to argue over their shares.

The only recent case of open fraternal conflict in Twisŏngdwi bears out this interpretation. The father died before property division, and his four sons had to divide their natal household's property among themselves. Moreover, the eldest son gave his younger brothers unusually small portions. Several years later, when one younger brother became ill, a lineage widow attributed his sickness to the spirit of his deceased eldest brother. Since the two brothers had argued while alive, she surmised that their mutual hostility continued after the elder's death. It is hardly surprising that the younger brothers later insisted that their eldest brother's son offer domestic ancestor rites at his house despite his Christian wife's objections.

Participation at Domestic Rites

Groups of closely related agnates, not the commemorated ancestor's own descendants per se, usually perform domestic rites. A ritual-performing group may be larger, smaller, or equal to the genealogical branch comprising the ancestor's descendants. But before describing the composition of these groups, we will first show how Twisŏngdwi lineage members perceive kinship distance.

Following the standard Korean practice (Lee Kwang-Kyu and Harvey 1973: 32–33), members of the Twisŏngdwi lineage measure the genealogical distance between two persons by counting ch'on. The distance between parent and child is one ch'on; and more remote kin can calculate their kinship distance by adding up the number of parent-child links in the genealogical path that unites them with a common ancestor. The distance between siblings, for example, is two ch'on because they are each one ch'on from their parents (see Figure 13). The distance between a man and his brother's son is three ch'on: two ch'on for the distance between brothers and one more for the distance between the brother and his son. A man and his father's brother's children, "first cousins" in American terminology, are four ch'on apart.

Theoretically, ch'on could be counted between any two people who share a common ancestor. In practice, however, they are rarely calculated beyond the range of third-cousin (eight ch'on) agnates, and even less where genealogical ties involve links through women. Most of our informants knew from memory their exact genealogical relationships with lineage mates within six or eight *ch'on*, but knowledge of more distant relationships varied from one informant to the next. Sometimes an informant would know the number of *ch'on* between himself and someone else but not their exact genealogical ties: he simply knew that his father's relationship with that person had been so many *ch'on* and that his own had to be one more than that number.

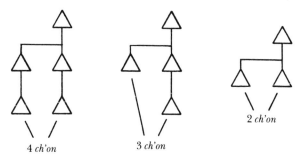

Fig. 13. Measurement of kinship distance.

Twisŏngdwi lineage members use *ch'on* not only to express genealogical distance but also to specify rights and duties between kin. Some say that all kinsmen within eight *ch'on* should participate in domestic rituals offered at each other's houses; others set the limit at six or ten *ch'on*. Most say that all kinsmen within eight *ch'on* of the deceased should wear at least a mourning hat at a funeral.

A fixed number of *ch'on* can also be used to define nonoverlapping genealogical segments (see Figure 14). Twisŏngdwi lineage members conceive of the ritual-performing segments of their lineage in just such terms, viewing each as a small kin group whose members are genealogically closer to each other than to any agnates outside their group.

By conventionally defining segments as fitting a fixed number of *ch'on*, lineage members can justify each group's fission with the passage of generations. The sons of an eight-*ch'on* segment make up a ten-*ch'on* segment, which ought eventually to divide into two (or more) eight-*ch'on* segments. Thus, Kwŏn Kap-sik figures that his segment will fission when all the members of his father's gen-

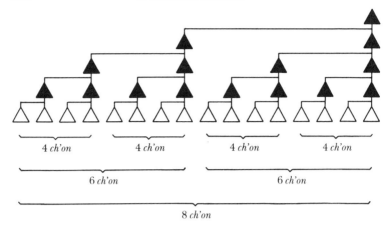

4 ch'on   4 ch'on   4 ch'on   4 ch'on

6 ch'on   6 ch'on

8 ch'on

Fig. 14. Kinship distance and genealogical segmentation.

eration pass away. The division of a segment, like the division of property among brothers, is viewed as a natural development that need not be precipitated or accompanied by ill will or quarreling.

Although genealogical distance provides the ideological charter for lineage segments, their actual composition is not always determined by it. Kwŏn Kŭn-sik and Kwŏn Sang-sik, for example, are eight-*ch'on* kinsmen who belong to different segments. Kwŏn Nam-su and Kwŏn T'ae-jun, on the other hand, are eight-*ch'on* kinsmen who belong to the same segment.

Figure 15 identifies the Twisŏngdwi lineage segments that jointly perform holiday rituals. Generally, all the village men of each segment, augmented by emigrant sons and brothers, participate in all of the holiday rituals offered at each other's homes. On New Year's Day and the Harvest Moon Festival, members of a segment gather and then visit their respective homes in turn. At each visit, they commemorate all the ancestors for whom the household head has primary ritual responsibility. The order of houses is determined by the generation-age status of the seniormost ancestor commemorated at each; thus each segment first assembles at the home of its primogeniture descendant.[10] The

---

[10] This appears to be the standard practice throughout Korea (e.g., Dix 1977: 120; Lee Kwang-Kyu 1977a: 21). Kim Taik-Kyoo (1964: 163), however, reports the reverse order of households in the lineage he studied.

homes of junior sons, who have no primary ritual obligations, are not visited at all.

The more households in a segment, the longer it takes to complete holiday rituals. This practical consideration tempers the rule of genealogical distance for the composition of the ritual performers. Segment III, the largest in Twisŏngdwi, assembles in its entirety only at the home of Kwŏn Pyŏng-u, its primogeniture descendant, then divides into two groups that perform their own rites. Informants explained that Segment III includes too many households for all its members to participate in each other's holiday rituals; it would take too much time. Under the present arrangement, all of the segments are able to complete their holiday rituals within two hours.

Just as segments can be too large, so can they be too small. After completing the rituals at his own house, Kwŏn Chŏng-su and his sons join the members of Segment VI, from which Kwŏn Chŏng-su's father had been adopted. By the time they arrive, Segment VI has already completed some of its rituals, but they join in the rest with the segment. It would be a pity, say informants, for Kwŏn Chŏng-su and his sons to spend the holiday by themselves.

Death-day rites usually involve fewer participants than holiday rituals. Fewer emigrant kinsmen return to the village on death-days; and even among Twisŏngdwi residents, a smaller group of agnates usually perform the rites. Younger brothers almost always participate in rites offered at the home of their father or eldest brother, and nephews (three *ch'on*) and first cousins (four *ch'on*) usually attend. Rarely do all the more distant agnates of a segment join the ritual participants, though often, some do.

Participation at domestic rites is affected by a number of considerations other than segment membership and genealogical distance. As we noted earlier, no lineage member bows to, or participates in a rite for, a kinsman of lower generation-age status. And Kwŏn Pyŏng-hwan no longer joins the other members of Segment III on holidays, because he now travels to Seoul to participate in rites offered at his son's home. Occasionally, too, a lineage member who is piqued at one or more of his agnates will invent an excuse and avoid the rites in their homes, but lineage members know each other too well to be deceived. One lineage member refrains from participating in all ancestor rituals, which

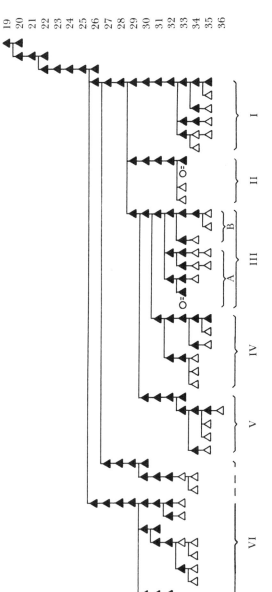

Generation

19
20
21
22
23
24
25
26
27
28
29
30
31
32
33
34
35
36

I   II   III   IV   V   VI

A   B

Fig. 15. Segments of the Twisõngdwi lineage. For names, see Figure 2.

informants attribute to a quirk in his personality. Finally, in one lineage family, the young daughters of the household head participated in a holiday rite by bowing together with their male kin at the appropriate moment. No one visibly encouraged them, but no one tried to stop them either.[11]

Obviously, ritual participation is not based solely on descent from the commemorated ancestor. Lineage members are expected to participate in domestic rituals for ancestors of their segment, not just their personal forebears. When they join in a rite for a first cousin's father, or a second cousin's grandfather, they commemorate ancestors of descent lines collateral to their own. This type of participation is common throughout Korea (Lee Kwang-Kyu 1977a: 7; Choi Jai-seuk 1966a: 130; Shima 1976: 75; Dix 1979: 59). On the other hand, some Twisŏngdwi lineage members do not participate in domestic rites for ancestors who are in fact their progenitors. Segment IV is descended from the thirtieth-generation ancestor commemorated on holidays at the home of Segment III's primogeniture descendant, yet no one of Segment IV participates in the rite. (Segment I is also descended from that ancestor by blood ties: its thirty-first-generation ancestor was an adopted son.)

In an insightful article on descent and ancestor worship in Korea, Lee Kwang-Kyu (1977a: 5–8) has pointed to a correspondence between limiting domestic commemoration to four generations and defining ritual-performing segments as eight-*ch'on* groups. As a result of using both principles, he suggests, each segment comes to commemorate a set of ancestors unique to its membership. Though this correspondence may be valid for an abstract model, the actual segments in Twisŏngdwi (Figure 15) show that demographic variation often prevents the manifestation of this ideal.

At any given domestic ritual, the composition of the performing group is based heavily on agnatic reciprocity, that is, members of each segment participate in rites for collateral kin because they are obligated to each other—not to the dead. Although segments themselves have few corporate functions, their members are held

[11] Participation by young females at holiday rituals may be more common in Seoul. Perhaps it is found more often among families that do not belong to local lineages. One of Biernatzki's (1967: 322) informants reported witnessing limited female participation at such rites in a village other than his own.

together by a web of interhousehold ties perpetuated by mutual help and economic cooperation. Ties between brothers are strongest; ties between first cousins are considerably weaker; and ties between second and third cousins are almost, but not quite, negligible.[12]

Lineage segments have no political functions. A dispute between two kinsmen does not mobilize the other members of their respective segments to act on their behalf. As we noted in Chapter 1, the major political divisions in Twisŏngdwi are determined by age, not by genealogy.

Some lineage segments have corporate economic functions, but these are usually insignificant. Only Segment VI jointly owns property, about 28 ares of paddy used to finance the annual lineage ritual for its twenty-sixth-generation male ancestor. Even this claim to property ownership lay dormant for several years, however, while the entire Twisŏngdwi lineage managed the parcel. Only after the possibility of selling some lineage-owned lands arose did Segment VI assert its exclusive rights to the parcel. In other Korean lineages, segments may regularly acquire ritual estates to finance rites for ancestors who pass beyond four generations (Cho Oakla, personal communication; Choi Jai-seuk 1966a: 96; Dix 1977: 450–51). Yet in these lineages as well, estates often merge into a general lineage fund as the segment that purchased the plot fissions and loses its corporate identity (e.g., Choi Jai-seuk 1966a: 84–130; see also Chapter 5).

At times other than holiday rites, whole segments are regularly visible only when repairing graves of recent ancestors in the spring of each year. When the earthen mound above the grave of an ancestor within four generations needs rebuilding, all the members of a segment are supposed to assemble for this task. Graves of more distant ancestors are repaired by the entire lineage.

The boundaries of a ritual-performing segment generally parallel its members' genealogical memories. All informants can trace their genealogical linkages and know the number of *ch'on* between themselves and other members of their segment. The

---

[12] Dawnhee Yim Janelli's mother often quoted a proverb to describe how rapidly affection attenuates as kinship distance increases: "One *ch'on* is a thousand *ri*" (*han-ch'oni ch'ŏl-li rago*). (One *ri* equals about four kilometers.) We have not heard this proverb elsewhere.

TABLE 4

Residence of Lineage Segments

Lineage segment	Number of households		
	Upper hamlet	Middle hamlet	Lower hamlet
I	5	0	0
II	0	0	3
III	3	4	0
IV	0	1	4
V	0	4	0
VI	2	7	0

primogeniture descendant of each segment, moreover, is called the "big house" by all of the other members. Genealogical ties to more remote agnates are often known only to the extent of identifying their segment.

Segment membership also corresponds roughly to hamlet affiliation, though no rule prescribes that members of a segment occupy the same hamlet. As Table 4 shows, Segments I, II, and V reside exclusively in the upper, lower, and middle hamlets, respectively. Nearly all of Segment IV lives in the lower hamlet, and most of Segment VI occupies the middle hamlet. Evidently, when younger brothers establish new households, or when the locations of existing households are changed, most lineage members prefer to live near their closest kin. Thus, members of the same segment are often neighbors and can assist each other more readily whenever a need arises.

Lee Kwang-Kyu has compiled some revealing statistics on mutual assistance between close agnatic kinsmen in another Korean lineage village. By counting visits between households, he found that members of the same generation visit more frequently than members of adjacent generations and that among agnates of the same generation, the frequency of household visiting drops sharply beyond the range of first cousins. He concludes: "In everyday activities, such as the possibility of borrowing farm tools, freely visiting on birthdays even without a formal invitation [when the host is expected to feed visitors], or candidly discussing the affairs of one's household, [such cooperation] appears to occur more within the narrow first-cousin [four-*ch'on*] range than within the entire ritual-performing segment [*tangnae*]" (Lee

Kwang-Kyu 1977a: 4). He adds that cooperation and mutual assistance between brothers is more generous than it is between cousins.

Our observations in Twisŏngdwi clearly support Lee Kwang-Kyu's findings. As we noted earlier, both Kwŏn Yŏng-sik and Kwŏn Sŏng-sik cultivated their brother's fields for them, but we did not observe one instance of such generosity between more distant kin. Indeed, one lineage member lamented that he had no brothers, for he felt that his cousins gave him little assistance. When Kwŏn Chae-sik opened a small general store and wine shop in competition with the one financed by the village Wives' Society, only his brother did not patronize the other shop. His first cousins used both shops, and more distant kin gave most of their business to the Wives' Society store.[13] Yet when Kwŏn Kŭn-sik's wife made a large amount of rice cake one evening, he sent portions to the most distant agnates of his segment as well as to his brothers and closest neighbors.

The correlation between agnatic reciprocity in ritual participation and mutual assistance in daily life is evident even in the exceptional cases. The only persons who admitted that they had deliberately eschewed their segment's holiday rites cited their kinsmen's lack of economic cooperation as the reason. And the lineage member with the "peculiar" personality, who never participates in ancestor rites, works and earns nearly all of his income outside the village. His household also cultivates one of the smallest landholdings in Twisŏngdwi. "I'm not a farmer," he once told us. No other lineage member made this claim.

Who Are the Ancestors?

Nearly all Twisŏngdwi lineage members agree that ancestors within four generations should receive domestic rites at the homes of their primogeniture descendants. They also agree that ancestors beyond four generations should be commemorated once a year with lineage rituals at their graves (see Chapter 5).

In fact, ritual obligations are not so easily defined. Recent research in China and Japan (Ahern 1973; A. Wolf 1974b; 1976; Wang S. 1976; Freedman 1970: 166; R. Smith 1974b) has shown

---

[13] The initial capital necessary to open the Wives' Society store was provided by loans from the members. If the store fails, the loans will not be repaid.

that domestic rites may also be offered to persons beyond the range of kin who ought to be commemorated by ideal rules. Very often, these "extra" persons are commemorated only on holidays and not on death-days (R. Smith 1974b: 129; A. Wolf 1974b: 154). A similar pattern can be seen in Twisŏngdwi. We will first examine the identities of these additional persons and then outline the general criteria by which they are included in domestic rituals.

No one in Twisŏngdwi could explain why domestic commemoration should end precisely at four generations.[14] Apparently the lack of a rationale allows variant interpretations and applications of this rule to questionable cases. Lineage members have no generally accepted procedure for commemorating ancestors whose four immediate generations of primogeniture descendants have died if other agnatic male descendants within four generations are still alive (see Figure 16). According to the *Sarye p'yŏllam*, an eighteenth-century work said to be one of the most authoritative ritual manuals of its day (Deuchler 1977: 5), the primogeniture descendant of such ancestors is not responsible for their commemoration (Lee Kwang-Kyu 1977a: 6). Instead, the surviving descendants within four generations ought to rotate this responsibility among themselves. Yet Lee Kwang-Kyu (ibid.) could not find an instance of this ideal prescription in Korea (but see Kim Taik-Kyoo 1964: 164) and the more popular of today's ritual manuals and etiquette books omit it. Evidently there is no generally accepted solution to this problem. In some Korean villages, moreover, only three generations of ancestors are commemorated with domestic rites (Osgood 1951: 119–21; Pak Ki-hyuk 1975: 68); in others, domestic rituals may be terminated before all descendants within four generations have died (Dix 1977: 58, 228).

[14] When pressed for an explanation of this rule, Kwŏn Pyŏng-ŏn's mother suggested that it derived from changes in residence. She noted that a house is often sold or otherwise passes from one family to another after four generations. As a result, the house of a primogeniture descendant is usually not the same as that of his ancestors beyond four generations; so these remote ancestors would not be able to return to their former homes if domestic rites were offered for them.

In exceptional cases, none of which are found in Twisŏngdwi, an ancestor (and his wife) may be granted a special privilege by the government or a Confucian academy and have a permanent tablet (*pulch'ŏnjiwi*). It entitles them to receive death-day rituals in perpetuity. For a description of this practice, see Janelli and Janelli (1978: 277–78).

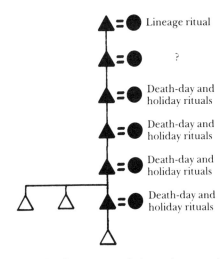

Fig. 16. Ritual statuses and elapsed generations.

Nor do the segments of the Twisŏngdwi lineage all deal with these interstitial cases in the same way. In Segment III, the thirtieth generation of ancestors now occupy this liminal position. They receive a domestic rite on holidays, but not on their death-days, at the home of their primogeniture descendant. Although that descendant is beyond four generations, he is still responsible for preparing the food offerings. The ritual presentation of wine, however, is made by one of the descendants within four generations of those commemorated. In Segment II, the same interstitial position is now held by the twenty-ninth generation of ancestors.[15] They receive a lineage ritual and no domestic commemoration. Kwŏn Pyŏng-nyŏl, the acting primogeniture descendant of Segment I, commemorates only three generations of ancestors on death-days and four on holidays. He justified his practice, which greatly surprised a few of his kinsmen of other segments, by claiming that he has no living uncles.[16]

[15] Domestic rituals in Segment II are offered at the home of a thirty-fourth-generation descendant who emigrated from Twisŏngdwi.

[16] Segments V and VI have no interstitial cases at this time. Segment IV, however, has a thirty-third-generation kinsmen who lives outside Twisŏngdwi. As informants recognized, his living could disqualify the twenty-ninth generation-ancestor (and his wife) of Segments III, IV, and V from the lineage rites they currently receive.

A few other persons, most of whom have no descendants at all, receive ancestor rituals only on holidays. A variety of motives have prompted their domestic commemoration.

Kwŏn Chŏng-su's commemoration of his great-great-grandfather and great-great-grandmother, who are depicted at the top of Figure 17, is an excellent illustration of the contingent ritual obligations of junior descent lines. Our attention here, however, focuses on the holiday ritual that Kwŏn Chŏng-su offers for a couple who died without descendants: his great-grandfather's elder brother and his wife. Clearly they are not his progenitors. When we asked why he offers a holiday ritual for these collaterals, Kwŏn Chŏng-su had a very practical explanation. Since rituals for other ancestors are offered at his home on holidays anyway, he noted, offering one more entails little effort. In fact, the additional holiday ritual requires only about ten more minutes and the preparation of two more bowls of rice-cake soup. Commemorating these ancestors on their death-days, by contrast, would add all the work required for two separate rituals.

Another case of offering holiday rituals to persons without issue also entails the addition of only one more rite to a lineage household's other holiday rituals. There, the household head provides a holiday ritual for his younger brother, but the actual presentation of wine is made by another brother who is junior to the deceased. Although it is easiest for the eldest brother's house-

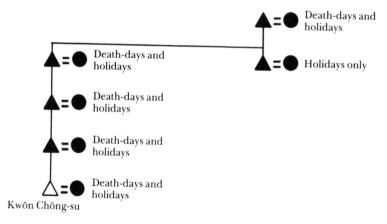

Fig. 17. Rituals offered by Kwŏn Chŏng-su.

hold to provide the ritual, only the deceased's genealogical inferiors can participate in the rite. In this case, however, only one place setting is arranged on the food-offering table. The brother's widow later remarried, and the family assumes that she will be cared for by her second husband's household.

Kwŏn Hae-su offers an extra holiday ritual to his paternal grandfather's sister (Figure 18). Her rite is the first to be per-

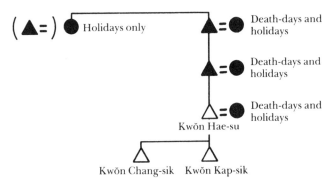

Fig. 18. Rituals offered by Kwŏn Hae-su.

formed at his house, though no one knows if she was an elder sister of Kwŏn Hae-su's grandfather and really deserves this preeminent position. Like all other women born into the Twisŏngdwi lineage, her name and the details of her birth and death are omitted from the Andong Kwŏn genealogy.[17]

An act of ancestral affliction started Kwŏn Hae-su's unorthodox ancestor ritual. We first learned of it by chance from his eldest son, Kwŏn Kap-sik. Our remark about the twelve-year age difference between him and his younger brother, Kwŏn Changsik, brought this case to light. Kwŏn Kap-sik explained that his mother had given birth to several other children during those twelve years, but none had lived to maturity. Upon consulting a shaman (*mudang*), she learned that their deaths had been caused by the unmarried sister of her husband's grandfather, who was unhappy because dying without descendants deprived her of ancestor rituals and care of her grave. After Kwŏn Hae-su's fam-

[17] Occasionally, a daughter of the lineage is indicated in the genealogy by the Chinese character for "daughter" (*yŏ*) and some biographical details about her husband.

ily began tending the grave and offering holiday rituals for her, Kwŏn Chang-sik was born and lived to maturity.

Kwŏn Kap-sik was dubious of the shaman's explanation for his family's misfortune, though he seemed to verify it with his account of the relevant events. After his father dies, he told us, he will open the grave that his family has been tending to see if a woman's skeleton is really buried there. In the meantime, he arranges two place settings on the food-offering table for her holiday ritual: though the woman died unmarried and was never given a posthumous marriage, an ancestor ritual for an unmarried person somehow seems inappropriate to him.

The only other instances we found of ancestor rites offered for persons other than agnatic forebears or offered on holidays only involved concubines and twice-married women.

If a woman enters into a union with a man who already has a legitimate spouse, she is unquestionably a concubine. She will later be commemorated by her mate's legitimate descendants, but only on holidays and on his death-day. A concubine's death-day rite, say lineage informants, is the responsibility of her own descendants.

We had no way of learning the actual ritual practices of concubines' sons or their views on ritual obligations. Their illegitimate status is an extremely touchy matter. All but one, moreover, have emigrated from Twisŏngdwi. We can guess that the concubines' sons who have left the village may commemorate both their parents on death-days and holidays, for commemorating only one would perpetuate knowledge of their illegitimacy. They also have other strategies, however: one concubine's son was said to have become a Christian, and he thereby had an excuse for not offering any ancestor rituals.

Some concubines are not commemorated at all in Twisŏngdwi, typically women whose unions were short and did not produce any offspring. Lineage informants usually assume that such women are cared for by sons that resulted from unions with other men.

Blurred with the status of concubines is that of twice-married women. Indeed, distinguishing a woman's second marriage from concubinage is often a very difficult matter. Individual cases are subject to varying interpretations and informally negotiated resolutions.

Informants feel that each ancestor should be commemorated

at only one household, though they recognize that a twice-married woman may eventually receive rituals at both the households with which she was affiliated. Deciding which one should offer her rituals is no easy matter. If only one of her unions resulted in male issue, those descendants will most likely offer all her rituals. The decision is far more difficult if a woman had sons by both husbands. Two half-brothers in a neighboring village were said to have fought over their mother's corpse to determine which would perform her funeral rites. (The winning son would have obtained a social acknowledgment of legitimacy for the union that produced him.) The case of a nonlineage Twisŏngdwi villager, whose widowed mother's second marriage to a childless widower produced another son, provided a set of circumstances to which none of our informants could offer a solution that other villagers would accept. Kwŏn Kŭn-sik knew it was futile even to try. "Cases like that are difficult," he said. "The descendants have to reach an agreement among themselves." In his opinion, the Twisŏngdwi villager should offer all the rituals for his own parents, and his half-brother should offer the rites for his father and his father's first wife; should the half-brother be unwilling to offer the rites for his father's first wife on her death-day, he should at least offer her a holiday ritual.

The above cases of holiday-only worship and rites for persons other than forebears all share three characteristics. First, each of these rites, like those for patrilineal forebears within four generations, is offered only for agnates. A mother's natal relatives, in-laws, or non-kin receive no ancestor rituals in Twisŏngdwi households. (A possible exception is the rite offered by Kwŏn Hae-su for his paternal grandfather's sister and her imaginary husband. An agnate by birth, the sister never lost her lineage affiliation through marriage. Whether or not her nonexistent husband constitutes an exception is a moot point.) Lineage members themselves stress agnatic ties as a criterion for entitlement to domestic commemoration. Some informants even say that a man's natural mother is entitled to ancestor rituals only because she is the wife of his father—it does not matter that she bore him. Their interpretation fits the facts better than any other. Some households commemorate both wives of a male ancestor, even if only one of the unions yielded offspring. The barren but legitimate wife receives rites not only on holidays but also on her death-day, her husband's death-day, and on the death-day of her husband's other wife. A barren wife who deserts her husband and thereby loses her agnatic tie receives nothing. A fertile wife who deserts her husband may be commemorated by the offspring of their union, but informants insist that she is not entitled to this privilege, and we know of no actual instances among the Twisŏngdwi kin group. In sum, lineage members recognize ritual obligations only toward those women who are related through male links.

The second characteristic shared by ancestors commemorated only on holidays is that they are not known to receive commemoration elsewhere. Indeed, the purpose of these rites is to provide for deceased persons who would not otherwise enjoy ancestor ritual offerings. Next of kin do not offer domestic rites for persons who have agnatic male descendants of their own.

Finally, in each of the above cases, both parents of the commemorated agnates were deceased. This may not be a requirement for domestic commemoration, but some evidence suggests that a living parent lessens a descendantless person's likelihood of commemoration. One informant said that as long as any man's parent is alive, his commemoration should be curtailed.

Twisŏngdwi lineage households perform domestic rites for very few persons other than their agnatic forebears within four generations, but ancestor rituals are only one of the ways of caring for them. Buddhist and shamanistic rites are available for a broader range of kin, many of whom do not meet the qualifications identified above, such as nonagnates, genealogical inferiors, and those whose parents are still living. When one lineage member's unmarried daughter died, her mother had her tablet installed in a Buddhist temple, where the resident monks care for it with periodic prayers and food offerings. Another lineage member, whose father is still living, had a tablet made for his eldest brother (who had died unmarried) and placed it in the care of a shaman when misfortunes in his household were attributed to the brother's spirit. Yet another lineage member had a shaman perform a posthumous marriage for a younger brother who had died unmarried in order to placate his spirit. Even maternal kin and in-laws, as well as agnates, may be given offerings at ancestor seances performed by a shaman. We will examine these ancestor seances in Chapter 6, after we take up the lineage rites performed for agnatic forebears beyond four generations.

❧ 5 ❧

Lineage Rituals

We have seen that the primary responsibility for mourning and domestic rituals is assigned to individual households via primogeniture. Entire lineages, by contrast, share responsibility for the rituals described in this chapter. Though "seasonal rituals" is a more literal translation of the Korean terms for these rites (*sije*, *sihyang*), we call them lineage rituals because they are corporately financed and offered by lineages.[1] Their performance at lineage-owned graves and ancestral halls, rather than in houses, further removes these rites from the domestic sphere of social life.

Lineage rituals are not motivated by a deep concern for the ancestors beyond four generations who are their recipients. Informants do not say that such remote forebears depend on their present offspring or even that they need to eat. Twisŏngdwi lineage members would not expect retribution from one whose lineage rite had been omitted, for misfortunes are never attributed to them.

Real-world social goals, rather than beliefs about the afterlife, prompt the offering of lineage rituals. Informants emphasize that the rites strengthen ties between agnates. Although assertion of social status, being a less laudable goal, is not mentioned as readily, informants are well aware that lineage rites serve to maintain the kin group's prestige. As one man said to his lineage

---

[1] The meanings of *sije* and *sihyang* are not entirely consistent throughout Korea. Usage here conforms to that of Lee Kwang-Kyu (1977a: 6, 8) and Twisŏngdwi informants. According to Korean dictionaries (e.g., Yi Hŭi-sŭng 1961: 1792, 1796), these terms refer to rituals offered (1) four times a year (once each season; such rituals are offered for the founder of the Andong Kwŏn kin group), or (2) in the tenth lunar month, before the graves of ancestors beyond four generations. One Korean government publication (Pogŏn Sahoe-bu 1973: 122), however, designates New Year's holiday rituals as "annual *sije*" (*yŏn-sije*). The corporate nature of *sije* or *sihyang* is not mentioned in either of these sources.

mates, "What will people think of us if we discontinue these rites?"

In the following pages, we will examine the goals of Korean lineages, how ancestor worship helps to attain these goals, and how the practice of ancestor worship results in more cohesive lineages than those found in China. We shall see how the different motivations for domestic and lineage rites are reflected in their responses to modern social changes.

Lineage Rites and Agnatic Solidarity

The observation that ancestor rituals strengthen kinship ties is commonplace in writings on East Asian ancestor worship (Hu 1948: 31; C. K. Yang 1961: 29–57; Kim Taik-Kyoo 1964: 160; Brandt 1971: 120; Hozumi 1913: 23; Yonemura 1976: 23). As Radcliffe-Brown (1952: 157–64) noted, the germ of this idea can be found in the writings of early Chinese philosophers. Neo-Confucianists in particular placed a high value on strong family and kinship ties, for maintaining an orderly society, and on ritual, for inculcating proper social sentiments (e.g., Chan 1967: 227–32; De Harlez 1889: 18, 24).

Twisŏngdwi villagers are not likely to mention a desire for agnatic solidarity in connection with domestic and mourning-period rites, because the participation of brothers and close cousins in them is simply another manifestation of the mutual assistance and cooperation expected of these kin in their everyday affairs. At lineage rites, by contrast, social solidarity is more consciously pursued and its desirability more often verbalized, especially at rites that bring together members of different local lineages. As Kim Taik-Kyoo (1964: 146) has observed, lineage rites may provide one of the few occasions at which more distant agnates can meet.

The five local lineages descended from Kwŏn Po have very little contact outside ritual contexts. The Twisŏngdwi kin group maintains close ties only with its kinsmen in Pangch'ukkol. The two lineages often send representatives to weddings and sixtieth-birthday celebrations in each other's villages. But when we needed to visit the Kaltam lineage to clarify a point about their genealogy, no one in Twisŏngdwi could give us precise directions to Kaltam village: no Twisŏngdwi lineage member had been

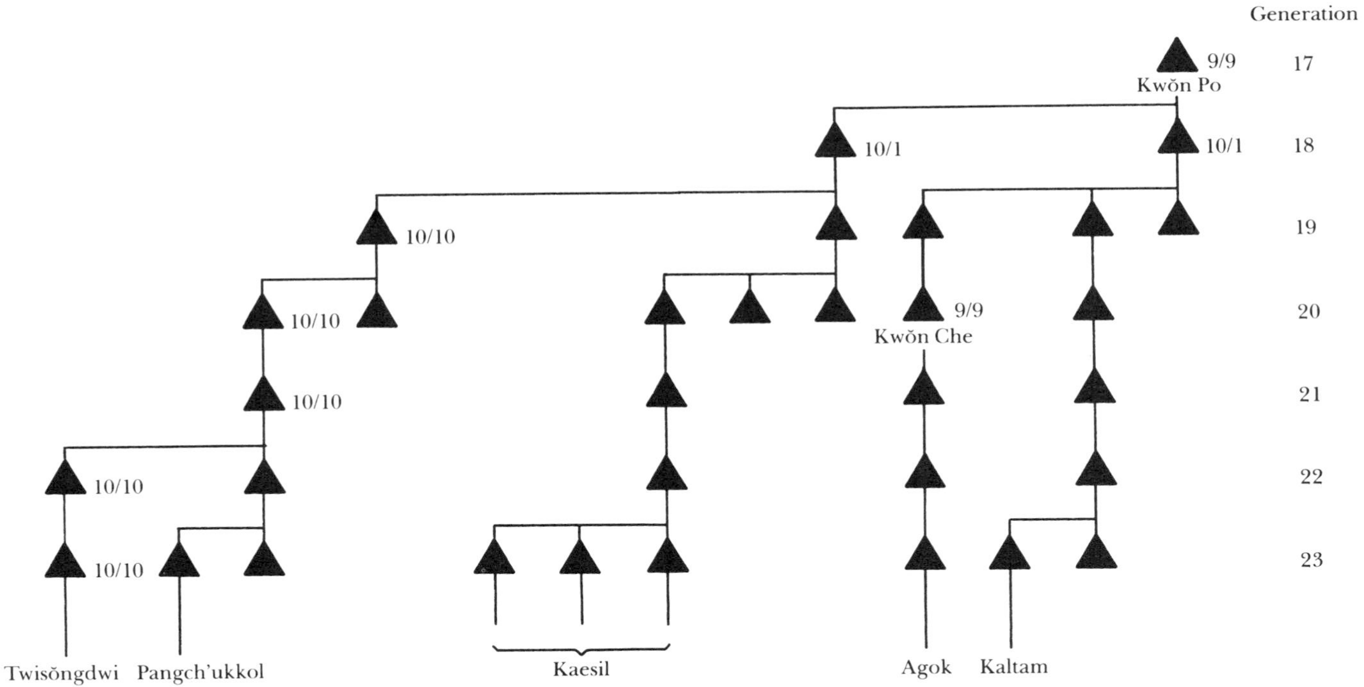

Fig. 19. Ancestors commemorated jointly by the Twisŏngdwi kin group and other local lineages.

there for over 30 years. Joint participation in a few lineage rituals, and rights in the estate that finances them, provide the only ties between Twisŏngdwi and Kaltam.

The use of ancestor rituals to strengthen agnatic ties can be a two-edged sword: whereas rituals for distant ancestors of an entire lineage serve to enhance the group's solidarity, those for less distant ancestors, from whom only one branch of a lineage is descended, may be used to differentiate or separate that branch from the others. In his admirable study of the Hahoe Yu lineage, rural sociologist Kim Taik-Kyoo (1964) describes a lineage divided into two major branches. The rivalry between these two branches is apparent not only in their statements and day-to-day activities, but also in their ancestor rituals. Though the two branches join together to commemorate a few common ancestors, each branch commemorates its exclusive ancestors separately.[2] Each owns and manages separate corporate estates, and each has adopted different arrangements for food offerings (Kim Taik-Kyoo 1964: 161), like contending political factions of the Yi dynasty.

A greater internal solidarity typifies the Twisŏngdwi lineage. Relations between the five lineages of Kwŏn Po's descendants are not as close as those within the Twisŏngdwi branch, but they are not marred by intense competition and conflict. In fact, participation in lineage rites is extended to include agnates who are not descendants of the commemorated ancestors. This practice, found only at some lineage rites in Korea (Choi Jai-seuk 1966a: 90–91; Biernatzki 1967: 210–13, 323–24, 331), is followed not only at many of the joint lineage rituals but also at rituals that the Twisŏngdwi kin group performs by itself.

Figure 19 identifies with a lunar-calendar date all the ancestors at whose rituals the Twisŏngdwi lineage participates with other kin groups. On the ninth day of the ninth month, representatives from all five lineages assemble to offer the annual ritual for Kwŏn Po and his wife, the seventeenth-generation ancestors of the five groups. They also commemorate Kwŏn Che and his wife, twentieth-generation ancestors of the Agok lineage, because

[2] The only exceptions were death-day rites before the permanent tablets (pulch'ŏnjiwi) of their famous ancestors, who lived about four hundred years ago. These rites were also attended by non-kin to honor these exalted persons (Kim Taik-Kyoo 1964: 160).

A lineage ritual for Kwŏn Pal and his wife, nineteenth-generation ancestors of the Twisŏngdwi and Pangch'ukkol kin groups.

their graves are near Kwŏn Po's. About three weeks later, representatives of the five lineages gather again to perform rituals for both pairs of their eighteenth-generation ancestors.[3]

The Twisŏngdwi lineage performs annual rites for its nineteenth and subsequent generations of ancestors on the tenth through thirteenth days of the tenth lunar month. On the first of these days, when the lineage commemorates its nineteenth through twenty-third generations of ancestors, it is joined by a delegation from Pangch'ukkol. The Pangch'ukkol kinsmen participate in all of the rituals performed that day, including those for the twenty-second and twenty-third generations of ancestors,

[3] In the early 1970's, the eighteenth-generation ancestors were each commemorated only by their own descendants. Informants said that relations between the branches then improved, and by the late 1970's the five kin groups resumed participating reciprocally in the rites for each other's eighteenth-generation forebears.

from whom they are not descended. By the same token, when the Pangch'ukkol representatives visit the grave of their own twenty-second-generation ancestors, they are joined by Twisŏngdwi lineage members. Because the grave of these forebears is near those of the formally commemorated ancestors, their descendants and their Twisŏngdwi kinsmen stop to offer a cup of wine as they pass by in a brief greeting. These and the other Pangch'ukkol ancestors are formally commemorated on the following day at the Pangch'ukkol lineage hall.

Extending agnatic solidarity while deemphasizing genealogical subdivisions is especially marked at the lineage rituals that the Twisŏngdwi kin group performs by itself on the next three days. Participants at each of these rituals are drawn from the entire lineage membership; thus the ancestors of the twenty-sixth and subsequent generations are commemorated by the entire lineage membership, even though each can count only a portion of the Twisŏngdwi lineage among his or her descendants. Both their own and collateral descent lines participate; moreover, the participating nondescendants are explicitly recognized—just as at death-day rites—when one of their number is chosen to act as second or third wine offerer. (The role of first wine offerer is reserved for descendants, though not necessarily the primogeniture descendant.) Kwŏn Kŭn-sik explained that appointing a wine offerer from the collateral descent lines is necessary to prevent a lineage ritual from looking as if it were the concern of only one segment. In sum, Twisŏngdwi lineage members offer lineage rites not as descendants of individual ancestors but as members of a corporate descent group.

This method of offering lineage rituals for ancestors beyond four generations reflects the absence of major genealogical divisions within the Twisŏngdwi kin group, as does the lineage's management of corporate property, which we describe below. The Twisŏngdwi lineage has chosen systems of ritual participation and estate management that reaffirm the ties of each member to all his local lineage mates in lieu of others that would enhance the solidarity of genealogical subdivisions at the expense of the lineage.

Twisŏngdwi lineage members may use lineage rites strategically to strengthen agnatic ties. A member who had emigrated to Seoul long ago is one example. His relations with his kin had been badly strained when he lived in the village, and he sought to improve them in his late years by contributing generously to village and lineage projects and by attending the annual rites. His strategy was perfectly obvious to his agnates, however: one wryly observed, "Now that he's old he comes to lineage rituals!"

Kwŏn Kŭn-sik also tries to use lineage rites to overcome social divisions within the lineage. Knowing that younger members are often reluctant to take part in the rites, he tries to encourage their participation by jockeying the assignments of ritual roles. Instead of limiting young men to the subordinate posts of ritual assistants, he told us, he chooses some to act as wine offerers from time to time.

Even though elders do not monopolize the important ritual roles, lineage rites cannot unite age divisions as effectively as they join genealogical branches. By reasserting the domination of lineage elders in a variety of ways, lineage rites exacerbate the political frustrations of younger lineage members.

The sequence of lineage rites, in order of descending generations, exemplifies generational seniority. The lineage visits each of its four cemeteries in turn, generally commemorating all the ancestors buried at each in the order of their respective generations. Only a few exceptions arise: three rites for ancestors whose graves are near those of more senior forebears are performed out of turn. Informants explained that the three rites are offered a bit prematurely but that this deviation from ideal principles saves them a lot of walking back and forth. Even such a practical concession thoroughly displeased an octogenarian widow of the lineage, however. The emigrant kinsman from Seoul, with tongue in cheek, sought to pacify her with the following words: "Suppose it is New Year's Day and you are on your way to greet some old people, but at the gate of the old people's house you meet a person younger than them. Of course you should greet the older persons first, but can you just ignore the younger person and look the other way? Should you wait until you come out of the old people's house before you even say hello?"

Lineage rites reinforce genealogical hierarchy in other ways as well. The subservient roles that younger men occupy remind them constantly of their inferior status. As ritual assistants, younger men must hand ritual objects to elders, pour wine for the elders to offer, and perform other similar acts. The occasional granting of a wine-offerer position to a young person hardly compensates for this age discrimination; moreover, at any rite where a younger man is selected as a wine offerer, any older kinsmen who also offer wine always precede him.

Elderly men not only occupy more prestigious positions and order the younger men about at ancestral rituals, they also display esoteric knowledge that they have acquired through years of ritual participation. They often correct the mistakes of younger men. Thus, lineage rituals enable elders to demonstrate their knowledge of tradition in an age when traditional wisdom is increasingly challenged. Naturally, elders are the most enthusiastic participants at lineage rituals. They want to maintain these rites in their present form. Younger men, on the other hand, are outspoken in pressing for ritual simplification, if not outright elimination. Most participate minimally, appearing only on the last day of the rites. One thirty-nine-year-old ran off when he was called on to join the ritual performers. "I'm too young to perform lineage rituals," he said.

Status Assertion

Status assertion has long been the main function of Korean lineages (Choi Jai-seuk 1966a); indeed it may well have been one of the incentives that prompted their formation, sometime in the mid-Yi dynasty (see pp. 10–11). In Korea during the Yi dynasty, status assertion was no mere vanity. Government-appointed officials were not usually natives of the regions they administered, and they seldom concerned themselves with village activities. As a result, powerful local elites regulated the affairs of their immediate vicinity. In the social turmoil that followed the Japanese invasions, the Yi government even encouraged the formation of local gentry (yangban) advisory councils to help rural magistrates administer their districts (Kawashima 1980). Even without government sanction, however, local elites enjoyed informal power at the magistrate's court by virtue of their latent entitlement to public office, their contacts with other office-holders, and their knowledge of neo-Confucian etiquette and legal procedures. Gentry status also carried legal exemption from military service and its equivalent tax.

The Japanese invasions also provide a benchmark for assessing changes in Korea's class system. In the first two centuries of the

Yi dynasty, gentry status usually had to be revalidated continually through success at government examinations (Ch'oe Yŏng-ho 1974: 629–31). After the invasions, however, gentry status came to be theoretically ascribed to agnatic descendants of former gentry. We say "theoretically" because household registers compiled by local magistrates during the eighteenth century evince considerable social mobility and manipulation of status indicators (Henthorn 1971: 207; Shin 1978; Somerville 1976–77).

As ancestry became the main basis for asserting gentry status during the latter half of the Yi dynasty, genealogical publications grew in number and importance. They were not simply means of identifying forebears or tracing long-lost relatives out of idle curiosity, nor did they serve merely to identify agnates who were potential political allies; genealogies now became vital instruments for establishing social credentials. Persons who were ignorant of their ancestry were automatically assigned to the low rungs of the social ladder. Not surprisingly, the temptation to falsify genealogies was considerable, and genealogical manipulation was not unknown. A descent line could be fitted into a gentry genealogy by posthumous "adoption" or outright forgery. It is difficult to assess how frequently lineages resorted to such practices, but recent ethnographies (see Biernatzki 1967: 316, 455; Dix 1977: 446–55) as well as historical documents (Song Chanshik 1976) suggest that genealogical manipulation has long been a useful aid to social mobility. A local magistrate's report of 1799 depicts such chicanery:

[Commoners who acquire a little wealth] raise money and treasures among their clansmen [lineage mates] and contrive a forged genealogical record. . . . By changing the names of their ancestors, they falsely represent themselves as members of another clan. . . . When one of their clansmen is subjected to the military tax, they all rush to the court of the yamen, clothed in the gentleman's robe, wearing the courtier's shoes, brandishing their clan's genealogical record which is wrapped up brilliantly in a silk cloth as if a treasure. Examined, the genealogical record reveals that all of the clansmen are descendants of noted sages and virtuous scholars as well as meritorious courtiers. [Song Chan-shik 1976: 48–49]

As the above report shows, the theoretically hereditary ascription of class membership motivated entire lineages to claim gentry status. Gentry privileges were not supposed to crosscut lineage memberships in Yi-dynasty Korea, as they did in late imperial China (Beattie 1979: 70); thus the members of a Korean local lineage had a common interest in advancing, or at least maintaining, their social standing. Status assertion became a corporate function.

In rural communities like Twisŏngdwi, lineage membership was almost essential for maintaining gentry standing. The Andong Kwŏn, like most other kin groups, updated its genealogy by asking its component branches to report their additions. An individual family or small branch that had severed contacts with agnates would in all likelihood be omitted.

Lineages are still important for maintaining social status in rural Korea because they provide institutional backing for their members' claims to gentry origins (Goldberg 1973–74: 165; Shima 1978: 2), as our Twisŏngdwi informants were keenly aware. A person who settles in a region where his local lineage is unknown is often denied the prestige he is accorded at his original home, said informants. They cited the case of a villager who had migrated from another province and now worked as a hired laborer in Twisŏngdwi. This man had been gentry in his natal village, they conceded, but he was not gentry in Twisŏngdwi because he had migrated there to work as a hired hand. Four years earlier, the man's mother had told us that her husband's natal kin group was indeed a gentry lineage; and his family's behavior was as genteel as that of most other families in Twisŏngdwi. When he returns to his natal lineage and village, moreover, he is probably accorded gentry status just as emigrant members of the Twisŏngdwi lineage are, regardless of occupation, whenever they return.

Although each legitimate member of a local lineage is unquestionably entitled to his kin group's standing in its local region, the status of the kin group itself is not entirely secure. Each lineage advances its best claims to prestige and counterclaims against its rivals. Through this competition, local lineages continually renegotiate their relative standings. In the Andong region, for example, the Munhwa Yu cite their greater number of officeholders to claim higher status than the Hahoe Yu, who respond that none of the Munhwa Yu ancestors had been as famous as their own Yu Sŏng-nyong (Kang Shin-pyo, personal communication). Among the Hahoe Yu, who are divided into two competing branches, the descendants of Yu-Sŏng-nyong use his achievements to assert higher status than the descendants of his elder brother. The other branch claims seniority of descent to advance its own position (Kim Taik-Kyoo 1964: 168–69).

Securing appropriate marriage partners was another traditional strategy for maintaining a lineage's social standing (Deuchler 1977: 9–12). Yet the Twisŏngdwi kin group does not intermarry with an apparently prestigious lineage located less than ten kilometers to the southeast, one descended from the prominent Yi-dynasty statesman Chŏng To-jŏn. Its members keep Chŏng To-jŏn's ancestor tablet permanently (*pulch 'ŏnjiwi*), a special privilege granted by the Yi government, and have enshrined it in a conspicuous building on a hill overlooking their village. Perhaps their status is too high for intermarriage with the Twisŏngdwi kin group; however, our informants explained that members of the Chŏng lineage had once worked as servants for some of the Tanyang U, a kin group with whom the Twisŏngdwi lineage regularly intermarried.[4] Our informants thereby implied that the Chŏng lineage was a notch lower than the U, and that marriage with them would have tarnished their own prestige. In sum, each local lineage advances its own assets and stresses different criteria by which prestige ought to be awarded in an effort to raise its standing.

Genealogies, bureaucratic positions of ancestors, and marriage alliances were not the only means by which class membership and relative standings of local lineages were negotiated. A lineage could also assert its claim to superior status by a strategy found among many societies: behaving as high-status people are supposed to behave. For one thing this meant keeping a strict sense of dignity and decorum. For example, until recently lineage members used not to carry funeral biers, because such work was thought unworthy of gentry; formerly the task was performed by hired men from a neighboring village who advanced no claims to gentry status. Again, even in the mid-1970's some lineage members were a little embarrassed about the formation of a farmers' band in Twisŏngdwi, for musical performance and pub-

---

[4] Perhaps the avoidance of intermarriage originated in the well-known animosity between Kwŏn Kŭn and Chŏng To-jŏn, the most prominent leader of the early Yi anti-Buddhist campaign (Kalton n.d.). As we noted in Chapter 1, Kwŏn Po's father was a second cousin of Kwŏn Kŭn. Twisŏngdwi informants did not mention the legend of Chŏng To-jŏn's illegitimacy (Hahm Pyong-Choon 1967: 116).

lic entertaining were regarded as lower-class behavior. And years ago, recalled some informants, lineage members would not even let children sing.

Upper-class behavior was also expected to be righteous. Moral worth became closely associated, if not equated, with social worth, and those competing for status and prestige could use moral qualities to support their claims or deny those of a rival. Filial piety and female chastity, including celibacy of widows, became particularly important indicators of a group's moral and social standing. A noteworthy activity in these areas by a lineage member or his wife affected the prestige of his entire kin group. In 1974, the Twisŏngdwi lineage erected a monument to a lineage widow who had not remarried after the death of her husband. They placed it beside the road that runs through the village, where it is visible to all who pass.

In the status competition that prevailed until very recently in Korea, and which still affects rural areas today, lineage rituals were another important device for asserting a kin group's social standing. We can identify at least four ways in which these rites enhance the prestige of a kin group today.

First, lineage rituals confer status because they advertise a lineage's existence, which alone is prima facie evidence of gentry status. In popular thought, though not always in fact, only gentry organize lineages and perform lineage rites (Shima 1978: 2; Brandt 1971: 118; Pak Ki-hyuk 1975: 146). As Kwŏn O-sik once commented about a household in a neighboring village, "They're gentry—they perform lineage rituals."

Second, because lineage rites are offered for distant ancestors, they demonstrate that the participants have deep genealogical roots in their community, that they are not "coming-and-going people." Migrants and newcomers in rural Korea are usually suspect: they may be illegitimate descendants, debtors escaping their creditors, or persons expelled from their natal village because of some immoral conduct (see Brandt 1971: 208–9). At the least they have been poor, because no wealthy man would have a reason to leave his natal village and settle in another. Also, one never knows whether migrants will stay long enough to repay any social obligations they might incur.

Third, lineage rituals confer status because they are an expression of filial piety. Precisely because they are less common and

A lineage ritual at Kwŏn Haeng's grave, located near the city of Andong. Kwŏn Haeng is the founder of the entire Andong Kwŏn kin group. His descendants participating in this rite are drawn from throughout the Republic of Korea.

obligatory than domestic rites, lineage rituals confer more prestige upon their participants. Those performing the rites are doing more than what is demanded of them, and more than many of their neighbors are doing. They are commemorating ancestors so distant that their ritual care could easily have been terminated long ago. Even though those ancestors do not need the food offerings, performing the rites demonstrates that participants remember their indebtedness to forebears.

Finally, lineage rituals confer prestige by giving a lineage an occasion to display publicly opulence, erudition, and other trappings of Korean gentry. Food offerings and ritual equipment are costly. Chanting the ritual text to the ancestors demands mastery of Chinese characters and proper intonation. Other exacting ritual procedures require familiarity with etiquette books or ritual manuals. The more carefully accomplished the performance, the greater the pride performers feel in having taken part. Though domestic rituals share these same status implications, there is clearly greater emphasis on status and prestige at the lineage rituals. The food offerings at the thirty-odd lineage rituals offered by the Twisŏngdwi kin group each cost about three or four times as much as those presented to the ancestors on death-days and holidays; the equipment used at lineage rituals is far more elaborate and expensive; and the ritual procedures at lineage rites are more complex and more fastidiously observed.

Ritual Estates and Lineage Organization

By looking to the motives and strategies of corporate ancestor worship, Maurice Freedman (1958, 1966) greatly advanced the analysis of lineage organization in southeastern China. The internal structure of local lineages in this region, argued Freedman, resulted from using ancestor worship to further two goals: asserting status and maximizing income. Lineages that included wealthy members subdivided asymetrically into sublineages of varying genealogical depth (see Figure 20) because such a structure enabled a wealthier sublineage to assert higher status and retain more of its income. Wealthier segments set themselves apart, ritually and economically, from their poorer and less prestigious kin by establishing their own corporate estates, and sometimes erecting additional ancestral halls, for the exclusive worship of their own ancestors. These corporately owned estates usually produced more revenue than was needed for ritual purposes, and the surplus accrued to their owners. By creating a separate ritual trust rather than contributing to the entire lineage's fund, a lineage's new segment not only asserted a higher social standing through demonstration of its wealth, but also restricted the income from its corporate property to its own members. As a result, Freedman surmised, the greater the economic differentiation of a local lineage, the greater its number of separate estates. Poor local lineages were not internally segmented, be-

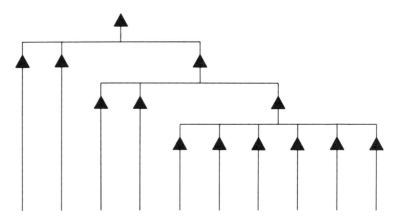

Fig. 20. An asymmetrically segmented Chinese lineage (Potter 1968: 25). Each ancestor depicted is the focal point of a separate property-owning corporation.

cause such subdivision would have served no purpose. This innovative analysis, based primarily on library research, was subsequently confirmed by the fieldwork of Jack Potter (1968), Hugh Baker (1968), and James Watson (1975b: 35–36).

Freedman's analysis provides a useful point of departure for analyzing corporate worship and lineage organization in Korea. Following Freedman's lead, we will try to show how motives and strategies for ancestor worship generated the lineage structures found in Korea, but we shall depart from his analysis by arguing that ownership of corporate property offers a poor index of Korean lineage organization.

Though agnatic groups sought to assert status in Korea, as in China, Korean lineages gained little prestige from the mere demonstration of wealth. Indeed, given the extreme corruption and avarice of local officials during the Yi dynasty (see Han Woo-keun 1971: 256–61), wealth could easily be "taxed" away unless well protected by political power. To obtain major social benefits in Korea, wealth had to be turned into such intangible assets as office-holding, erudition, marriage alliances (Peterson 1979), and notable ancestry. Korean lineages expended their resources on all of these. Some groups petitioned the government, erected monuments, printed books, and, more recently, constructed mu-

seums to gain added recognition for their forebears (Kim Taik-
Kyoo 1964: 167; Choi Jai-seuk 1966a: 111–13). Others, as we
have seen, tried to buy their way into prestigious genealogies.
Although Chinese genealogies trace their descent groups to
humble origins, stressing that the hard work of early ancestors
eventually brought prosperity and success to descendants (see
M. Yang 1945: 138; Lo 1972: 17–18; Beattie 1979: 111–12), Koreans take no pride in the achievements of ancestors who rose
from poverty and obscurity.

The importance of ancestry to a lineage's prestige affected Korean lineage organization in two ways. First, it motivated local
lineages to retain—or at least claim—memberships in larger agnatic groupings in lieu of becoming completely autonomous.
Such memberships deepened a local lineage's genealogical roots,
established its descent from more office-holders and famous per-
sonages, and vouched for its genealogical claims. For a local lineage like the Twisŏngdwi Kwŏn, whose exclusive ancestors had
rarely held offices, affiliation with a larger and more prestigious
agnatic organization backed its claims to status, just as membership in a local lineage supported the claims of individual families.
Clusters of local lineages like that composed of Kwŏn Po's descendants are common in rural Korea. Each comprises several
local descent groups and is maintained through joint ancestor
worship (see Biernatzki 1967: 34–355; Choi Jai-seuk 1966a:
85–95; Kim Taik-Kyoo 1964: 145; Lee Kwang-Kyu 1975:
110–17; Lee Man-Gap 1960: 72). These regional clusters in turn
maintain memberships in national-level kin groups, like the Andong Kwŏn. Some of these groups, each with a common surname
and place of origin (*pon*), are now said to include more than a
million members, their component lineages and individuals
spread throughout Korea (Biernatzki 1967: 499–503; Brandt
1971: 108–9; Choi Jai-seuk 1966a: 145; Lee Mun Woong 1976:
88).[5]

Second, the greater importance of ancestry than wealth as a
basis for asserting status affected the internal structure of Ko-

---

[5] A few of these national groups ought to be called "clans." Though their members too possess a common surname and place of origin, these groups lack common property, a unified genealogy, or any other corporate activity (Fortes 1953:
25; Freedman 1966: 18–22; Fried 1970).

rean lineages. Illustrious ancestry, rather than economic success, was far more likely to motivate a lineage branch to establish its own corporate estate and worship its own ancestors exclusively. In the native Korean view, the descendants of a very famous ancestor are especially prone to establish their own segment (Choi Jai-seuk 1966a: 140; Lee Man-Gap 1970: 341; Lee Kwang-Kyu 1975: 118–42); and ethnographic data substantiate this opinion (Janelli and Janelli 1978: 283).

The paucity of office-holders among the Twisŏngdwi lineage's exclusive ancestors precluded this potential source of factionalism, and the continued scarcity of office-holders in more recent generations gave the entire lineage a precarious hold on its gentry status; therefore, the entire lineage membership had a common stake in simply maintaining their gentry standing. No genealogical branch had good reason to differentiate itself from its agnates.

In addition to the great importance of ancestry to a group's status, one other reason explains why differences in wealth per se were unlikely to promote internal segmentation in a Korean lineage. A small, wealthy group of close agnates lacked any economic incentive for creating a corporate trust separate from the lineage's property, because surplus income from corporately owned property in Korea was not divided among its owners but was used to advance collective interests.[6] The economic benefits derived from this property, therefore, were not diluted as the number of owners increased.

In Twisŏngdwi, economic benefits from corporate property are either enjoyed by its cultivator or deposited into the lineage's common fund. Because rents on lineage-owned land are somewhat below the going market rate, cultivators earn a slightly greater reward for their labor than they would enjoy from land rented on the open market. The amount of surplus income varies from one parcel to the next, however. Rents on ritual estates consist of standardized food offerings, but the size and quality of

---

[6] Apparently this was also true of the T'ungch'eng Chang (Beattie 1979: 119), one of the most eminent Chinese lineages of the Ch'ing dynasty (Lo 1972: 22). It would be interesting to know if such lineages were as internally segmented as the less politically prominent but more commercialized groups of southeastern China.

estates vary. Generally, estates for rituals of the most distant ancestors, created when rice yields were lower, are larger and more lucrative to cultivators than recently created ritual estates. Other plots of lineage-owned property, not assigned to the rite of any ancestor, are rented out in return for an annual payment of rice.

Informants are well aware of the economic value of cultivation rights in lineage-owned land. Although these rights may not be subcontracted, they are sometimes sold for a consideration by one lineage member to another. Unless the lineage has specific cause for revoking them, cultivation rights are retained by the same household and passed on from father to son.

Cultivation rights in lineage-owned land are not necessarily granted to a descendant of the ancestors whose ritual that land finances. Some lineage lands are even cultivated by nonagnates, though the Twisŏngdwi lineage has kept the choicest plots for its own members. The ritual trust for Kwŏn Po, on the other hand, was purposely given to a nonagnate. Kwŏn Kŭn-sik explained that this strategy eliminated a potential source of friction between the five local kin groups: should it become necessary to reprimand the cultivator for neglecting his responsibilities, his local lineage would inevitably take his side against the other four. In many other Korean lineages, members did not cultivate any of their kin group's ritual estates (Biernatzki 1967: 387; Lee Man-Gap 1970: 343; Choi Jai-seuk 1966a: 106–7).

Aside from the food offerings, which are consumed by the ritual participants or taken home at the end of the day, the Twisŏngdwi lineage's corporate property earns about ten sacks (*kama*) of rice a year (about US $600 in 1978). Out of this revenue, the lineage pays for the transportation expenses of the delegation it sends to the rituals for its seventeenth- and eighteenth-generation ancestors, expenses of renovating the graves of these ancestors, wages of workers hired to assist with the lineage's own rituals, and nominal salaries for the lineage's officers. It also pays for tombstones to mark ancestral graves, a gift of a few gallons of wine for any lineage member who celebrates a sixtieth birthday, additional land for ritual estates as more ancestors pass beyond four generations, and maintenance of the lineage's ritual equipment. Any remaining funds are normally lent out at interest to one of the kin group's members; otherwise, the lineage deposits its money in a bank.

Evidence from elsewhere in Korea confirms that corporate estates brought their owners little or no economic benefit (see Choi Jai-seuk 1966a: 101–7). Some lineages used part of their property to assist their primogeniture descendant (*chongson*) because his household had special ritual responsibilities or acted as the kin group's symbol to the outside world (Choi Jai-seuk 1966a: 103–4; Lee Man-Gap 1970: 343–44; Kim Taik-Kyoo 1964: 147). Other lineages supported the education of a promising descendant in the belief that his success would enable him to become a patron and benefit the entire kin group. Most lineage members, however, received nothing. In the village of Hahoe Iltong, a now-defunct organization, whose name (*ŭijangso*) may be etymologically related to the charitable estates of Chinese lineages (Kim Taik-Kyoo 1964: 158; see also Twitchett 1959), did not restrict its benefits to lineage members. Its major purpose was paying the taxes of the whole community, but it appears to have been motivated by other than charitable interests: it was founded by the Hahoe Yu lineage shortly after one of its members was paddled at the local government office for embezzling the villagers' tax payments.

Because income from a corporate estate is not distributed to its owners in Korea, ownership rights are normally unimportant to lineage members; therefore they do not define the precise share of every agnate. In official land registers, lineage-owned plots are recorded quite haphazardly: sometimes they are registered in the name of the primogeniture descendant of the ancestor whose ritual they finance, sometimes in the name of the lineage treasurer or manager (*ch'ongmu, yusa*), and sometimes in the name of the cultivator. Such practices underlie several recent legends about men who sold lineage land without their lineage's knowledge (e.g., Lee Man-Gap 1970: 344) and sometimes absconded with the funds. In recent years, Kwŏn Kŭn-sik has begun to protect lineage land by registering plots in the names of several lineage members, a stratagem that apparently is his own innovation.

This lack of precision in ownership rights extends beyond the legal registration of corporate property; lineage members as well lack a consensus as to exactly who or which segment owns how much of the estates (see also Kim Taik-Kyoo 1964: 144; Shima 1979: 63). They rarely need precise definitions of ownership rights; when rights must be defined, they emerge through negotiation, persuasion, and manipulation. A few examples from Twisŏngdwi demonstrate this process at work.

In 1977, Kwŏn Po's descendants decided to refurbish his (and his wife's) grave. The treasurer of this five-lineage group, a member of the Agok branch, asked each of the local lineages to contribute one-fifth of the costs. He thereby claimed, by implication, that each local lineage had equal rights and obligations to the ritual estate of Kwŏn Po. Kwŏn Kŭn-sik, however, maintained that the Twisŏngdwi and Pangch'ukkol lineages made up a single branch (*p'a*), that Kwŏn Po thus had only four branches of descendants, and that each branch should pay one-fourth of the costs. By his reasoning, the Twisŏngdwi and Pangch'ukkol lineages would each pay one-eighth. He based his argument on symmetry: Kwŏn Po's descendants divide into two major branches at the eighteenth generation, and both divide again at the nineteenth generation (see Figure 21). Evidently, one of the participants at Kwŏn Po's 1973 lineage rite shared this view, for he too had spoken of Kwŏn Po's descendants as forming four branches.

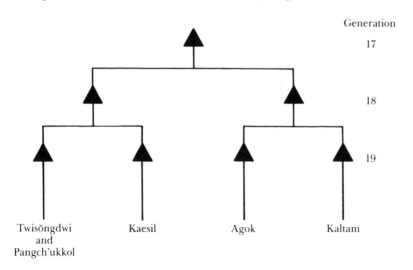

Generation

17

18

19

| Twisŏngdwi and Pangch'ukkol | Kaesil | Agok | Kaltam |

Fig. 21. Perception of genealogical relationships (Twisŏngdwi version).

Kwŏn Kŭn-sik won the argument for the two lineages. He first approached the treasurer of the Pangch'ukkol lineage and obtained his support, which likely was not a difficult task, since both kin groups stood to gain by a victory in the appeal. Thus united, Twisŏngdwi and Pangch'ukkol won their case before the other three lineages.

Another dispute, this one entirely within the Twisŏngdwi lineage, arose during our fieldwork that involved a parcel of cultivable land allegedly set aside by a childless ancestress about a century ago. She and her husband are the thirtieth-generation ancestors of Segment I. Although this couple was given an adoptive descendant, a few lineage elders claimed that the woman had feared that her and her spouse's ancestor rituals might not be performed and had set aside a small plot of land to finance their rites. Although the agreement was only oral, said the elders, the land was later to be given to the lineage to finance the couple's lineage ritual. Therefore, the lineage would not have to provide a ritual estate for this couple from its own corporate property after four generations had elapsed. Kwŏn Pyŏng-nyŏl, the acting primogeniture descendant of Segment I, denied this story and instead claimed that he had received the plot as part of his father's household property.

When we learned of these competing claims, the ancestress and her husband were in a ritual limbo. Since they had passed beyond four generations, Kwŏn Pyŏng-nyŏl offered them no domestic rituals, and the lineage treasurer refused to provide an estate for their lineage ritual; thus the two ancestors received no rites at all. Eventually an amicable compromise was reached: Kwŏn Kŭn-sik dropped the lineage's claim to the contested land and Kwŏn Pyŏng-nyŏl agreed to provide the annual food offerings for their lineage ritual.

The last example of renegotiation of a ritual estate arose more recently. In 1973, the Twisŏngdwi lineage's property appeared to include a small parcel of land for the twenty-sixth-generation ancestor of Segment VI. This estate was included in the lineage's land records along with the rest of its corporate property, and everyone seemed to agree that it was indeed lineage land. The village chief's land records offered neither confirming nor contradictory evidence since at that time they did not distinguish a cultivator's personal property from lineage estates.

When we returned to Twisŏngdwi four years later, we found that the village chief's records had been amended to indicate which plots of land the lineage (*chongjung*) owned. Next to the small plot, however, was a notation indicating that it was the exclusive property of a sublineage (*so chongjung*). This sublineage is comprised of Segment VI, the descendants of the ancestor whose ritual it finances.[7]

Why did the villagers become concerned during the intervening four years with identifying corporate property in their land register? And why did one segment press its claim to separate ownership of an estate, a claim that had apparently lain dormant for several years? The answers lie in the lineage's recent decision to sell some of its ritual estates. Local industrialization has raised land prices to the point where the lineage can no longer buy new ritual estates for the ever-greater number of ancestors beyond four generations. As a result, the lineage has decided to build a large ancestral hall where they will henceforth perform the rituals for all their ancestors beyond four generations. The hall's construction is to be financed by the sale of ritual estates, since they will no longer be needed to finance separate grave rituals. In brief, the sale of ritual estates has now become likely, and the lineage members are responding to this new circumstance by pressing claims to ownership rights that were previously unimportant. In the case of the one small parcel, the lineage treasurer acquiesced in the ownership claims of Segment VI. He maintains, however, that this plot will have to be given to the lineage anyway when the new hall is built, because the ancestor commemorated with the estate will be commemorated in the hall. After all, he argues, it would be ridiculous to exclude only that ancestor and commemorate all the others.

These three cases illustrate how ownership rights to ritual estates may be continually renegotiated. Decisions are made only when circumstances require them, and outcomes are determined not by the strict application of socially accepted norms but by a person's persuasive ability. In future years new claims may well arise, and property rights of the lineage and its members will be

---

[7] One member of Segment VI, a leader of the young people's faction, was village chief briefly during the mid-1970's (see Chapter 1). Perhaps he was the person who amended the land records.

affected accordingly. For example, a ritual estate was established prematurely by an emigrant lineage member for his great-great-grandfather and great-great grandmother, and in return they receive a lineage ritual undistinguishable from any other. Theoretically, grants Kwŏn Kŭn-sik, the lineage member could reclaim the estate when those two ancestors pass beyond four generations; at present, however, no one expects that to happen.

The volatility of ownership rights in ritual estates is not matched by instabilities in other social rights and obligations. Whether Segment VI owns its own estate or not, it still performs its holiday rituals corporately, joins with the other Twisŏngdwi segments at all lineage rituals, asserts neither greater nor lesser status, and receives neither more nor less annual income. Even the disputes do not seem to affect relations between genealogical branches. For example, Segment I did not rally behind Kwŏn Pyŏng-nyŏl in support of his case: Kwŏn Wŏn-sik, an elder of Segment I, sided with the Twisŏngdwi treasurer. Thus, to see corporate property rights as the sole definer of lineage organization in Korea would attribute an importance to land ownership that it does not deserve. The organization of Korean lineages depends more on status than on economics.

Ritual Change

Pervasive social and economic changes in rural Korea, coupled with a government-sponsored campaign to simplify rituals, have generated strong pressures to alter lineage rituals. The Korean government recommends that lineage rites be eliminated (Pogŏn Sahoe-bu 1973: 115–30). These pressures for change were especially apparent during our 1973–74 fieldwork, when the government's campaign was at its height, but they persisted during the following years as well. In 1973, after the rituals for Kwŏn Po and Kwŏn Che, representatives of the five local lineages held their usual business meeting to discuss matters of common interest pertaining to the rituals and the corporate property that finances them. That year, the discussion centered on a proposal to discontinue the annual rites and sell the kin group's ritual trust. Those who favored the proposal pointed to the government's ritual-simplification campaign, and argued that proceeds from the sale of the corporate estate could be used to educate promising descendants of the formerly commemorated ancestor— an alternative form of filial piety, one informant explained. Those who opposed the plan argued that the whole kin group would lose prestige if the rites were discontinued, and that the five lineages would lose the only occasion on which they all get together. No one mentioned the welfare of the ancestors.

These arguments are especially revealing, considering the context in which they were presented. With the fate of two lineage rituals hanging in the balance, supporters of the rituals marshaled what they saw as the most compelling reasons for continuing them: to assert status and reaffirm agnatic ties. Whereas informants were quick to point to the needs of the dead when justifying domestic rituals, no such considerations crossed their minds for ancestors who lived so long ago.

The pressures that threatened the annual rites for Kwŏn Po and Kwŏn Che also threaten the rituals for the Twisŏngdwi lineage's exclusive ancestors. Class structure and status hierarchy in rural Korea are changing, especially in the rapidly industrializing vicinity of Twisŏngdwi. As ancestry becomes less and less important for determining status, a household's well-being depends increasingly on its own merit rather than the standing of its lineage. Nowadays little consideration is given to the ancestry of potential marriage partners, as most young persons select their own spouses. Moreover, we have seen how the domination of the lineage elders is openly contested. Finally, rising land prices and greater employment opportunities have led many to question the investment of so much time and money in lineage rituals.

The Pangch'ukkol lineage yielded to pressure for change in 1973; their solution was to build a lineage hall, where they enshrined all of the exclusive ancestors who had formerly received separate grave rituals, and to commemorate them there in one grand ceremony each year. The main advantage of the new method, they explain, is that it saves time and money: whereas commemorations had cost thirty sacks of rice a year, the new procedures cost only ten, and the kin group no longer has to buy more land and add more rituals as new ancestors become eligible for lineage commemoration.

The Twisŏngdwi kin group will also build a lineage hall. Younger men constantly pressed the lineage elders—especially the lineage treasurer—to consent to its construction. The elders knew they could not prevent the hall, but they held out as long as they could.[8] In the meantime, they used lineage funds to place tombstones at the graves of each of their ancestors beyond four generations; they feared that when lineage rituals are performed in the hall rather than at individual graves, future descendants will not have any occasion to visit the graves and will forget their locations.

The social and economic changes that had such drastic consequences for lineage rituals seem to have little or no effect on domestic rites. Emigration to Seoul must have reduced participation at death-day and holiday rites, but informants never mentioned a reduction in the number of participants. They frequently commented, however, on the paucity of kinsmen, especially younger men, at lineage rites. Years ago, say Twisŏngdwi villagers, the lineage elders made all the young men participate in the annual rituals. Today's younger lineage members are not so docile and do not acquiesce so readily to the demands of senior agnates. Except perhaps for fathers and their own sons, the genealogical hierarchy carries less import than it did in the past.

Three more reasons can be cited for the domestic rites' greater immunity to social change. First, public status assertion is not as important at domestic rites, so changes in class structure or criteria for class membership affect them little. Second, domestic rites are based in part on beliefs about the afterlife and the need to provide sustenance to the recently deceased. And finally, agriculture is still the major source of income for most Twisŏngdwi households, and members of the groups that perform domestic rituals continue to cooperate in their day-to-day activities. Changes in religious belief, occupation, inheritance practices, and the development of Korean households and lineage segments, not changes in Korean class structure, can threaten domestic rituals. Only one informant ever suggested that domestic rites be changed at all. He said he was perfectly willing to go along

[8] Rising land prices prohibited the acquisition of more ritual estates as more ancestors passed beyond four generations, and most elderly opponents of the lineage hall eventually died or retired from lineage leadership. We returned to Twisŏngdwi in 1981 and found that the lineage had finally sold some of its estates and begun construction of the hall.

with the government's recommendation that death-day rites be limited to two generations (Pogŏn Sahoe-bu 1973: 117); but he was also the lineage member who earned nearly all his income outside the village and who never participated in any ancestor rites.

⚜ 6 ⚜

Shamans and Ancestors

In addition to formal ancestor worship, Twisŏngdwi villagers have another major system of beliefs and rites for dealing with the dead. Folklorists politely term this other religious system "the traditions of shamans" (*musok*), but villagers call it "superstition" (*misin*). In this chapter, we will describe the shamanistic traditions, explore their relationship to ancestor worship, and finally, attempt to identify the social basis of shamanistic beliefs about ancestors.

Shamanistic Rites

At shamanistic rites called *kut*, ancestors are propitiated along with an assortment of local and household deities. Typically, a village household hires a few professional shamans to come and perform a *kut* when an ancestor or deity is thought to have caused a serious illness or other misfortune.

Offerings made to placate supernatural beings at *kut* consist primarily of food and money; sometimes a set of clothing is offered for a dead relative to use. Part of the food is consumed by participants during the rite; but most of the food, the money, and the occasional sets of clothing are kept by the shamans as part of their compensation.

Kut are performed far less often than ancestor rituals, but each *kut* consumes far more time and money than a domestic or lineage rite. A given household rarely offers more than one in several years. A *kut* begins about mid-afternoon and runs until mid-morning of the following day. In 1978, the average cost of a *kut* was a few hundred U.S. dollars, about twenty times the expense of a typical death-day offering.

Kut are dramatic and entertaining: shamans take turns beating drums and gongs, singing mythical narratives, performing comic skits, and impersonating supernatural beings. Speaking through the mouth of a shaman, deities act like corrupt and rapacious officials. They denigrate the quality of food presented to them, feign insult at the size of their offerings, and demand more and more money as they sing and dance about. Villagers refuse to be intimidated; they cajole, negotiate, and match wits with the deities, pleading for good fortune and trying to hold on to their cash. Some of the participants too play musical instruments or dance. Everyone has a good time.

A portion of every *kut* is performed by one of the shamans especially for ancestors. This highly dramatic seance is far more serious than the exchanges with deities. Ancestors lament their discomforts in the afterlife, complain about their grave locations, or grieve over the mistreatment and neglect they suffered as elders at the hands of their living kin. Playing on the sympathies of their listeners, ancestors plead for a little more money, another cup of wine, or a different gravesite. The seance is usually performed in the early hours of the morning and is clearly one of the most important parts of every *kut*: informants say as much themselves, and many participants leave and return to their homes when the seance is finished.

Most of the participants at a *kut* are women over 40; few younger women are present. Men of the sponsoring household, together with their closest kinsmen and neighbors, usually attend the early evening segments of a *kut* but then retire to the "across room" or leave the house altogether. No male villager participates in ancestor seances. At one seance, the head of the sponsoring household was physically present, but he lay on the floor, covered with a blanket, and appeared to sleep throughout the event.

The women who attend a *kut* are drawn primarily from the sponsoring household's closest neighbors and kin; most live in the same hamlet or belong to the same ritual-performing segment. Usually, a few other women attend, especially some elderly lineage wives who take a special interest in these rites. Though no one's presence is formally required, one woman was criticized for absenting herself from an ancestor seance held at a household of her own hamlet and ritual-performing segment. The woman, an eldest son's wife, was apparently reluctant to face her dead mother-in-law. The old woman, who had committed suicide seven months earlier, made a dramatic appearance at the seance.

A male shaman (center, foreground) transmits the words of dead relatives at an ancestor seance.

Like Buddhism, shamanism provides a means of caring for a broader range of kin than does ancestor worship (Kendall 1979: 159–91). In their discussions of shamanistic rites, informants often extend the word "ancestor" (*chosang*) to a few nonagnatic deceased kin, including maternal relatives and in-laws, and even to descendants. At one Twisŏngdwi seance, a separate table of food offerings was set out for four "humble ancestors" (*yat'ŭn chosang*), family members who had died unmarried. Yet another table was set out for the parents of the household head's paternal grandmother. Though they were not agnatic kin, explained informants, this couple had no son and spent their final years in their daughter's home. As in Japan and China (Wang S. 1976: 365; Kerner 1976: 206), one finds in Korea both an extension of the word "ancestor" beyond its primary meaning and a willingness to care for close relatives who have no proper descendants of their own. In Twisŏngdwi, such nonagnates never receive formal ancestor rituals.

Neither shamans nor Twisŏngdwi villagers can define precisely which agnates and forebears eat at the main food-offering table. One wine cup is supposed to be placed there for each of these deceased kin, but participants usually disagree about the number necessary. At one seance, the village women could not agree whether ancestors within six or eight *ch'on* ought to be given wine cups, or whether these genealogical boundaries ought to be drawn according to blood or adoptive ties. Just before another seance, the shaman from the neighboring village kept telling the housewife of the sponsoring household, "Put more." During the seance, a few ancestors commemorated by other ritual-performing segments appeared unexpectedly, and the housewife had to add still more cups to the table. Some informants say that when a seance is held for ancestors, "they all come." In fact, deceased kin beyond six or eight *ch'on* rarely appear.

The dead who speak at a seance are a genealogically more diverse (Kendall 1979: 159–91) but generationally shallower group of kin than those who receive ancestor rituals. Ancestors beyond a few generations, even if they still receive domestic rites, do not speak unless they are personally known to some of those present. Although nonagnates may appear more commonly in nonlineage villages (see Kendall 1979), they speak rarely in Twisŏngdwi. In one such instance, a daughter of the lineage was addressed by her dead husband. This woman had married into a neighboring village and still lived there as a widow, but had returned to Twisŏngdwi to participate in a *kut* offered at the house of her brother's second son (case number 12, p. 159).

Because ancestors do not identify themselves and appear in no particular order, participants must infer which one is speaking as they listen to the words of the shaman. Of course, specific clues make the task much easier: as soon as the shaman said, "Mom, I'm here" (*Ŏmma, naega wassŏ*), everyone seemed to recognize the dead son of the elderly woman for whose illness the *kut* was offered. Shamans do not always provide kinship terms and other such explicit guides, however, and participants often ask each other which ancestor is speaking. There came a point at one seance when no one could figure out which ancestor was complaining about his or her grave site. Out of desperation, one of the village women approached the shaman, tapped her on the shoulder, and asked, "Who is it?" The shaman replied with an air of annoyance, "Don't ask me now. Wait and see." Even after the seance was completed, participants disagreed over which ancestors had come and spoken.

Given the inference-discussion-consensus process used to identify ancestors at a seance, it is hardly surprising that close kin of the sponsoring household speak most frequently. No one is likely to identify a long-dead ancestor about whom she knows nothing. Furthermore, since most participants are drawn from the same ritual-performing segment, and are more likely to reach consensus about someone known to all, close agnatic kin naturally are identified almost to the exclusion of other deceased relatives.

The shaman, too, contributes to the identification process. When the shaman from the neighboring village performs a seance, more ancestors, and more distant ancestors, appear. Familiar with the histories of most Twisŏngdwi lineage families, he can provide more details about the ancestors he impersonates. Shamans who come from afar rely more heavily on generalized complaints, which any of several ancestors could conceivably utter. The seance at which the village women could not guess who was complaining about his or her grave site was performed by a shaman from Suwŏn who was visiting Twisŏngdwi for her first time.

By identifying ancestors and listening to their complaints, participants gain information that helps them determine the cause of the illness or misfortune that prompted the *kut*. Ancestor seances never provide enough information for unequivocally fixing the cause of a misfortune, however. Too many supernaturals voice grievances that conceivably could have motivated the affliction, and none ever admits to having been the perpetrator. Instead, both deities and ancestors want more offerings and reproach the living. Any of the supernaturals may promise to bring good fortune or to heal an afflicted person, tell the members of a household that their situation will soon improve, or imply that it will by telling them not to worry. But none of these statements is enough to ascertain who or what caused the misfortune. As a result, even after a *kut* is finished, participants come away with different conclusions.

Encounters with ancestors at shamanistic rites evoke responses, much like Thematic Apperception Tests, Rorschachs, or other projective tests used by clinical psychiatrists (Kim Kwang-iel 1973; Janelli and Janelli 1979). Whether interpreting inkblots or a shaman's utterances, individuals reveal a good deal about themselves and their interpersonal relationships. Each seance participant also exposes her views of relations between others in the community. When the mother-in-law who had committed suicide appeared at a seance, the village women expressed great sympathy; many felt she had not been treated well by her household. Yet a dead son's appearance elicited little pity from his own mother when he appeared at the *kut* offered to relieve her suffering. According to village gossip, he had not been a model son; and one informant claimed to have heard from others that the son himself had caused the woman's illness (case number 6, p. 158). As we shall see, the affective qualities of particular social relationships or variant perceptions of them emerge more clearly when villagers attribute misfortunes to the intervention of dead kin.

Participants also expose their emotions at ancestor seances. As elsewhere in Korea (Rhi Bou-yong 1970: 18), women in Twisŏng-dwi are sometimes moved to tears by the laments or reproaches of the dead—a sharp contrast to the restrained and formalized behavior of the men at ancestor rituals. Moreover, these emotional outpourings are intrinsic to the success of a seance. One shaman boasted of her abilities by telling us that she could make a lot of people cry; evidently, eliciting the emotions of participants is seen by shamans as a major goal.

The free release of normally controlled emotions is perhaps one reason why shamanism is something of an embarrassment for everyone involved. *Kut* lack the assertion of status so integral to ancestor worship and evoke none of the pride with which lineage members discuss their ancestor rituals. Shamans traditionally were assigned to one of the lowest strata of Korean society; even today, their occupation confers no prestige or even respect. As we noted above, shamanistic rituals and associated beliefs about ancestral affliction are labeled *misin*, which bears the same negative connotation as "superstition," its closest English equivalent.

Ancestral Affliction and Related Beliefs

Instances of ancestral affliction were not easy to find. It took a good deal of persistent questioning to elicit the examples described below. When providing us with these data, informants did not display the same enthusiasm they had shown for their ancestor rites.

Reticence concerning ancestral affliction is partly due to embarrassment about such matters. Some events or circumstances are public knowledge in the village, but the afflicted families are understandably reluctant to advertise them. When discussing the illness of a woman in another lineage household, for example, Kwŏn Chŭng-sik's mother noted that the sick woman's family would not care to admit that her illness had been caused by the spirit of her niece who had died unmarried (the woman's husband's brother's daughter). Admitting that would hurt the woman's chances of finding a good husband for her own daughter, our informant reasoned. A prospective husband's parents would worry about the girl's spirit jealously following the new bride to their home and causing trouble there.

Potential embarrassment is not the only reason that ancestral affliction is a difficult topic for research. Many informants are reluctant to accept the idea that ancestors are hostile. Some denied that ancestors would ever harm their own descendants, but knew specific instances when they had. Others granted the theoretical possibility of the dead afflicting their offspring or other close kin but were hesitant to accept that explanation in specific cases. The attitude of Kwŏn Kap-sik, described in Chapter 4, was typical. A shaman had told his mother that several of her children had died because of her grandfather's sister's discontent, but Kwŏn Kap-sik wanted to verify that the skeleton in the grave was a woman's. Other informants, too, were unwilling to commit themselves to a shaman's explanation of a particular misfortune, although, like Kwŏn Kap-sik, they were equally unwilling to disregard it entirely.

The opinions of shamans do not appear to convince anyone about ancestral affliction. The shaman from the neighboring village, for example, merely suggests explanations of misfortune and does not try to impose his interpretations on clients. He is hardly in a position to do so: shamans are openly suspected of fakery and their abilities are often doubted. Some informants noted that when a family visits a shaman a few weeks after a death in order to determine the reincarnated form of the deceased, they prefer to consult one who lives some distance away. A distant shaman could not counterfeit that divination, our informants reasoned, because he (or, more typically, she) would not know the history of the deceased's family.

We had no way of knowing what shamans really believed, but they obviously spoke of ancestors more harshly than our Twisŏngdwi informants did. The shaman in the neighboring village, for example, had not one kind word to say about the dead and was never reluctant to blame them for misfortunes. (He also told us that more misfortunes were caused by ancestors than by deities or the ghosts of unrelated persons.) Twisŏngdwi informants expressed a different view. Though they did not attribute instances of good fortune to the acts of benevolent ancestors, they insisted nonetheless that ancestors were more benevolent than harmful.

Not only may informants disagree with a shaman's explanations, they often disagree with each other's allegations as well, especially when these involve affliction by their own parents or other close kin. The case of one lineage member's misfortune well illustrates this diversity of opinion.

This lineage member was spraying his crops one day when he collapsed, apparently from the fumes of the chemicals he was using. He has since suffered from dizziness and been unable to work. One woman told us that his inability to work was being caused by his father's younger brother. This uncle's wife had deserted him at about the time of the Korean War, and he was later murdered by some soldiers stationed near the village. A second woman said that the man's misfortune had been caused by his father, who must have been angered when some workers accidentally leveled part of the earthen mound on his grave. A third woman thought that the partial leveling of this grave had motivated the father to cause only the accident and initial illness. The illness's persistence, she claimed, resulted from the man's not having received proper medical treatment for the devastating effects of his intensive army training; his father's first wife then made his condition much worse because she was not being given any ancestor rituals.[1]

The lineage member himself did not subscribe to any of these explanations but told us that his misfortune was caused by (1) not wearing a protective mask while spraying, and (2) improper relocation of his paternal grandfather's grave. The accident had occurred on his grandfather's death-day, he noted, but the grandfather himself had not caused the misfortune; rather, the precise timing and location of his grandfather's reburial had brought it about.

In addition to the above case, and the ancestral affliction of Kwŏn Kap-sik's family discussed in Chapter 4, we recorded fourteen other allegations of ancestral intervention in the affairs of the living. In enumerating them, we follow our informants' practice of extending the term "ancestor" to all deceased kin, including nonagnates, siblings, and descendants.

1. One lineage member admitted that his mother had made him extremely ill because he had had her remains exhumed and cremated. (He had sold the land on which she was buried to a company that wanted it for a factory site.)

2. A few months after an elderly lineage woman committed suicide, her eldest son's unmarried daughter suffered a nearly fatal accident. A leak in the heating system allowed carbon mon-

---

[1] The Andong Kwŏn genealogy makes no mention of this first wife. Apparently her union with the afflicted man's father was of short duration.

oxide into her room while she slept and left her unconscious for days.

Some village women guessed that the suicide had caused the granddaughter's accident. And at an ancestral seance held a few months later in another household, the dead grandmother complained bitterly about the hard life she had led.

3. A few years after that incident, the suicide's son became sick after eating a wild bird. A shaman attributed the sickness to his mother's inability to enter the otherworld. (Suicides, polluted by their act of self-destruction, cannot enter the otherworld for a few years after death, nor can others who die before their allotted life span, such as executed criminals or those who die in automobile accidents. Until they can enter the otherworld, they are ill disposed and likely to afflict the living.) First the afflicted son denied that a dead mother would harm her own children, but then, with a puzzled expression, he asked, "But my mother made me sick, didn't she?" He then noted that his mother could not have made him sick if he had not eaten the wild bird. He seemed to find some satisfaction in knowing that she was not entirely to blame; nevertheless he sponsored a *kut* to placate her.

The shaman's diagnosis was admitted very reluctantly by the dead woman's sister-in-law (the husband's brother's wife), with whom she had apparently enjoyed a warm relationship. The sister-in-law attributed her nephew's illness to the "ancestor(s),"[2] saying that the shaman had not identified any particular one. Only when pressed for a more specific identification did she admit to surmising (*nae pogienŭn*) that her sister-in-law had been the afflicting spirit. (She denied outright that her sister-in-law had caused the earlier carbon-monoxide accident.)

4. A lineage woman told us that her first son died in childhood, shortly after her husband's family had failed to perform a death-day rite for one of their ancestors (she could not recall which one). Someone later told her that omitting the rite had caused her child's death.

5. A lineage woman blamed her daughter-in-law's dead parents for her son's illness and a few other minor misfortunes in his household (for example, one of their children cut his fingers on

---

[2] *Chosang*, the term she used, can refer to one or more ancestors

a farm tool). The daughter-in-law's parents had been executed during the Korean War, she noted, and thus were likely to afflict the living. (The relationship between this informant and her daughter-in-law was especially difficult.)

6. An elderly lineage widow and a female shaman both ascribed the widow's illness to the ancestors of her household. The ancestors afflicted her because they wanted a *kut*, said both informants, though neither named a specific ancestor. A woman of another lineage household told us she had heard that the widow's dead son had caused her illness.

7. One lineage member fought often with his wife, and his household suffered a series of minor misfortunes. An elderly woman of another lineage family attributed these difficulties to his ancestors, noting that his circumstances had improved after the ancestors had received a *kut* at his home. Ancestors often cause trouble between a descendant and his wife, she said, just as living parents do (*sijip sari sik'inŭn kŏt ch'ŏrŏm*).

The same informant ascribed a subsequent illness of the same lineage member to his elder brother, who had died in a traffic accident. The two brothers had fought over the division of their father's property (see Chapter 4), so naturally the deceased brother was hostile toward his younger sibling, she said. The dead man's deceased wife was helping him to afflict his brother, she added, since wives usually assist husbands in their endeavors.

8. A man ascribed the second illness in the preceding case to the afflicted man's dead grandfather. The grandson had made a lot of money, he said, so the grandfather felt it was time for him to spend some of it and offer a *kut*. (The informant headed one of the wealthiest households of the lineage; perhaps he was voicing one of his own concerns.)

9. Shortly after a man's grave had been moved next to his wife's grave, his eldest son's unmarried daughter became lame, and the husband of another daughter was involved in a traffic accident. One lineage man attributed these misfortunes to the ancestor's anger at being moved from what had apparently been a good grave location.

10. A lineage widow imputed her own and her eldest son's concurrent illnesses to her dead husband's and other ancestors' desire for a *kut*. About six weeks later, when she was still ill, she was less certain about which ancestors were responsible, but she

surmised that her husband and his parents were the most likely cause. They had been fed and entertained as guests when *kut* were offered at other ancestors' homes, she reasoned, so they must now be embarrassed because they could not reciprocate. Her two sons, however, opposed her wish to sponsor a *kut*, probably because of its expense.

11. A lineage woman gave two different reasons to explain why a five-year-old boy of another lineage household was ill. At first she said the ancestors made the child sick because they wanted a *kut*. His family had planned to offer one during the preceding spring, she noted, but they postponed it and then the boy became ill. (Like several other informants, this woman told us that each household should offer a *kut* every few years as a preventive measure; but few families actually offer them until a misfortune occurs.)

The woman later told us a more specific reason for the child's illness. His family had sold the land on which the boy's great-grandfather had been buried to a firm that needed space for a chicken farm. After the grave was relocated, she reasoned, the great-grandfather afflicted the boy out of anger at being moved from a good site.

She went on to observe that ancestors are not like living people. Their minds were different, she said, for no living person would ever harm his or her own descendants.

12. The eldest brother of one lineage family suffered from insanity and died at the age of nineteen. Several years later, according to two lineage informants (a man and a woman), the deceased afflicted two of his relatives: his youngest brother, who headed his own household in Twisŏngdwi, and his father's married sister, who lived in a nearby village. The brother and aunt shared the cost of a *kut* for him, and also had a tablet made for him for a shaman to care for in her shrine. After these measures had been taken, neither family had any further difficulties.

13. A lineage youth who suffered from epilepsy was killed by a train. His parents later experienced spells of insanity, until they had a shaman perform a posthumous marriage for their son. The lineage woman who told us of this incident blamed the son for the parents' illness.

14. One elderly lineage member told us that he had moved his grandparents' grave several times before he found a good site.

In the meantime, his grandparents kept appearing in his dreams, and some of his own and his younger brothers' children died.

Though different informants seldom corroborate each other, the above cases nevertheless manifest a shared set of beliefs about the afterlife and about the motivations that prompt the dead to afflict their living kin. These same beliefs are also evident at ancestor seances, in oral literature, and in various comments we heard in Twisŏngdwi. Although etiquette manuals and other written texts used by informants make no mention of these matters, Twisŏngdwi lineage members seem to share a common ideology to explain why the dead afflict the living.

First of all, the deceased exist in the physiological state they were in at the time of death. Dead children never become adults, as they do in China (Jordan 1972: 140–55; A. Wolf 1974b: 148). Posthumous marriages, for example, are performed only for those who died at a marriageable age, never for those who died as children, regardless of how many years have passed since their deaths. Children who die before adolescence, say informants, do not afflict the living, even in later years.

Similarly, those who die in old age remain aged; they are never imagined in more active stages of their lives, as they may be in some Taiwanese villages (Ahern 1973: 217–18). We have already seen in Chapter 4 a folktale that depicted an ancestor who had died in advanced old age as quite feeble.

The dead even retain the physical disabilities they suffered from at the time they died. At one seance, when a shaman spoke the words of a lineage member who had been partially paralyzed by a stroke, he kept one side of his body rigid to imitate the handicap. At another seance, a lineage member's mother did not appear because she had been bedridden prior to her death and could not travel. One of the other ancestors explained that they had brought a cart to collect her food offerings and would bring them to her later.

Just as the physiological conditions of the dead are unchanged, so their basic needs are the same as those of the living: the dead need food, shelter, clothing, money, and—for unmarried adolescents and young adults—sex. Tables of food and wine offerings and sometimes new sets of clothing are prepared for the dead at shamanistic rituals. And the dead themselves, speaking through the shaman, may plead for another cup of wine, ask for a little more money, or perhaps complain of discomfort in their present grave sites. As we have seen, the desire for food offerings and discomfort in grave sites figure prominently in accounts of ancestral affliction.

Though our Twisŏngdwi informants did not mention the sexual needs of the dead in the allegations listed above, other evidence shows that such needs are not entirely ignored. An elderly lineage widow—our informant least inhibited about discussing sexual matters—ascribed her temporary urinary disorder to an unmarried female ghost who was longing for sex. She reasoned that the malevolent dead often afflict the living with sufferings similar to their own. Korean oral narratives also mention the sexual frustrations of the unmarried dead (Choi In-hak 1979: 135; Dorson 1975: 287), and posthumous marriages may well be performed with the sexual needs of the dead in mind. Certainly they do not serve to continue a descent line or provide an heir to offer ancestral rituals, for Twisŏngdwi informants said that posthumously married persons cannot be given adoptive descendants.[3]

Physiological needs of the dead are not the only basis for their acts of affliction. Their emotional dispositions, which may have physical correlates, are also important. Many of the dead who are hungry for ritual offerings died prematurely, have no descendants of their own, or perished in tragic circumstances. Feeling unfairly deprived of their allotted life span and the rewards of human existence (ŏgurhada), such persons afflict their closest kin out of resentment and must be propitiated with shamanistic rituals. In general, those who die with a pressing desire cannot find peace in the afterlife until that desire is satisfied.[4]

Another point of agreement among informants is that ancestors never kill a person outright, though they may send an illness that can result in death if not properly treated. (They may, however, kill an infant or a young child in order to vent a grievance against its parents, as infants and children are viewed as only potential persons and not as real members of a kin group or community.) In the case cited as number 2 above, for example, the

[3] In some other Korean villages, however, heirs may be adopted to a posthumously married couple (Lee Kwang-kyu 1977a: 10).

[4] From a village in the northern part of Kyŏnggi Province, Kendall (1979: 181) reports that a woman who had died craving a fancy rice cake was thought to maintain that desire in the afterlife. Choi In-hak (1979: 135–41) cites several folktales in which a ghost seeks vengeance for offenses or injuries suffered during its lifetime.

suicide's sister-in-law firmly rejected the explanation of the charcoal-gas incident given to us by other village women. The dead grandmother could not have caused this misfortune, argued her sister-in-law, because ancestors only make people sick. They do not, she insisted, try to kill someone suddenly.

The varying opinions in case number 2 illustrate how the same facts can be interpreted differently despite a shared set of beliefs. Since the granddaughter did not actually die from the gas, the village women could logically attribute the accident to her deceased grandmother without implying that she had wanted to kill her descendant. But the deceased's sister-in-law, by emphasizing that the accident had been nearly fatal, could dismiss by a *reductio ad absurdum* her co-villagers' assertion of ancestral affliction: to blame the dead woman for this near-fatality was to imply that she had been *trying* to kill her victim.

The social relationships between particular persons, rather than differences in beliefs or knowledge, seem to account for the acceptance or rejection of ancestral hostility as the cause of this misfortune. We think the sister-in-law found her own opinion more satisfying because of her strong affection for the deceased woman. This sister-in-law was the informant who told us that in the early years of her marriage she had slept in the same room with the now-deceased woman in order to avoid her husband's sexual advances. And in case number 3, we saw that she was reluctant to blame the same dead woman for a later illness in the family. Yet this informant provided us with six other accounts of ancestral affliction in her own and other lineage families; indeed, she was our most prolific source of information about ancestral hostility.

The belief that ancestors do not kill mature descendants or next of kin is a logical consequence of the motives imputed to afflicting ancestors. Informants stress that ancestors send punishment or misfortune because they want something from the persons they afflict. Killing the people on whom their welfare depends would be contrary to their interests.

Ancestors almost always afflict their own descendants or next of kin, for these are the persons from whom the dead may expect the best care or the largest offerings. Deceased persons with no close living kin afflict strangers because they have no kin of their own to satisfy their needs. Such "wandering ghosts" (*kaekkwi*) are regarded and treated as beggars: they receive a bowl of gruel and perhaps a few coins, deposited at a crossroads. Like ogres and monsters in many other societies, Korean ghosts are sometimes a bit dim-witted. Offerings for them are left at a crossroads to confuse their sense of direction and thereby hinder them from finding their way back to their victim's home. As one informant explained, the dead naturally afflict their closest kin, for they could hardly expect very good treatment from strangers.

Another reason the dead afflict the households of their closest kin is that those people are more likely to have offended or injured them. They are the ones who omitted the ancestor's death-day rite, moved his or her grave to a poorer location, or drove the ancestor to commit suicide. A dead lineage member naturally afflicted his younger brother, explained an elderly woman (case 7): they had fought over property division before the elder brother died, and their mutual hostility continues today.

Ancestor Worship and Shamanism

Ancestor worship and the shamanistic treatment of the dead not only are distinguishable from each other, but are each separate, internally coherent systems. Unlike Buddhism in Twisŏngdwi, neither is a mere assemblage of vague, disconnected beliefs and practices.

In several recent studies of folk religion in Asia, the interrelations of variant beliefs and rites have drawn a good deal of attention and controversy. Some authors, noting that the various beliefs and practices of an individual, a local community, or an entire society usually appear to be inconsistent (Yoder 1974: 7–8), seek to explain the origin and perpetuation of these inconsistencies (Spiro 1967; A. Wolf 1974a; 1974b; R. Smith 1974a; 1974b). Others maintain that seemingly irreconcilable beliefs and practices are actually related parts of an overall system to which they belong (Tambiah 1970; Freedman 1974b; Hicks 1976: 19; Hori 1968: 10–11; Dix 1980). We will try to show that both views are partially valid in Twisŏngdwi. Some of the differences between ancestor worship and shamanistic propitiation are only different means for achieving diverse but not incompatible objectives. Other differences, however, seem to represent a fundamental inconsistency in beliefs about ancestors.

The separation of ancestor worship from shamanism is obvious. Kwŏn O-sik did not even mention ancestor seances (*chosang kut*) when we asked him to enumerate the rites of ancestor worship. Ritual manuals and etiquette books likewise ignore shamans and seances. And several ethnographers (Akiba 1957; Brandt 1971: 23; Dix 1980: 47; Kendall 1979: 159–91) have pointed to various differences between the two ritual systems. Terminology also differentiates ancestor worship from shamanism. "Ancestor rituals" (*chesa*) belong to "ancestor worship" (*chosang sungbae*) or "Confucianism" (*yugyo*), whereas *kut* belong to "superstition" (*misin*), at least according to Twisŏngdwi villagers. Shamans sometimes claim that their religion is a branch of Buddhism (*pulgyo*).

Although seances and ancestor rites are assigned to separate categories, we have no evidence that Twisŏngdwi villagers see any contradiction or opposition between them. Both have one major goal in common: feeding ancestors. Ancestor seances too "could be called ancestor worship," Kwŏn Sang-sik once suggested, but he was offering us his personal insight in contradistinction to generally accepted terminology.

Because ancestor rites and seances have a similar purpose, they may once have been viewed as competing alternatives. The following legend, recorded by Im Pang (1640–1724), suggests that such a view may have existed during the middle years of the Yi dynasty. According to James S. Gale (1913: 157), the missionary who translated the narrative, the government official described in the legend is Ch'oe Yu-wŏn, a political figure who held office during the first two decades of the seventeenth century.

There was a minister in olden days who once, when he was Palace Secretary, was getting ready for office in the morning. He had on his ceremonial dress. It was rather early, and as he leaned on his arm-rest for a moment, sleep overcame him. He dreamt, and in the dream he thought he was mounted and on his journey. He was crossing the bridge at the entrance to East Palace Street, when suddenly he saw his mother coming towards him on foot. He at once dismounted, bowed, and said, "Why do you come thus, mother, not in a chair, but on foot?"

She replied, "I have already left the world, and things are not where I am as they are where you are, and so I walk."

The secretary asked, "Where are you going, please?"

She replied, "We have a servant living at Yong-san, and they are having a witches' [shamans'] prayer service [*kut*] there just now, so I am going to partake of the sacrifice."

"But," said the secretary, "we have sacrificial days, many of them, at our own home, those of the four seasons, also on the first and fifteenth of each month. Why do you go to a servant's house and not to mine?"

The mother replied, "Your sacrifices are of no interest to me, I like the prayers of the witches. If there is no medium we spirits find no satisfaction. I am in a hurry," said she, "and cannot wait longer," so she spoke her farewell and was gone.

The secretary awoke with a start, but felt that he had actually seen what had come to pass.

He then called a servant and told him to go at once to So-and-So's house in Yong-san, and tell a certain servant to come that night without fail. "Go quickly," said the secretary, "so that you can be back before I enter the Palace." Then he sat down to meditate over it.

In a little the servant had gone and come again. It was not yet broad daylight, and because it was cold the servant did not enter straight, but went first into the kitchen to warm his hands before the fire. There was a fellow-servant there who asked him, "Have you had something to drink?"

He replied, "They are having a big witch business on at Yong-san, and while the *mutang* (witch) was performing, she said that the spirit that possessed her was the mother of the master here. On my appearance she called out my name and said, 'This is a servant from our house.' Then she called me and gave a big glass of spirit. She added further, 'On my way here I met my son going into the Palace.' "

The secretary, overhearing this talk from the room where he was waiting, broke down and began to cry. He called in the servant and made fuller inquiry, and more than ever he felt assured that his mother's spirit had really gone that morning to share in the *koot* (witches' sacrificial ceremony). He then called the *mutang*, and in behalf of the spirit of his mother made her a great offering. Ever afterwards he sacrificed to her four times a year at each returning season. [Gale 1913: 159–61]

Aside from feeding ancestors, other goals of ancestor rites and *kut* are disparate, but they are not contradictory. The purposes of ancestor worship, say informants, are to promote agnatic solidarity, repay obligations to forebears, and inculcate filial piety. Shamanism attempts to ward off or alleviate suffering by placating a broader range of supernaturals; participants at *kut* also want to have a good time. One could argue that by ignoring the goals of ancestor worship, shamanism implicitly threatens them, but our informants apparently did not view the two ritual systems in such terms. Instead, shamanism basically acquiesces to the social order consciously promoted by ancestor worship: even at seances, most participants come from agnatically related households; separate eating tables are provided for agnatic kin, nonagnatic kin, and genealogical inferiors; and the rites acknowledge that a family's greatest obligations are to its closest agnatic kin. Unlike "animism" and Buddhism, the practical and ethical religions of Burma (Spiro 1967), Korean shamanism and ancestor worship are not antithetical. Shamanism is not directed toward goals that are condemned by neo-Confucian morality (Kendall 1979: 166–69).

The inconsistency between shamanism and ancestor worship lies not in their goals or ritual procedures, but in their belief systems. Ancestor worship idealizes ancestors. At ancestor rites, the dead conform to the perfect image of retired elders: though benevolently inclined, they have neither strong personalities nor great power. They passively await the offerings on which their welfare depends and accept them as expressions of indebtedness proffered at the initiative of their offspring. According to a metaphor common in literary sources, forebears are the roots of a tree and descendants are its leaves and branches. Each automatically nourishes the other. Even the food offered at ancestor rites is later eaten by participants. Shamanism, by contrast, portrays ancestors as self-interested, afflicting their kin to enhance their own comfort or satisfy their desires. Ancestors demand costly sacrifices purely for their own welfare. A family that sponsors a *kut* does not even consume its food offerings after the rite. In sum, ancestor worship idealizes ancestors and their mutual dependency with their closest living kin. In shamanism, ancestors are threatening, and their dependency on their closest relatives channels their acts of affliction toward them. This dual personality of ancestors has been noted in other Korean villages as well (Dix 1979: 69–71)

In recent years, much effort has gone into assessing the general degree of benevolence or malevolence attributed to ancestors in China and Japan. We will not attempt such an appraisal of ancestors in Twisŏngdwi. Ancestor worship and shamanism present very different images of ancestors, and we have no means of combining them into a general average. Instead, we will try to identify the social experiences that underlie both images.

That the two conceptions of ancestors are incompatible, not merely different, is suggested by informants' contradictory assertions about ancestral affliction. As we have seen, some informants claimed that ancestors never harm their descendants, but then provided specific instances. Others admitted that ancestors afflicted descendants but were reluctant to provide cases. We surmise that these contradictions are not always apparent because the conflicting statements were usually evoked in different contexts. We have seen how one informant (in case 3) was caught by surprise when we juxtaposed the two ideas and he realized that mothers sometimes afflict their sons. Informants also invoked a variety of apparently idiosyncratic rationalizations, some of which were contradicted by their other statements: ancestors are generally benevolent, even though only instances of affliction and none of benevolence were cited; the dead may afflict some of their living kin, but not their own descendants; ancestors do not harm offspring but "send punishments." Such interpersonal variation also suggests that individuals often come to their own terms with a fundamental ideological contradiction.

Interpersonal variation shows one general characteristic: women incline toward the more negative view of ancestors, while men profess the idealistic conception more strongly. This is evident not only in women's participation in ancestor seances, where the image of the demanding and self-interested ancestor is openly acknowledged, but also in the data women gave us. More than two-thirds of our cases of ancestral affliction were provided by women, and women gave us our two versions of the folktale depicting ancestral hostility (see Chapter 4). Men were much less promising sources of information about ancestral affliction. We will argue below that this general difference between the beliefs of men and women arises from their different social positions vis-à-vis the ancestors who are dependent on their household.

Explanations of Ancestral Hostility

Beliefs about ancestral hostility have received a good deal of attention in anthropological and psychoanalytic writings. The literature is replete with hypotheses that attribute such beliefs to social experiences of the living. Many of the earlier hypotheses, derived from Freudian theory, argue that repressed hostility among living kin prompt them to blame misfortunes on the activities of their dead relatives. More recently, Arthur Wolf (1974b) has offered a cognitive rather than psychoanalytic explanation: he suggests that attributes of supernatural beings are directly modeled upon conscious perceptions of social relationships. We shall review these two approaches and try to determine how well each can explain allegations of ancestral affliction in Twisõngdwi.

Freud, in *Totem and Taboo* (1950: 60–63), maintained that social relationships generally characterized by conscious affection almost always entail a measure of unconscious hostility as well. Individuals commonly have some desire for their loved ones to die and derive a measure of satisfaction from their deaths. But this unconscious hostility and satisfaction generate feelings of guilt, and guilt anxiety needs to be alleviated. One common way of doing this is to project one's feelings of hostility onto the dead. Survivors need not feel so guilty if they can convince themselves that the dead person is hostile toward them. In sum, people in many societies come to believe that they may be harmed by the dead because this belief serves a valuable psychological function: reduction of guilt anxiety.[5]

It is important to note that repression and the unconscious are essential to Freud's theory. If feelings of hostility toward loved ones could be openly acknowledged, maintained Freud (1950: 62), there would be no psychological need to attribute hostility to relatives in the afterlife.

Freud's theory was later reformulated by Meyer Fortes, primarily in his analyses of ancestor worship among the Tallensi of West Africa (1949; 1959; 1961; 1965). Though Tale fathers and eldest sons are openly affectionate, noted Fortes, their relationship is also marked by a latent rivalry: an eldest son cannot attain jural and ritual autonomy until his father's death. Only then does he gain custody over ancestor shrines and replace his father as the head of the domestic group. As a result, every eldest son has good albeit unconscious reason to wish for and derive satisfaction from his father's death.

Fortes departs from Freud's analysis by regarding belief in ancestral authority, rather than belief in ancestral hostility, as the major defense mechanism for coping with guilt. Upon a father's death, the son lessens guilt anxiety not by projecting his hostile feelings onto his dead father, but by attributing his father's former authority to the now deceased parent. By artificially pro-

---

[5] Whether or not such latent functions can be used to explain the existence of a custom or religious belief has been the subject of great controversy in folklore, anthropology, and philosophy of science. For a discussion of the issue, see Oring (1976), Hempel (1959), Jarvie (1973), and Enç (1979).

longing his subordination in this way, the son can reassure himself that he did not really profit from his father's death after all. Belief in ancestral affliction, says Fortes, functions merely to convince and remind descendants of their continued subjection.

In support of this thesis, which he extends to China and Japan (1961; 1976), Fortes claims that ancestors are always just. They afflict (1) only those over whom they could legitimately exercise authority,[6] and (2) only when their own rights or moral norms are violated. In both Africa and East Asia, maintains Fortes,

ancestors are not believed to afflict their descendants indiscriminately or even capriciously. They are believed to punish descendants for such wrongdoings as ritual neglect (e.g., not "feeding" them) or moral transgressions. In other words, ancestors are supposed to exact the services they are *entitled* to from identified responsible descendants and to adjudicate their moral and ritual conduct. [1976: 13, original emphasis]

Moreover, argues Fortes, the image of ancestors stresses their jural authority, not their whole personalities, because belief in the survival of ancestors' rights over descendants, not the perpetuation of their personal idiosyncracies, has functional value.[7]

The concreteness and rigor of Fortes's analysis mark a major advance over Freud's more nebulous formulation. Fortes links specific genealogical relationships with an identifiable source of hostility, a limited range of motives for affliction, and a salient attribute of ancestors. In so doing, he not only combines social and psychoanalytic modes of analysis, but he also makes Freud's theory testable by providing a hypothesis specific enough for falsification. We shall pursue these points below.

Jack Goody created a different hypothesis out of Freud's theory from his study of ancestor worship among the LoDagaa of West Africa (1962). Goody's hypothesis was subsequently tested on Taiwanese data by Emily Ahern (1973). In Goody's view, intergenerational conflict results primarily from competition over

[6] Fortes (1976: 5) acknowledges, however, that although beliefs in ancestral authority are rooted in the filio-parental relationship, they may also be projected onto preceding generations of forebears.

[7] Fortes posits that belief in ancestral authority has social as well as psychological functions, but a full discussion of the former would take us too far afield (see Calhoun 1980). Our reasons for rejecting Fortes's hypothesis as an explanation of ancestral affliction in Twisŏngdwi, set forth below, are unaffected by the presence or absence of these social functions.

property rights rather than jural authority. Because property among the LoDagaa is transmitted only upon the death of a holder, the succeeding generation is tempted to wish for their seniors to die. But after a death occurs, the heir feels guilty for his former hostility toward the deceased. Evidently,[8] this guilt is alleviated by projecting onto the dead eternal rights to property and a desire to receive via sacrifice a share of its material benefits. Acts of affliction, therefore, serve to remind heirs of their predecessors' continuing economic rights.

In formulating his hypothesis, Goody too attempts to link specific social relationships with particular motives for ancestral affliction. "In the main," he argues, "it is those from whose death one benefits [through inheritance] that one fears as ancestors" (Goody 1962: 410). Among the LoDagaa, an individual is afflicted primarily by those who formerly held rights to his property. Thus, Goody's hypothesis, like Fortes's, is falsifiable.

Other writers (Opler 1936; Gough 1958) have attempted to make Freud's theory testable for yet other societies. Indeed, each new set of enthnographic facts seems to have generated an additional Freudian hypothesis. We shall limit our discussion to Fortes's and Goody's formulations, however, since these have been most prominent among analyses of ancestor worship in East Asia.

Neither hypothesis has been enthusiastically embraced in China or Japan.[9] Whether or not these explanations of ancestral hostility are valid for the African societies in which they originated,[10] they are either inapplicable or entail too much controversy for easy acceptance in East Asia. One disagreement centers on whether or not Chinese sons gain significant economic, ritual,

---

[8] Goody does not detail the causal mechanism that relates conflict over property to belief in ancestral affliction among the LoDagaa. Thus, Ahern (1973: 191–92) interprets Goody to mean that instances of ancestral affliction merely reflect fear of retaliation from those dead persons toward whom one had hostile feelings. Our interpretation, on the other hand, is based on Goody's claim (1962: 22–25) that he is building upon the theory set forth by Freud in *Totem and Taboo*.

[9] Griffin Dix (1979: 201–40) has discussed the relevance of some Freudian and Fortesian ideas in relation to Korean ancestor worship. He argues that an emphasis on love and concern for ancestors evidences a "reaction formation" to unconscious hostility toward parents, a thesis he finds only partly similar to Freud's or Fortes's ideas (1979: 238, 240).

[10] For Africanists' criticisms of Fortes's and Goody's hypotheses, see McKnight (1967) and Kopytoff (1971). For a recent defense of Fortes, see Calhoun (1980).

or jural rights by their father's death (Freedman 1966: 148–53; 1967: 93–96; 1970: 5; Ahern 1973: 196–99). In Japan, sons evidently obtain their full complement of rights during their father's lifetime (Nakane 1967: 16–21). Another controversy entails whether or not guilt is important in either China or Japan, particularly in relations with ancestors (Benedict 1946: 222–25; De Vos 1973: 144–64; R. Smith 1974b: 130; Eberhard 1967; Ahern 1973: 212–13; M. Yang 1945: 89). Yet other controversies surround the image of ancestors in both societies. Some authors say ancestors are benign; others say they may be capricious and hostile (Hsu 1948; Yanagita 1970; A. Wolf 1974b: 164–68; Freedman 1967: 92–102; Ahern 1973: 200–202; R. Smith 1974b: 124–26). Nor is it entirely clear whether or not ancestors are concerned with justice and the enforcement of jural norms (Otake 1980; Jordan 1972: 170; R. Smith 1974b: 147–48).

Despite the obvious rivalry of fathers and eldest sons for household headship (including control of household property), the overt expression of guilt in the chief mourner's costume, and the several reported instances of ancestral affliction, neither Fortes's nor Goody's hypothesis is applicable to Twisŏngdwi. As we have seen, in Twisŏngdwi the eldest son is expected to come into full de facto control of his household and perhaps even ritual responsibilities prior to the death of his father. Twisŏngdwi ancestors, moreover, do not enforce jural norms or their rights to property. They are far more selfish. Even an ancestor who receives all the formal rites he or she is entitled to may afflict a descendant in order to obtain a *kut*. Finally, ancestors do not strike only their own descendants or those who inherited their property. Even if we exclude four cases of affliction by childless kin to whom the word "ancestor" is extended, other true ancestors afflicted a brother (case 7), a mother (case 6), and a daughter's family (cases 5 and 9).

We could modify Fortes's or Goody's hypothesis or otherwise draw upon Freudian theory to construct a new hypothesis to match the facts of social organization and folk belief in Twisŏngdwi. Perhaps an eldest son and daughter-in-law wish unconsciously for his parents' deaths to be rid of the onerous task of feeding and caring for them. Perhaps, too, survivors alleviate the resulting guilt by prolonging their obligation to feed, clothe, house, and provide pocket money for parents after they die. Occasional acts of affliction would then serve to convince or remind survivors that they are still subject to the cantankerous demands of elders. Afflictions sustained by junior sons or instigated by deceased kin other than parents could be disregarded as outside the scope of the hypothesis. Alternatively, instances in which a Twisŏngdwi villager was afflicted by a deceased person who was not of the household's senior generation could be interpreted as "left-over" hostility: that is, hostility between successive generations of the same household is too intense for all of it to be projected onto its true objects (Gough 1958: 468–69). Or perhaps one could view all deceased kin, or even all supernaturals, as generalized parental figures (Whiting and Child 1953; Lambert et al. 1959). The possibilities are endless. In sum, our data demonstrate that neither Fortes's nor Goody's hypothesis is a valid explanation of ancestral affliction in Twisŏngdwi; however, the Freudian theory emerges unscathed.

Theories are abandoned not because they are disproved but because they are found wanting: a theory ultimately loses favor because it cannot easily account for new discoveries (Kuhn 1970). The Freudian theory's ability to adapt to new ethnographic evidence, however, appears to derive more from its malleability than from its validity. The concepts of repression and the unconscious create an ambiguous relationship between what an ethnographer observes and what may actually exist: overt behavior may usually be interpreted either as a telltale sign of emotions pent up in the unconscious or as a release of those emotions. Similarly, if overt manifestations of a particular emotion are absent or rare, their absence or paucity may be attributed either to a weakness of the emotion or to its repression (McKnight 1967: 13). In consequence, Freudian theory can provide hypotheses to account for almost any conceivable set of facts. If Twisŏngdwi ancestors never afflicted their kin, for example, we could invoke Freudian theory and explain that openly acknowledging complicity in the death of parents, as evidenced by the mourning costume, obviated any need for dealing with guilt by means of projection. And if ancestors did afflict their kin but there were no overt signs of guilt, we could as readily claim that the survivors' guilt was unconscious—or simply not revealed to others (Ahern 1973: 213).

So it is with the difference between men's and women's views of ancestors. That women see ancestors in a more hostile light than their husbands do can be explained according to Freud's theory by positing that a woman has more hostility toward her husband's parents than he does, as evidenced by her more frequent conflict with them. Presumably this greater hostility generates greater guilt anxiety and hence a greater need to project hostility onto the dead. But if it were men who viewed ancestors as more malevolent, we could alternatively reason that men have greater *repressed* hostility and guilt anxiety than their wives. The paucity of overt conflict between a son and his parents could then be interpreted not as evidence of less hostility but as evidence of the stronger repression of this emotion demanded of sons by the moral imperatives of filial piety.

Fortunately, there is another approach to explaining ancestral affliction. Its theory is simpler than and thus, by Occam's razor, preferable to Freud's, because it does not require unconscious mechanisms. In a seminal paper entitled "Gods, Ghosts, and Ancestors," Arthur Wolf (1974b) advances the view that Chinese beliefs about supernatural beings literally express Chinese conceptions of social reality. A villager's beliefs about deities reveal the peasant's view of government officials; characteristics and behavior attributed to ghosts are those of beggars or bandits; and the image of ancestors reproduces perceptions of parents and other kin. In addition to its epistemological advantages, we find that this cognitive approach explains ancestral hostility in Twisŏngdwi better than psychoanalytic theory for three reasons: It comes much closer to the expressed views of our informants; it provides a more complete account of our data; and it can explain much of the interpersonal variation in allegations of ancestral hostility. We will discuss each of these reasons in turn.

In many societies of the world, ethnographers have observed that ancestors are like elders, parents, or other living kin. This view has been advanced most forcefully by Igor Kopytoff (1971), writing about African societies. His essay has sparked a lively controversy among Africanists (see Brain 1973; Sangree 1974; Uchendu 1976; Calhoun 1980), primarily because the forcefulness of his writing style has created the impression that he overstates his case (see Kopytoff 1981). Neither Kopytoff, Wolf, nor we would argue that the dead are undifferentiated from the living;

in Twisŏngdwi, some of the ritual procedures at ancestor rites (arrangement of foods, for instance) are deliberate reversals of behavior appropriate toward parents and other elder kin. On the whole, however, similarities far outweigh differences, and the same social relationships apply to both the living and the dead. One deals with ancestors and living kin in similar ways; and ancestors in turn treat their living relatives as they did when they were alive. In Twisŏngdwi, death does not entail as radical a transformation as it does in Western societies (or ought to according to Freud's theory).

Evidence of the fundamental correspondence between ancestors and living kin is abundant in Twisŏngdwi. The parallels between sixtieth-birthday celebrations and ancestor rituals; similarities between formal greetings to elders, holiday rites, and grave visits on New Year's Day; the importance of the age-generation hierarchy for regulating relations between agnates as well as participation in domestic rites; the images of deceased kin evident at ancestor seances, in folktales, in allegations of affliction, and in general beliefs about the afterlife—all support informants' assertions that ancestors are like elders or other living kin. Nor does all of this behavior result from the bland Confucian prescription that dead parents be treated as if they were alive. An ancestor's affliction of a descendant is just like a parent hitting a child, explained Kwŏn Chŭng-sik's mother, swatting the air at waist level for effect. Individual ancestors, moreover, have the same basic needs, retain the same likes and dislikes, suffer the same infirmities, and harbor the same grievances as they had at the time of death. They are still enmeshed in their former social relations and have the same rights they formerly enjoyed. The woman who told us that her son's family had been afflicted by his wife's parents (case number 5 above) actually spoke with indignation: after all, she pointed out, the couple had a son of their own to satisfy their needs.

Our second reason for preferring a cognitive approach is its applicability to a wider range of belief. Affliction by agnatic forebears, other "ancestors," and ghosts all articulate a common set of ideas about the afterlife and the dependency of the dead upon the living. Compared with African societies (Gluckman 1937; Fortes 1965: 126–29; Kopytoff 1971: 129), eschatology and affliction are more closely connected in East Asia. It seems arbitrary to single out ancestral afflictions for explanation by one hypothesis. In Twisŏngdwi, an adult offspring who dies prematurely afflicts his or her parent for the same reason that a parent who dies prematurely afflicts his or her child: both are resentful and want to be comforted with a *kut*. Even wandering ghosts afflict the living because they have the same needs as everyone else.

Our third reason for adopting a cognitive approach is that it explains an important part of the wide interpersonal variations in villagers' allegations of ancestral affliction. As Wolf observes, different people have different social relationships with any particular person. Hence, they can be expected to have different images of that person as a supernatural being. "My ancestors," noted Kwŏn O-sik, "are evil spirits [*kwisin*] to somebody else" (see also A. Wolf 1974b: 172–74). A peasant and a bureaucrat are not likely to share the same view of a deity.

Though Wolf argues that different social relationships are likely to give rise to different images of a person turned ancestor, he does not pursue this line of analysis within families or kin groups. Perhaps members of a given family or lineage in northern Taiwan, where Wolf conducted his fieldwork, do not hold noticeably different images of their dead kin. In Twisŏngdwi, however, the various social relations within a family evidently give rise to different perceptions of the same ancestor. Thus, we can combine Wolf's cognitive approach with some of the specificity of Fortes's genealogical analysis.

As we have seen, women generally espouse a more hostile view of ancestors than their husbands. This difference would be predicted by a cognitive explanation of religious ideas. As we argued in Chapter 2, a woman usually has a less cordial relationship than her husband with his parents and agnates. The wife was never nurtured by his parents in her childhood; they made the early years of her marriage especially difficult and were often a source of anguish in later years; and her affiliation with all his agnatic kin is never certified until her death. In sum, the ancestors—the deceased parents—of the Twisŏngdwi lineage are usually not persons from whom in-married women ever expected much affection. One could anticipate that women would comment less favorably about these ancestors than would their husbands.

We should not expect every woman to express harsher sentiments about every ancestor, however. When misfortune is attributed to her son (case number 6), or to a sister-in-law with whom she had enjoyed a particularly warm relationship (cases 2 and 3), a woman may be more reluctant than a man to acknowledge affliction. In most cases, moreover, informants are not victims but third persons, with their own opinions of the afflicting ancestor and their own perceptions of the relationship between the ancestor and the victim. Finally, any particular social tie is modified by idiosyncratic events as well as the personalities of those involved. Some people, as we have seen, are not as mutually supportive as the rest of their lineage mates (case 7).

As a broad generalization, however, a cognitive theory unambiguously predicts that women in Twisŏngdwi ought to view ancestors more negatively than men. Any evidence that men hold the harsher view of ancestors could not be reconciled with this theory. In the next chapter, we will pursue this difference between men's and women's social relations and religious beliefs in China and Japan.

Only two pieces of evidence seem incongruent with this cognitive explanation. Some Twisŏngdwi women, echoing the words of shamans, say that "an ancestor's hand is a hand of thorns" (*chosang soni kasi sonida*) (cf. Kendall 1979: 169), and they say that people's minds change when they die. Yet we recorded no instance of a person injured by a thorny hand nor any cases where an ancestor afflicted living kin because his or her mind had changed, though we specifically asked informants for examples. Twisŏngdwi villagers are not inclined to ascribe an affliction to an ancestor unless they can impute a reasonable motive to the deceased. We conjecture that statements about thorny hands and changing minds are rationalizations, like the claim that each person has three souls. These ideas may be invoked when the community's consensus or other evidence leads individuals to a conclusion that they find dissatisfying. In short, these slogans may well provide informants with an out. Without specific cases, however, we cannot pursue this idea further.

※ 7 ※

Ancestor Cults in
East Asia Compared

Students of Korean society have long stressed its Confucian character. American observers (Osgood 1951: 332; Peterson 1974: 28) are fond of saying that Koreans "out-Chinese" the Chinese in their devotion to Confucianism. Their solecism has no equivalent in the Korean language, but it certainly captures an important part of the Korean self-image. A recent survey of Korea, issued by the Republic of Korea's Ministry of Culture and Information (Korean Overseas Information Service 1978: 200) expresses a similar view: "In Korea, Confucianism was accepted so eagerly and in so strict a form that the Chinese themselves regarded the Korean adherents as more virtuous than themselves, and referred to Korea as 'the country of Eastern decorum [*tongbang yeŭi chi kuk*],' referring to the punctiliousness with which Koreans observed all phases of the doctrinal ritual."

Discussions of ancestor worship are especially likely to evoke observations about the influence of Confucianism in Korea. Twisŏngdwi informants were echoing popular opinion when they told us their ancestor rites are Confucian. The ritual manuals and etiquette books that they and other rural villagers readily consult are heavily indebted to Chu Hsi's *Book of Family Ritual*, regarded as one of the classic texts of Chinese neo-Confucianism.[1]

Neo-Confucian ritual prescriptions are not so strictly observed outside the "country of Eastern decorum." In Japan, Buddhism continues to exert a far greater influence than neo-Confucianism on ancestor worship (R. Smith 1974b). Buddhist priests, for example, are commonly hired to recite sutras at Japanese funerals and death-day rites, and Buddhist images frequently adorn domestic altars in private homes. In China, Buddhism has not en-

[1] Ironically, this manual may be a forgery (Chan 1976: 556).

joyed supremacy for centuries, but similar practices are occasionally reported. Taoist priests and other deities are sometimes found in place of Buddhist accouterments (Hsu 1948: 52, 183–84; Day 1940: 29–31; Jordan 1972: 94; Ahern 1973: 164), and from a Korean perspective Chinese ancestor worship appears to have a distinctly materialistic or commercial orientation that is hardly in keeping with the spirit of neo-Confucian orthodoxy. Effigies of houses, automobiles, electric fans, automatic rice cookers, and a variety of other worldly goods, as well as vast sums of imitation money, are burned as offerings for the use of the dead in the afterlife. Lineage members may tender competitive bids for a contract, to provide ritual food offerings for their ancestors (Baker 1968: 95). Finally, ethnographies of China and Japan make no mention of neo-Confucian manuals dictating procedures at ancestor rituals.[2]

The influence of Chinese neo-Confucianism on Korean ancestor worship has been overemphasized, however. During the early Yi dynasty, Korean intellectuals modified neo-Confucian ritual procedures to make them more congruent with native traditions (Deuchler 1977: 9–17; 1980a; n.d.). As a result, Korean ritual manuals and etiquette books are no mere imitations of Chu Hsi (Chang Chŏl-su 1973–74: 80–81); many ritual practices in present-day rural Korea, in fact, cannot be traced to either Chinese or Korean versions of these publications.

The social arrangements involved in ancestor rites, like the shamanistic domain of the ancestor cult, are particularly remote from neo-Confucian ritual prescriptions. In the preceding chapters, therefore, we have sought alternative explanations for these ritual practices and beliefs. The development cycle of the family, inheritance practices, the structure and functions of lineages, agnatic solidarity, and the positions of the sexes—all exerted a greater influence than neo-Confucianism on the beliefs and social aspects of the ancestor cult in Twisŏngdwi.

In this chapter we will review our findings and attempt to extend our analysis to China and Japan. By comparing worship practices and beliefs about ancestral hostility in Korea and its neighbors, we will try to show how differences in both domains of the ancestor cult reflect variations in social relations among the

[2] Chu Hsi's *Book of Family Ritual* is frequently mentioned in Chinese genealogies, however (Liu 1959a; de Bary 1959: 37).

living. These comparisons not only lend support to our analysis of Korea but offer new insights into the folk religion of the other two societies as well. After first examining formal ancestor rites, we then turn to the personalities attributed to dead forebears.

Ancestor Rites

The most obvious influence of social organization on ancestor worship can be seen in the basic correspondence between property inheritance or household succession on the one hand and the allotment of ritual obligations on the other. In China, where all sons normally inherit equal shares of property, and none succeed to the headship of their parents' household, each descendant is equally obligated to his forebears. As Arthur Wolf puts it, "Responsibility for the dead falls equally and fully on all their descendants. . . . If agnates do not worship their ancestors collectively, they must worship them separately" (1976: 346–47).

This Chinese pattern of ritual obligations comes close to neo-Confucian prescriptions. In Chu Hsi's *Book of Family Ritual*, brothers are told that they ought to worship together; but if they live so far apart that common worship is impractical, then each should offer his own rite (De Harlez 1889: 134).

In Japan, by contrast, ritual obligations are vested in corporate households, not descent lines. Whoever succeeds to the headship of a household inherits all of its property; and only members of a household worship its preceding heads, their spouses, and its deceased dependents. This is the prevalent practice throughout contemporary rural Japan (R. Smith 1974b: 163; Nakane 1967: 6–7; Ooms 1976: 63), and we shall use this pattern as our point of reference. Japanese folklorists and other scholars have detailed a myriad of temporal and regional variations in succession, inheritance, and ritual obligations. But as far as outsiders can tell, attempts to correlate these variations are still inconclusive.[3]

[3] The ritual practices of rural groups termed *dōzoku* by Japanese social scientists often seem to resemble Korean practices more closely than those of other Japanese households (Yonemura 1976; R. Smith 1974b: 163, 173; Nakane 1967: 106; Brown 1968: 115, 126; Yanagita 1970: 29–30). These groups do not recruit all their members through agnatic links, but are functionally similar to the ritual-performing segments of Korean lineages. Unfortunately, however, both the structure and functions of *dōzoku* have been subjects of sharp disagreement among students of Japan. Thus, a group that one scholar calls a *dōzoku* may not be so labeled by another. The contested issues may never be resolved (R. Smith 1974b: xvii–xviii). Or perhaps *dōzoku* is not a useful analytic category.

The Korean pattern for allocating ritual obligations has similarities to both the Chinese and Japanese systems. Each son receives a share of his parents' (and earlier agnatic forebears')
property and is obligated to participate in their rites. Yet the eldest son receives the largest share of their ancestors' property and
succeeds to the headship of their household, and in return he is
expected to bear most of the costs of the rituals and to offer these
rites at his home. Other descendants are obliged to join him
there, but if they must be absent for any reason, they do not offer,
nor are they obliged to offer, rites of their own. The Korean system of ritual obligations, therefore, does not follow Chu Hsi's
recommendations, but instead reflects (1) obligations generated
by both inheritance and household succession and (2) a compromise between equal inheritance and primogeniture.

But the Korean system of household succession and property division does more than structure ritual obligations. It also
strengthens ties between close agnates. Because the father, rather
than his sons, determines respective shares of inheritance, Korean brothers are spared the bitter disputes over property division that sour fraternal relations in China. Forced to wait until
their parents' deaths to divide their natal household's property,
Chinese brothers are left to work out the details of the division
among themselves. The result is usually a bitter squabble over
their respective shares, and outside arbitrators are often brought
in to resolve these disputes. A Chinese proverb says, "Though
brothers are so closely akin each keeps his own money" (Scarborough 1964: 215; A. Smith 1914: 25). No similar proverb has been
reported from Korea. Yet the case of the four brothers in
Twisŏngdwi, whose father died prematurely and who later
fought over division of his property, shows that fraternal relations in Korea can deteriorate when brothers divide property
among themselves. The same moral can be drawn from the case
of the lineage member who took control of his deceased brother's
household and then sought a grave site that would geomantically
benefit himself at the expense of his deceased brother's son:
jointly held property and its division can generate conflict between close agnates in Korea as well as China. Normally, however,
the timing of property division prevents such conflict.

By assigning unequal shares to their sons, Korean fathers further strengthen ties between close agnates. Farm households can

benefit from economic cooperation even when their sizes and economic standings are more or less equal (see Potter 1968: 78), but economic inequality fosters interdependence. Whereas the wealthier household has a relative surplus of capital goods, the poorer household has a relative surplus of labor. Thus, the frequent cooperation and mutual assistance among Korean brothers, and to a lesser degree among other members of a ritual-performing segment, are grounded in both sentiment and economic advantage.

The timing and inequality of property division in Korea, which prompt the solidarity of close agnates, combine with lineage functions that strengthen ties between a still wider range of agnates. Members of a local lineage usually have a common interest in advancing their claims to gentry status, for in the eyes of the neighboring communities as well as the central government, members of the same local lineage share the same status and gain, retain, or forfeit its privileges. In late imperial China, by contrast, the legal privileges of gentry status cut across local lineage membership (Beattie 1979: 70).

The extraordinary strength of agnatic solidarity produced by this unique combination of inheritance practices and lineage functions is reflected in the Twisŏngdwi lineage's ancestor rites. Agnatic solidarity can be seen in reciprocal participation at rites for collaterals, the exclusion of women from funeral processions and domestic rites, the identities of deceased kin who receive ancestor rites, and the adoption of ritual heirs. We will briefly review these in turn, contrasting each with cognate practices in China and Japan.

Reciprocal participation in the rites of collaterals is a tradition unique to Korea and one, moreover, that is not ordained by neo-Confucian writings. In China, individuals participate in a rite only if it commemorates a person to whom they owe a ritual obligation (Potter 1970b: 126–27; Baker 1979: 88; Ahern 1973: 247; A. Wolf 1976: 344; Gallin 1966: 146–47; Jordan 1972: 100).[4] In Japan, individuals may participate in death-day rites offered by other households, but their participation is clearly motivated by affection for the deceased and not by ties to collat-

---

[4] Because of affective attachments, Chinese families sometimes offer rites to deceased persons who would otherwise be neglected (A. Wolf 1976: 355, 363). Such affection does not motivate participation in rites offered by collaterals, however.

eral agnates per se. Neighbors and a wide variety of nonagnatic kin may participate at these same rituals (R. Smith 1956: 91; Hozumi 1913: 57). In Korea, by contrast, agnatically related local lineages may regularly participate in lineage rites for each other's ancestors; members of a local lineage may join in lineage rites for each other's ancestors; and the entire membership of a ritual-performing segment may participate in all of the domestic rites offered at its constituent households. Furthermore, these practices, which Twisŏngdwi informants interpret as reaffirmations of agnatic solidarity, find no mention in ritual manuals. Though neo-Confucianist writers valued agnatic organization, they also urged that participation in ancestor rites be used to clarify lines of descent (Chan 1967: 227–32). The Korean practice extends the reaffirmation of agnatic solidarity well beyond neo-Confucian dictates.

A similar conclusion is suggested by the exclusion of women from funeral processions and domestic rites. Japanese women normally walk in funeral processions; Chinese women may or may not; but Korean women rarely do. The ethnographic data also suggest that local variations of this custom in China and Korea may be related to the relative importance of agnation in each community. This correlation is uncertain because accounts of funeral practices are not always accompanied by assessments of lineage organization. On the whole, however, the exclusion of women at rites certainly correlates with the relative strengths of agnation in the three societies.

The roles of women at domestic rites provide an even more striking contrast. In China and Japan, women may play greater roles than men in domestic worship (Freedman 1967: 97; 1970: 175; M. Wolf 1972: 15; Hsu 1948: 185; Feuchtwang 1974a: 115; Gallin 1966: 148–247; R. Smith 1956: 91; 1974b: 118; Yonemura 1976: 196; Hozumi 1913: photos facing 58 and 70).[5] In contemporary rural Korea, by contrast, women are normally excluded from domestic rites (Dix 1977: 252; Kendall 1979: 161–62; Biernatzki 1967: 322; Osgood 1951: 119). Yet women appear to have

---

[5] Limited evidence (Kulp 1925: 147; Baker 1979: 80) suggests, however, that their ritual roles may be more circumscribed in villages where agnatic organizations are especially significant. Baker (1968) conducted his fieldwork in a lineage-dominated New Territories village, and is apparently generalizing from his own observations there when he notes (1979: 80) the exclusion of women from formal rites in China.

been more actively involved in ancestor worship during the Koryŏ and early Yi dynasties (Kim Yung-Chung 1977: 49; Deuchler 1980b: 652; Lee Kwang-Kyu 1977a: 13–16), before agnation assumed its present importance.

The exclusion of women from funeral processions and domestic rites in present-day rural Korea cannot be attributed to neo-Confucian influence. In neo-Confucian ideology, the use of ritual to inculcate proper social sentiments among family members receives far greater emphasis than descent-group solidarity. Thus, the participation of women in funeral processions and domestic rites is clearly prescribed in Chu Hsi's Book of Family Ritual; it even ordains that women present the second of the offerings at domestic ancestor rituals (De Harlez 1889: 97–99, 138–39). Korean manuals are silent about women in funeral processions (e.g., Ross 1879: 337), but usually repeat Chu Hsi's prescriptions for the second wine-offerer. In fact, however, women rarely serve as second wine-offerers except in a few elite kin groups in the conservative Andong region (Lee Kwang-Kyu 1977a: 20). In sum, agnatic unity is stressed at the expense of family ties in most Korean villages, and this imbalance cannot be blamed on neo-Confucianism.

The identities of ancestors who receive formal ancestor rites provide another index of agnation in East Asia. As we noted in Chapter 4, ancestor rites in China and Japan are not uncommonly offered for persons who are neither agnates by birth, women who become agnates by marriage and death, nor fictive agnates by adoption. The majority of these "ancestors" are natal kin of persons who married into the households where they are commemorated. Often they are maternal forebears with no descendants of their own. Usually they are commemorated somewhat differently from ordinary ancestors; often their individual death-day rites are omitted, but they are commemorated along with the other ancestors on holidays.

In Twisŏngdwi, holiday rites are also offered for descendantless kin, but these kin are always limited to agnates or concubines who could claim a wife-like affiliation. A wife's natal kin and maternal kin receive no ancestor rites from her husband's kin group.

Not all Korean communities exclude nonagnates from ritual commemoration as rigidly as Twisŏngdwi. A few instances of lineage rites for nonagnates have been reported (Kim Taik-Kyoo 1964: 153; Biernatzki 1967: 249–51), but these rites perpetuate obligations that began during the first half of the Yi Dynasty, before the formation of local lineages and the transformation to present-day inheritance practices.

Domestic commemoration of nonagnates was also common during the early Yi period (Lee Kwang-Kyu 1977a: 14), but its current status is very poorly documented. Most students of Korean society have assumed that formal ancestor rites are offered only for agnatic forebears (see Moon Seung-Gyu 1974; Kendall 1979: 159–91; Lee Kwang-Kyu 1977a). Such oversight is understandable. Twisŏngdwi informants were unlikely to mention cases of holiday-only worship even when asked to identify the persons they commemorated with domestic rites, and only a few ritual manuals provide ritual texts for recitation at rites for nonagnates (e.g., *Sarye ŭijŏl* n.d.: 114–18).

Despite the apparent paucity of nonagnatic commemoration throughout Korea, the practice has been cited among the Hahoe Yu lineage (Kim Taik-Kyoo 1964: 163): "Agnatic forebears within four generations are normally those who receive domestic rites, but in this village it is said that instances of commemorating maternal ancestors are not few, . . . and I even heard of a household where rites were offered for a mother's mother's parents." This domestic commemoration of nonagnates among the Hahoe Yu is almost ironic. Located in the heart of the Andong region, the Hahoe Yu are apparently among the most thoroughly Confucianized and prestigious lineages of Korea. They are one of the few kin groups that follow Chu Hsi's prescription that second wine-offerers be women (Lee Kwang-Kyu 1977a: 20), and they have been cited, by ourselves and others, as a model of Korean lineage organization (see Brandt 1971: 213; Han Sang-Bok 1977: 57; Janelli and Janelli 1978).

We suggest that precisely because the Hahoe Yu lineage is such an elite and prestigious kin group, it should be taken as a model for only a limited number of Korean lineages. With a secure grasp on gentry status, different segments of the Hahoe Yu turned on each other. Rivalry between segments was rampant. Within the lineage, differences in the official positions earned by respective ancestors became a basis for status competition; different segments of the lineage owned and managed their own corporate estates. This weakening of agnatic solidarity was evidently reflected in turn in the commemoration of nonagnates. It would be interesting to know if a weakening of agnatic solidarity in other Korean communities—which could have resulted from different inheritance practices or an absence of claims to gentry status— is also reflected in a higher incidence of nonagnatic commemoration, greater ritual roles for women, or a lower incidence of reciprocal participation by collateral kin.

Adoption practices are our fourth and final gauge of agnatic solidarity in East Asia. Though a variety of adoption practices are known, we are concerned here only with those instances that relate to ancestor worship. These occur when the adoption perpetuates a descent line or household and thereby provides an heir to perform ancestor rituals.

Confucianists sought to eradicate nonagnatic adoptions throughout East Asia. As the following legend shows, their disapproval of nonagnatic succession has a two-thousand-year history. This story was first recorded by the Confucian philosopher Tung Chung-shu (second century B.C.). It was later quoted by the neo-Confucianist Ch'en Ch'un (1153–1217) and cited as a guide for settling litigation over inheritance in Wang Hui-tsu's (1731–1807) *Administrative Precepts for Local Officials* (Van der Sprenkel 1962: 144–46, 152–53). The anecdote is obviously a literary version of the legend Kwŏn Tŏk-su's widow told us to demonstrate the disadvantages of adoption in Korea (see Chapter 2). The literary Chinese variant, however, is used to remonstrate against nonagnatic adoption.

There was a family paying sacrifice to its ancestors, praying for the spirits to descend. After the whole ceremony was finished, the chief celebrant told the others: "What I saw just now was very strange. There was an official dressed in official robes, wanting to go forward and yet hesitating—he dared not proceed. There was also at the same time a ghost, with untidy hair and exposed arm,[6] holding a butcher's knife, who bravely marched forward and accepted the sacrifices. What sort of spirit was this?" he asked. He himself was not able to explain the reason for this, but there was an old man who said that in this family some time before, as there had been no heir, a son from a butcher's family with a different surname [a nonagnate] had been taken as heir; that was why

---

[6] Van der Sprenkel (1962: 153) provides the following explanation in a footnote: "To a Chinese this signifies complete déshabillé."

the man conducting the sacrifices could only recall ancestors of the butcher's family to come forward, while he had no means of communicating and making contact with ancestors in the line he was supposed to be continuing, as he was not of their blood. [Van der Sprenkel 1962: 153]

After relating the story, Ch'en Ch'un observes: "Nowadays there are quite a lot of people who take as heir a boy related through the female line." He thoroughly denounced the practice (Van der Sprenkel 1962: 152–53).

Evidently swayed by neo-Confucian ideology, the Ming (1368–1644) and Ch'ing (1644–1912) dynasties of China and the Tokugawa government (1603–1868) of Japan all sought to eradicate nonagnatic adoptions (Ch'ü 1961: 37; Dore 1958: 145, 446; Jamieson 1921: 13–24; McMullen 1975), but none of them succeeded. In Japan, forbidding succession to nonagnates generated a major difficulty because a potentially dangerous power vacuum was created whenever a politically powerful family was unable to obtain an agnate for adoption. As a result, adoption laws had to be liberalized (Dore 1958: 446). In China, laws against nonagnatic adoption remained on the books into the Republican era (Escarra 1940: 86–87), but conflict between agnates proved too powerful an obstacle to their observance (Watson 1975a; Wolf and Huang 1980: 209–13). Chinese lineages imposed their own sanctions against nonagnatic adoption (Liu 1959b: 48–77) with greater success (Wolf and Huang 1980: 203, 208–15).

Both Chinese and Japanese families can exercise several options when adopting a nonagnate. Evidently the most common entails a practice that can be called "uxorilocal marriage": a son-in-law marries into his wife's home, inherits her parents' property or succeeds to the headship of their household, assumes responsibility for the ancestor rites of their descent line or household, and later assigns his wife's natal surname to one or more of his offspring. Some statistical comparisons from the first half of this century show that uxorilocal marriages were especially common in Taiwan and various parts of mainland China, where they amounted to 15 percent or more of all marriages (Wolf and Huang 1980: 13–14, 123–26, 337). In Japan, they accounted for about 5 percent of all marriages (Dore 1958: 446). Finally, uxorilocal marriages were rare in the northern part and the lineage-dominated southeastern region of China (Wolf and Huang 1980: 333–35, 351–52). We will return to these regional variations below, when we discuss the personalities attributed to ancestors by men and women throughout East Asia.

In Korea, statutes prohibiting nonagnatic adoption were promulgated during the earliest years of the Yi dynasty, evidently under the impetus of neo-Confucianism and in imitation of the Ming legal code (Peterson 1974: 35; Deuchler 1980a: 88; Kim Yung-Chung 1977: 90, 101); in fact, however, nonagnatic adoptions were common until the seventeenth century. Men may have also gone to live at their wives' natal households at marriage (Deuchler 1977: 8, 15–16), but the effects of this practice on early Yi descent and household succession are unknown. At any rate, the change in adoption practices was contemporaneous with the formation of local lineages and the pattern of primogeniture that prevails throughout Korea today. Nowadays, nonagnatic adoption has become so rare—perhaps extinct—that few Koreans know that it ever existed at all (Peterson 1977; but see Bae Kyung Sook 1973: 63).

Later Yi dynasty and modern rural adoption practices have been interpreted as another expression of the Korean devotion to neo-Confucian orthodoxy (Peterson 1974: 28); in our view, however, these adoption practices reflect the solidarity of living agnates, a solidarity grounded primarily in fraternal affection, mutual assistance and economic cooperation, and advancement of social interests. Korean adoption practices changed only when residence patterns, property inheritance, and lineage functions generated this agnatic unity. Eighteenth-century household registers and local magistrates' reports, moreover, as well as contemporary ethnographic accounts, show that many individuals were ready to forsake their own ancestors and latch on to another descent group when their social aspirations conflicted with agnatic loyalty. Finally, we can find nothing in Confucian or neo-Confucian ideology that dictates giving eldest sons to elder brothers and younger sons to younger brothers. This Korean practice has been devised primarily for the sake of maintaining respective shares of inheritance and, as we have seen, it may be set aside if the economic statuses of the natural and adopting fathers do not accord with their respective ages: a wealthier but younger brother is evidently reluctant to surrender his eldest son to an older but poorer sibling.

In sum, rural Koreans are hardly compulsive Confucianists. Perhaps a few are social philosophers, but their social philosophies are predicated on perceptive understanding of family, lineage, and status-group organization. Moreover, correlations between inheritance, family development cycle, and lineage functions on the one hand, and ancestor-worship practices on the other— correlations which appear to be valid throughout East Asia regardless of the relative strength of neo-Confucian ideology in the three societies—argue that social organization rather than ideology has exerted the greater influence on Korean ancestor worship. In the following section we will try to show how similarities and differences in East Asian family structures are also reflected in men's and women's images of ancestors.

Ancestral Hostility and Benevolence

Informants' reluctance to acknowledge ancestral hostility appears to be the main reason why assessing the personalities of ancestors in East Asia has been so difficult. "In Japanese ideals," wrote David Plath, "the living and the departed are full of mutual affection. . . . So strong is the feeling that the household dead are friendly and supportive, that antagonism is not easily verbalized and must be glimpsed obliquely" (1964: 309–10). One Japanese informant provided Robert Smith with a vivid and detailed example of ancestral affliction but then denied ever having heard of such a case (R. Smith 1974b: 124). And a Tokyo resident questioned by Ronald Dore revealed by the wording of her response a reluctance to believe in ancestral hostility: " 'Some people say,' said one woman, thus giving a hint of her skepticism about this, her suggested reason for worshipping at the *butsudan* [ancestral altar], 'that if anything happens in your house it is because you haven't taken enough care of, say, the second generation, or the third generation' " (Dore 1958: 318).

Evidence from Taiwan indicates that Chinese informants are no more willing than Koreans or Japanese to acknowledge ancestral affliction. "In general, it was difficult to get people to speak of the harm their ancestors had done to them," noted Emily Ahern (1973: 200) in her richly documented account of ancestral hostility among residents of a village in northern Taiwan. Arthur Wolf detected the same unwillingness during his fieldwork in the same region: "[There is] a conflict between an ideal that says the ancestors are always benevolent and a fear that they are in fact punitive. Asked if they believe that their ancestors would punish them for neglect, people usually insist that they would not. But when they suffer a series of misfortunes, most people give serious consideration to the possibility that the ancestors are responsible" (A. Wolf 1974b: 165).

The views of Francis Hsu, a Chinese anthropologist, provide the most striking example of reluctance to acknowledge ancestral hostility. For three decades, Hsu has repeatedly insisted that Chinese ancestors never harm their offspring (1948: 194, 210; 1963: 45; 1975: 56; 1979: 527). At first glance, Hsu's position appears almost irrational. Two classic ethnographies, both written by native Chinese and familiar to Hsu (1948: 3, 68; 1967: 351, 353), easily refute the claim that Chinese never attribute harm to their ancestors:

A family's fortune or misfortune is largely controlled by spirits of the ancestors. When the spirits are pleased, the family will receive blessings; but when they have been antagonized, disaster inevitably comes. [M. Yang 1945: 45]

Misfortunes and sickness are sometimes, not always, explained as the warning of ancestor spirits for some action that they do not approve, such as non-observance of the periodic sacrifice, damage to the coffin shelter, selling of land or house, etc. [Fei 1939: 78]

Yet Hsu offers plausible reasons why descendants ought to regard their ancestors as benevolent. The welfare of each generation is so intimately bound up with that of its predecessors, argues Hsu, that mutual hostility is inconceivable.

A major Chinese cultural postulate is father-son identification and continuity of generations. The father automatically bequeathed his wealth to his sons and was duty bound to see all his children married and well placed. In turn, sons were responsible for the pleasure and welfare of parents in life and after death. Socially, the mutual sharing of their statuses was even more automatic. . . . The father's prestige determine[d] the son's social position when the son [was] young; the order [was] reversed when the son [came] of age. . . . Because of such manifestations of the Chinese premise of father-son identification, I concluded that Chinese did not have to fear harm by the spirits of their ancestors. The mutual bond between them was culturally defined as too automatic to leave room for such harm. [Hsu 1979: 527]

We propose to reformulate rather than reject Hsu's analysis. Intergenerational dependence and identification do not explain why ancestors are always benevolent but instead why they ought to be always benevolent. In other words, we will argue that these two variables generate the stereotype of the benevolent ancestor common to Korea, China, and Japan. We will also attempt to explain why this ideal image is not equally popular among all East Asians.

Mutual dependency and identification of successive generations are recurrent themes in the literature on East Asia. Japan specialists, heavily influenced by psychoanalytic and culture-and-personality theories, emphasize indulgent childrearing practices and emotional attachments as the causes of close bonds between parents and children (Doi 1973; De Vos 1973: 46–52; Befu 1971: 151–66; Kiefer 1970: 69). Young Japanese children are said to acquire a strong sense of dependence on parents because they find them a thoroughly reliable source of emotional gratification and comfort. Boys are said to identify especially with their mothers. In later years, attempts to establish similar relationships with other persons meet with mixed success (Doi 1973; Nakane 1970; De Vos 1975: 50).

China specialists, by contrast, usually point to ideological and social factors as determinants of intergenerational dependence and identification. Family structure and solidarity, social and economic reciprocity, filial piety, and continuity of descent are typically cited as the major causes (C. Yang 1959: 90–92; Baker 1979: 26–48; Fei 1939: 28).

These differing explanations overemphasize the social and cultural differences between China and Japan. To be sure, Japanese childrearing is generally more lenient than that of China (Barry and Paxson 1971: 479; Barry et al. 1977: 202–3); and in Japan, only one child may retain a lifelong membership in his parents' household. But significant similarities between these two societies can also be advanced. Notions of filial piety and reciprocity underlie intergenerational dependence in Japan (Lebra 1979) as well as China; indulgence of children during the first year of life is nearly equal in both societies (Barry and Paxson 1971: 479; see also M. Wolf 1972: 57–65); and both Chinese and Japanese sons are said to be *emotionally* dependent on their mothers, but *socially* dependent on their fathers (Sofue 1971: 284–85;

Hsu 1975: 105). Thus, the different explanations of China and Japan specialists owe more to the theoretical orientations of the analysts than to empirical differences between the two societies. Korea specialists, at any rate, have employed ideology, social structure, and childrearing to explain intergenerational dependence and identification in Korea (Kim Jae-ŭn 1974: 54–60; Brandt 1971: 138, 172–73; Hahn Dongse 1972; Harvey and Chung 1980: 148; Dix 1977: 195–201; Hahm Pyong-Choon 1975: 340).

The ethnographic literature on East Asia, and our observations in Twisŏngdwi, therefore, all provide evidence of reluctance to acknowledge ancestral hostility, on the one hand, and intergenerational dependence and identification on the other. Our argument for a *causal* relation between these variables would be greatly strengthened, however, if their consistent association could be demonstrated in other ways as well.

Two other sets of data appear to offer evidence in support of our hypothesis. The first is a cross-cultural study of childrearing practices and the malevolence or benevolence attributed to supernatural beings. The second is found in the different images of ancestors held by men and women in East Asia.

In a cross-cultural study of 62 nonliterate societies, Lambert, Triandis, and Wolf (1959) found statistically significant relations between beliefs about supernatural beings and childrearing techniques. Those societies in which misfortunes were less often attributed to supernatural beings shared two characteristics: (1) high indulgence of children during infancy, and (2) little encouragement of independence or self-reliance in later childhood (approximately five to twelve years of age). Conversely, those societies in which misfortunes were more often attributed to supernatural beings were characterized by less indulgence during infancy and greater encouragement of self-reliance or independence during later childhood.

Either indulgence during infancy or lack of independence training during later childhood (or both) could foster the pervasive intergenerational dependency and identification found throughout East Asia. The cross-cultural study does not provide unambiguous support of our hypothesis, however, because "infancy" is inconsistently said to comprise "the first year of a child's life and as long thereafter as the treatment of the infant remains approximately constant," the first five years of a child's life, and "approximately to a year and a half" (Lambert et al. 1959: 162–63, 163, 168). Thus, one could cite the indulgence afforded infants during the first year and a half of life as a cause of intergenerational dependence and identification, and ultimately the benevolent stereotype of ancestors found throughout Korea, China, and Japan; but Emily Ahern (1973: 214–15), citing this same study, suggests that harsh treatment of children aged one-and-a-half to three in one Taiwanese community may be the cause of its residents' beliefs in ancestral hostility. The cross-cultural findings concerning independence training in later childhood, on the other hand, point more clearly to a connection between intergenerational dependence and ancestral hostility.

Differences between men's and women's images of ancestors provide the most systematic evidence for our argument. Toward both her natal parents and parents-in-law, a woman probably develops some measure of dependence and identification. She receives some of the same nurturant treatment as her brothers; and her social status and economic welfare too are dependent on the social position and property of her husband's parents. Yet men have a lifelong relationship with only one set of parents; a woman divides her loyalties between two. And her membership in her natal and her marital household is subject to revocation through marriage and divorce respectively. Like women in Twisŏngdwi, women in both China and Japan are more independent of the senior generation than either their husbands or their brothers (M. Wolf 1972: 41; Beardsley et al. 1959: 209).

In forming her conceptions of ancestors, a woman's relationship with her husband's parents is usually more important than her ties to her natal parents, for they normally become the ancestors with whom she must deal. As we have seen, her relationship with these persons is typically more conflict-laden than her husband's. And she never receives from her parents-in-law the nurturance and support that they showered upon her spouse in his childhood years. Thus, we can predict that, compared with their husbands, women in East Asia ought to be less susceptible to the stereotype of the benevolent ancestor and generally more willing to acknowledge ancestral hostility. In fact, this is precisely what we found in Twisŏngdwi. The ethnographic literature from

China and Japan point to, and regional variations support, this interpretation.

In Japan, spirit mediums are said to be the persons most likely to identify ancestors as the cause of misfortunes (Plath 1964: 310; Dore 1958: 318–19; R. Smith 1974b: 125). But descriptions of the ancestor seances that these mediums perform indicate that most of their clients are women (Blacker 1975: 155, 160; Hori 1968: 211). New Religions are the only other Japanese institutions where ancestral malevolence is a prominent theme; and most of their members are women as well (R. Smith 1974b: 124; Dore 1958: 319–20; Kerner 1976; Lebra 1976).

Writing of China, Maurice Freedman surmised that "to the limited extent that ancestors can intervene detrimentally in the lives of their descendants, it is women who are probably the agents for the unfavorable interpretation of ancestral behavior" (1970: 174; 1967: 97–98). Although Freedman provides no evidence to support this statement, descriptions of Chinese ancestor seances are certainly consistent with his claim. One such description is found in J. J. M. De Groot's account of female spirit mediums (Classical Chinese: *wu*; Korean: *mu*, as in *mudang*) in southeastern China. Another is a literary document describing practices in northern China, which De Groot quotes in his account. According to both these sources, female spirit mediums are typically employed by women in cases of family illness to determine whether or not ancestors are content (De Groot 1964: 1330–33).

An ancestor seance held in a village near Canton (Potter 1974) bears many similarities to those we observed in Twisŏngdwi. The female shaman, for example, did not name those whose voices she transmitted but provided a few general clues from which her audience inferred each spirit's identity (Potter 1974: 213). The spirits often voiced grievances, and the participants were apprehensive of the harm these spirits could inflict. Most important, however, were the different degrees of participation of men and women. Though both sexes were present, women played a far more active role. Only women addressed the dead in the several conversations quoted by Potter (1974: 208–13).

It is instructive to contrast this seance in southeastern China with Emily Ahern's account of communication with the dead in a northern Taiwanese village (1973: 229–35). The Taiwanese villagers did not use shamans as intermediaries but traveled to the other world personally to see and speak with their ancestors, most frequently with parents. Says Ahern (1973: 220), "The ancestor is contacted in the otherworld not out of fear that his dissatisfaction there may lead to trouble for the living but rather out of a desire to perpetuate cherished relationships." And her descriptions of these encounters with the dead, unlike Potter's, include no overt expressions of hostility or fear. But her data also show that men of the village, not women, typically visit the otherworld (1973: 217–18, 229–30).

The difference in men's and women's inclinations to accept the possibility of ancestral affliction is not equally pronounced throughout East Asia, nor should it be. When a man marries uxorilocally and assumes ritual obligations toward his wife's progenitors, his dependency on and identification with his "ancestors" and their idealized, benevolent image is considerably diluted; and he may well be more willing than his wife to acknowledge their hostility.[7] Perhaps it is only accidental, but Yanagita Kunio, who was less reluctant than Francis Hsu to acknowledge ancestral affliction, was also an uxorilocally married husband (Ch'oe Kilsŏng 1980: 185).

In Twisŏngdwi, as we have seen, men never assume obligations toward their wives' ancestors, and this appears to be generally true throughout Korea. Even the sons-in-law who married into Twisŏngdwi maintain their own households and commemorate only their own agnatic forebears. In Korea, therefore, men's and women's conceptions of ancestors stand in sharpest contrast. Freedman's research focused on the lineage-dominated villages of southeastern China, the type of village from which Potter's description comes. In these communities, and in the northern Chinese locations mentioned by De Groot's literary source, uxorilocal marriages are rare. In these regions as well, therefore, fidelity to agnatic descent maintains systematic differences between men's and women's dependence upon and identification with those persons who later become their "ancestors." These sys-

[7] Assessing their respective beliefs is complicated because uxorilocally married men may bring the tablets of their own parents into their wife's household. Thus, the "ancestors" an uxorilocally married man worships may include some of his own as well as his wife's forebears.

tematic differences in social experiences are in turn reflected in men's greater reluctance to acknowledge ancestral hostility or to attribute misfortune to ancestral intervention. In Japan, uxorilocal marriage is somewhat more common, and differences between men's and women's beliefs are not so obvious. In northern Taiwan, uxorilocal marriages are far more frequent. Combined with a variety of adoption practices and other complexities in the assumption of ritual obligations (A. Wolf 1976; Wang S. 1976), this high rate of uxorilocal marriage appears to have obliterated the systematic differences between men's and women's beliefs found elsewhere in East Asia. Other than the ancestor seances, at which men betray no trace of belief in ancestral hostility, neither Emily Ahern's nor Arthur Wolf's rich data include any evidence suggesting that men's and women's images of ancestors differ in any way. In sum, the lower the rate of uxorilocal marriage, the sharper the difference between men's and women's reluctance to acknowledge ancestral hostility.

If we had not conducted our research in a Korean village like Twisŏngdwi, we would probably not have noticed that men and women in many East Asian communities hold different beliefs about ancestors. Nor could we have identified some of the consistent relations between inheritance practices, family and household organization, lineage functions, and ancestor rites in Korea, China, and Japan. A Korean village in which agnatic descent is so faithfully observed offers a new and therefore valuable vantage point from which to view the effects of social organization on cults of the dead in East Asia.

Reference Matter

Bibliography

Ahern, Emily M. 1973. The Cult of the Dead in a Chinese Village. Stanford: Stanford University Press.

Akiba, Takashi. 1957. A Study on Korean Folkways. *Folklore Studies* 16: 1–106.

Andong Kwŏn-ssi sebo. 1961. Taejŏn: Hoesangsa.

Bae, Kyung Sook. 1973. Women and the Law in Korea. Seoul: Korean League of Women Voters.

Baker, Hugh D. R. 1968. A Chinese Lineage Village: Sheung Shui. Stanford: Stanford University Press.

———. 1979. Chinese Family and Kinship. New York: Columbia University Press.

Ball, J. Dyer. 1912. The Chinese at Home. New York: Fleming H. Revell.

Barry, Herbert, III, and Leonora M. Paxson. 1971. Infancy and Early Childhood: Cross-Cultural Codes 2. *Ethnology* 10: 466–508.

Barry, Herbert, III, Lili Josephson, Edith Lauer, and Catharine Marshall. 1977. Agents and Techniques for Child Training: Cross-Cultural Codes 6. *Ethnology* 16: 191–230.

Beardsley, Richard K., John W. Hall, and Robert E. Ward. 1959. Village Japan. Chicago and London: University of Chicago Press.

Beattie, Hilary J. 1979. Land and Lineage in China: A Study of T'ung-Ch'eng County, Anhwei, in the Ming and Ch'ing Dynasties. Cambridge: Cambridge University Press.

Befu, Harumi. 1962. Corporate Emphasis and Patterns of Descent in the Japanese Family. In Robert J. Smith and Richard K. Beardsley, eds., Japanese Culture: Its Development and Characteristics. Chicago: Aldine.

———. 1971. Japan: An Anthropological Introduction. New York: Harper & Row.

Benedict, Ruth. 1946. The Chrysanthemum and the Sword: Patterns of Japanese Culture. Boston: Houghton Mifflin.

Biernatzki, William Eugene. 1967. Varieties of Korean Lineage Structure. Ph.D. dissertation, St. Louis University.

Blacker, Carmen. 1975. The Catalpa Bow: A Study of Shamanistic Practices in Japan. London: George Allen and Unwin.

Brain, James. 1973. Ancestors and Elders in Africa: Further Thoughts. *Africa* 43: 122–33.

Brandt, Vincent S. R. 1971. A Korean Village: Between Farm and Sea. Cambridge, Mass.: Harvard University Press.

Brown, Keith. 1968. The Content of Dozoku Relationships in Japan. *Ethnology* 7: 113–38.

Buchanan, Daniel Crump. 1965. Japanese Proverbs and Sayings. Norman: University of Oklahoma Press.

Calhoun, C. J. 1980. The Authority of Ancestors: A Sociological Reconsideration of Fortes's Tallensi in Response to Fortes's Critics. *Man* (n.s.) 15: 304–19.

Cha, Jae-ho, Chung Bom-mo, and Lee Sung-jin. 1977. Boy Preference Reflected in Korean Folklore. In Sandra Mattielli, ed., Virtues in Conflict: Tradition and the Korean Woman Today. Seoul: Samhwa.

Chan, Wing-tsit (trans.). 1967. Reflections on Things at Hand: The Neo-Confucian Anthology Compiled by Chu Hsi and Lü Tsu-ch'ien. New York and London: Columbia University Press.

———. 1976. The Study of Chu Hsi in the West. *Journal of Asian Studies* 35: 555–77.

Chang, Chŏl-su. 1973–74. Chungguk ŭiryega Han'guk ŭirye saenghwal e mich'in yŏnghyang: *Chuja karye* wa *Sarye p'yŏllam* ŭi sangnyerŭl chungsim ŭro. *Munhwa illyuhak* 6: 67–83.

Chang, Dae Hong. 1962. The Historical Development of the Korean Socio-Family System Since 1392: A Legalistic Interpretation. Ph.D. dissertation, Michigan State University.

Ch'en, Kenneth K. S. 1964. Buddhism in China: A Historical Survey. Princeton: Princeton University Press.

———. 1973. The Chinese Transformation of Buddhism. Princeton: Princeton University Press.

Cho, Oakla. 1979. Social Stratification in a Korean Peasant Village. Ph.D. dissertation, State University of New York at Stony Brook.

Ch'oe, Kil-sŏng. 1978. Han'guk musok ŭi yŏn'gu. Seoul: Asea munhwasa.

———. 1980. Ilbonhak immun: munhwa illyuhakchŏk sigak. Taegu: Kyemyŏng University Press.

Ch'oe, Yŏng-ho. 1974. Commoners in Early Yi Dynasty Civil Examinations: An Aspect of Korean Social Structure, 1392–1600. *Journal of Asian Studies* 33: 611–31.

Choi, Hochin. 1971. The Economic History of Korea: From the Earliest Times to 1945. Seoul: The Freedom Library.

Choi, In-hak. 1979. A Type Index of Korean Folktales. Seoul: Myong Ji University Publishing.

Choi, Jai-seuk. 1966a. Tongjok chiptan ŭi chojik kwa kinŭng. *Minjok munhwa yŏn'gu* 2: 75–146.

——. 1966b. Han'guk kajok yŏn'gu. Seoul: Minjung sŏgwan.

——. 1972. Chosŏn sidae ŭi sangsokche e kwanhan yŏn'gu: punjaegi ŭi punsŏk e ŭihan chŏpkŭn. *Yŏksa hakpo*, Nos. 53/54: 99–150.

——. 1976. Family System. In Chun Shin-Yong, gen. ed., Korean Society. Korean Culture Series 6. Seoul: International Cultural Foundation.

Ch'ü, T'ung-tsu. 1961. Law and Society in Traditional China. Paris and La Haye: Mouton.

Chung, Bom Mo, James A. Palmore, Lee Sang Joo, and Lee Sung Jin. 1972. Psychological Perspectives: Family Planning in Korea. Seoul: Hollym.

Clark, Charles Allen. 1932. Religions of Old Korea. New York: Fleming H. Revell.

Cohen, Myron L. 1976. House United, House Divided: The Chinese Family in Taiwan. New York and London: Columbia University Press.

Cormack, Mrs. J. G. 1935. Everyday Customs in China. Edinburgh and London: Moray Press.

Dallet, Charles. 1954. Traditional Korea. New Haven: Human Relations Area Files.

Day, Clarence Burton. 1940. Chinese Peasant Cults: Being a Study of Chinese Paper Gods. Shanghai: Kelly and Walsh, Ltd.

de Bary, Wm. Theodore. 1959. Some Common Tendencies in Neo-Confucianism. In David S. Nivison and Arthur F. Wright, eds., Confucianism in Action. Stanford: Stanford University Press.

Dégh, Linda. 1977. Biologie des Erzählguts. In Kurt Ranke, ed., Enzyklopädie des Märchens: Handwörterbuch zur historischen und vergleichenden Erzählforschung, Vol. 1, Nos. 1/2. Berlin and New York: Walter de Gruyter.

——. 1979. Biology of Storytelling. Folklore Preprint Series, Vol. 7, No. 3. Bloomington, Ind.: Folklore Publications Group, Indiana University.

De Groot, J. J. M. 1964. The Religious System of China. 6 Vols. Taipei: Literature House.

De Harlez, C. 1889. Kai-li: Livre des Rites Domestiques Chinois de Tchou-Hi. Paris: Leroux.

Deuchler, Martina. 1977. The Tradition: Women During the Yi Dynasty. In Sandra Mattielli, ed., Virtues in Conflict: Tradition and the Korean Woman Today. Seoul: Samhwa.

——. 1980a. Neo-Confucianism: The Impulse for Social Action in Early Yi Korea. *Journal of Korean Studies* 2: 71–111.

——. 1980b. Thoughts on Korean Society. In Papers of the First International Conference on Korean Studies, 1979. Sŏngnam: The Academy of Korean Studies.

————. n.d. Ancestor Worship and Lineage Organization in Early Yi Dynasty Korea. Unpublished ms.

De Vos, George A. 1973. Socialization for Achievement: Essays on the Psychology of the Japanese. Berkeley and Los Angeles: University of California Press.

Dix, Griffin. 1977. "The East Asian Country of Propriety": Confucianism in a Korean Village. Ph.D. dissertation, University of California, San Diego.

————. 1979. How to Do Things with Ritual: The Logic of Ancestor Worship and Other Offerings in Rural Korea. In David R. McCann, John Middleton, and Edward J. Shultz, eds., Studies on Korea in Transition. Honolulu: Center for Korean Studies, University of Hawaii.

————. 1980. The Place of the Almanac in Korean Folk Religion. *Journal of Korean Studies* 2: 47–70.

Doi, Takeo. 1973. The Anatomy of Dependence. New York: Kodansha International.

Dore, R. P. 1958. City Life in Japan: A Study of a Tokyo Ward. Berkeley and Los Angeles: University of California Press.

Dorson, Richard M. 1962. Folk Legends of Japan. Rutland, Vt.: Charles E. Tuttle.

———— (editor). 1975. Folktales Told Around the World. Chicago and London: University of Chicago Press.

Dredge, C. Paul. 1976. Social Rules of Speech in Korean: The Views of a Comic Strip Character. *Korea Journal* 16 (1): 4–14.

————. 1978. What's in a Funeral? Korean, American-Mormon, and Jewish Rites Compared. In Spencer J. Palmer, ed., Deity and Death. Provo, Ut.: Religious Studies Center, Brigham Young University.

————. n.d. Korean Funerals: Ritual as Process. Unpublished ms.

Dundes, Alan, 1966. Metafolklore and Oral Literary Criticism. *The Monist* 50: 505–16.

Eberhard, Wolfram. 1937. Typen chinesischer Volksmärchen. FF Communications, No. 120. Helsinki: Suomalainen Tiedeakatemia Academia Scientiarum Fennica.

————. 1967. Guilt and Sin in Traditional China. Berkeley and Los Angeles: University of California Press.

Economic Planning Board. 1963a. 1960 Population and Housing Census of Korea. Vol. 1, Complete Tabulation Report, 11-3 Gyeonggi-Do. Seoul: Economic Planning Board.

————. 1963b. 1960 Population and Housing Census of Korea. Vol. 2, 20% Sample Tabulation Report, 11-1 Whole Country. Seoul: Economic Planning Board.

Embree, John F. 1939. Suye Mura: A Japanese Village. Chicago: University of Chicago Press.

Enç, Berent. 1979. Function Attributions and Functional Explanations. *Philosophy of Science* 46: 343–65.

Escarra, Jean. 1940. China Then and Now. Peking: Henri Vetch.

Fei, Hsiao-tung. 1939. Peasant Life in China: A Field Study of Country Life in the Yangtze Valley. New York: Dutton.

Feuchtwang, Stephan D. R. 1974a. Domestic and Communal Worship in Taiwan. In Arthur P. Wolf, ed., Religion and Ritual in Chinese Society. Stanford: Stanford University Press.

———. 1974b. An Anthropological Analysis of Chinese Geomancy. Vientiane, Laos: Vithagna.

Fortes, Meyer. 1949. The Web of Kinship Among the Tallensi. London: Oxford University Press.

———. 1953. The Structure of Unilineal Descent Groups. *American Anthropologist* 55: 17–41.

———. 1958. Introduction. In Jack Goody, ed., The Developmental Cycle in Domestic Groups. Cambridge: Cambridge University Press.

———. 1959. Oedipus and Job in West African Religion. Cambridge: Cambridge University Press.

———. 1961. Pietas in Ancestor Worship. *Journal of the Royal Anthropological Institute* 91: 166–91.

———. 1965. Some Reflections on Ancestor Worship in Africa. In African Systems of Thought: Studies Presented and Discussed at the Third International African Seminar in Salisbury, December 1960. London: Oxford University Press.

———. 1976. An Introductory Commentary. In William H. Newell, ed., Ancestors. The Hague and Paris: Mouton.

Freedman, Maurice. 1958. Lineage Organization in Southeastern China. London School of Economics Monographs on Social Anthropology, No. 18. London: Athlone Press.

———. 1966. Chinese Lineage and Society. London School of Economics Monographs on Social Anthropology, No. 33. London: Athlone Press.

———. 1967. Ancestor Worship: Two Facets of the Chinese Case. In Maurice Freedman, ed., Social Organization: Essays Presented to Raymond Firth. Chicago: Aldine.

———. 1970. Ritual Aspects of Chinese Kinship and Marriage. In Maurice Freedman, ed., Family and Kinship in Chinese Society. Stanford: Stanford University Press.

———. 1974a. The Politics of an Old State: A View from the Chinese Lineage. In J. R. Davis, ed., Choice and Change: Essays in Honour of Lucy Mair. New York: Humanities Press.

―――. 1974b. On the Sociological Study of Chinese Religion. In Arthur P. Wolf, ed., Religion and Ritual in Chinese Society. Stanford: Stanford University Press.

Freud, Sigmund. 1950. Totem and Taboo: Some Points of Agreement Between the Mental Lives of Savages and Neurotics. New York: W. W. Norton.

Fried, Morton H. 1953. Fabric of Chinese Society: A Study of the Social Life of a Chinese County Seat. New York: Praeger.

―――. 1970. Clans and Lineages: How to Tell Them Apart and Why: With Special Reference to Chinese Society. Bulletin of the Institute of Ethnology, Academia Sinica 29: 11–36.

Fung, Yu-lan. 1952. A History of Chinese Philosophy. Vol. 1: The Period of the Philosophers. Derk Bodde, trans. Second Edition in English. Princeton: Princeton University Press.

Gale, Rev. James S. 1898. Korean Sketches. New York: Fleming H. Revell.

―――(trans.). 1913. Korean Folk Tales: Imps, Ghosts, and Fairies. New York: E. P. Dutton.

Gallin, Bernard. 1966. Hsin Hsing, Taiwan: A Chinese Village in Change. Berkeley and Los Angeles: University of California Press.

Gamble, Sidney D. 1954. Ting Hsien: A North China Rural Community. New York: Institute of Pacific Relations.

Gifford, Daniel L. 1892. Ancestral Worship as Practiced in Korea. The Korean Repository 1: 169–76.

Gluckman, Max. 1937. Mortuary Customs and the Belief in Survival After Death Among the South-Eastern Bantu. Bantu Studies 11: 117–36.

Goldberg, Charles N. 1973–74. Yangban, sangnom kwa illyuhakcha: Illyuhakchŏk iron kwa cross-cultural studies rŭl pich'uŏbon Han'guk sahoe kyegŭp kwa tongjok chiptan chosa. Munhwa illyuhak 6: 161–67.

Goody, Jack. 1962. Death, Property and the Ancestors: A Study of the Mortuary Customs of the LoDagaa of West Africa. Stanford: Stanford University Press.

Gough, E. Kathleen. 1958. Cults of the Dead Among the Nāyars. Journal of American Folklore 71: 446–78.

Gray, John Henry. 1878. China: A History of the Laws, Manners, and Customs of the People. London: Macmillan and Co.

Hahm, Pyong-Choon. 1967. The Korean Political Tradition and Law: Essays in Korean Law and Legal History. Seoul: Hollym.

―――. 1975. Toward a New Theory of Korean Politics: A Reexamination of Traditional Factors. In Edward Reynolds Wright, ed., Korean Politics in Transition. Seattle and London: University of Washington Press.

Hahn, Dongse. 1972. Maturity in Korea and America. In William P. Lebra, ed., Transcultural Research in Mental Health: Volume II of Mental Health Research in Asia and the Pacific. Honolulu: University Press of Hawaii.

Han, Chungnim C. 1949. Social Organization of Upper Han Hamlet in Korea. Ph.D. dissertation, University of Michigan.

Han, Sang-Bok. 1977. Korean Fisherman: Ecological Adaption in Three Communities. Seoul: Seoul National University Press.

Han, Woo-keun. 1971. The History of Korea. Honolulu: East-West Center Press.

Harrell, Stevan. 1979. The Concept of "Soul" in Chinese Folk Religion. *Journal of Asian Studies* 38: 519–28.

Harvey, Youngsook Kim. 1979. Six Korean Women: The Socialization of Shamans. St. Paul, Minn.: West Publishing Co.

Harvey, Youngsook Kim, and Chung Soon-Hyung. 1980. The Koreans. In John F. McDermott, Jr., Wen-Shing Tseng, and Thomas W. Maretzki, eds., People and Cultures of Hawaii: A Psychocultural Profile. Honolulu: University Press of Hawaii.

Hempel, Carl G. 1959. The Logic of Functional Analysis. In Llewellyn Gross, ed., Symposium on Sociological Theory. New York: Harper & Row.

Henderson, Gregory. 1968. Korea: The Politics of the Vortex. Cambridge, Mass.: Harvard University Press.

Henthorn, William E. 1971. A History of Korea. New York: Free Press.

Hicks, David. 1976. Tetum Ghosts and Kin: Fieldwork in an Indonesian Community. Palo Alto: Mayfield.

Hori, Ichiro. 1968. Folk Religion in Japan: Continuity and Change. Chicago and London: University of Chicago Press.

Hozumi, Nobushige. 1913. Ancestor-Worship and Japanese Law. Third and Revised Edition. Tokyo: Maruzen Kabushiki-Kaisha.

Hsu, Francis L. K. 1948. Under the Ancestors' Shadow: Chinese Culture and Personality. New York: Columbia University Press.

———. 1963. Clan, Caste, and Club. Princeton: D. Van Nostrand.

———. 1967. Under the Ancestors' Shadow: Kinship, Personality, and Social Mobility in Village China. Revised and Expanded Edition. New York: Doubleday.

———. 1975. Iemoto: The Heart of Japan. Cambridge, Mass.: Schenkman.

———. 1979. The Cultural Problem of the Cultural Anthropologist. *American Anthropologist* 81: 517–32.

Hu, Hsien Chin. 1948. The Common Descent Group in China and Its Functions. New York: Viking Fund.

Ikeda, Hiroko. 1971. A Type and Motif Index of Japanese Folk-Literature. FF Communications, No. 209. Helsinki: Suomalainen Tiedeak-atemia Academia Scientiarum Fennica.

Jamieson, G. 1921. Chinese Family and Commercial Law. Shanghai: Kelly and Walsh.

Janelli, Dawnhee Yim. 1977. Logical Contradictions in Korean Learned Fortunetelling. Ph.D. dissertation, University of Pennsylvania.

Janelli, Roger L. 1975. Korean Rituals of Ancestor Worship: An Ethnography of Folklore Performance. Ph.D. dissertation, University of Pennsylvania.

Janelli, Roger L., and Dawnhee Yim Janelli. 1978. Lineage Organization and Social Differentiation in Korea. *Man* (n.s.) 13: 272–89.

————. 1979. The Functional Value of Ignorance at a Korean Seance. *Asian Folklore Studies* 38 (1): 81–90.

Jarvie, I. C. 1973. Functionalism. Minneapolis: Burgess.

Jordan, David K. 1972. Gods, Ghosts, and Ancestors: The Folk Religion of a Taiwanese Village. Berkeley and Los Angeles: University of California Press.

Kalton, Michael C. n.d. Early Yi Dynasty Neo-Confucianism: An Integrated Vision. Unpublished ms.

Kang, H. W. 1974. Institutional Borrowing: The Case of the Chinese Civil Service Examination System in Early Koryŏ. *Journal of Asian Studies* 34: 109–25.

Kang, Younghill. 1931. The Grass Roof. New York and London: Charles Scribner's.

Kawashima, Fujiya. 1977. Lineage Elite and Bureaucracy in Early Yi to Mid-Yi Dynasty Korea. In James B. Palais and Margery D. Lang, eds., Occasional Papers on Korea, No. 5. New York: Joint Committee on Korean Studies of the American Council of Learned Societies and the Social Science Research Council.

————. 1978. Historiographic Development in South Korea: State and Society from the Mid-Koryŏ to the Mid-Yi Dynasty. *Korean Studies* 2: 29–56.

————. 1980. The Local Gentry Association in Mid-Yi Dynasty Korea: A Preliminary Study of the Ch'angnyŏng Hyangan, 1600–1838. *Journal of Korean Studies* 2: 113–37.

Kendall, Laurel. 1977. Caught Between Ancestors and Spirits: Field Report of a Korean Mansin's Healing Kut. *Korea Journal* 17 (8): 8–23.

————. 1979. Restless Spirits: Shaman and Housewife in Korean Ritual Life. Ph.D. dissertation, Columbia University.

Kerner, Karen. 1976. The Malevolent Ancestor: Ancestral Influence in a Japanese Religious Sect. In William H. Newell, ed., Ancestors. The Hague and Paris: Mouton.

Kiefer, Christie W. 1970. The Psychological Interdependence of Family, School, and Bureaucracy in Japan. *American Anthropologist* 72: 66–75.

Kim, Jae-On. 1977. The Idea of Chastity in Korean Folk Tales: A Study of a Popular Ideal and Its Social Implications. In James B. Palais and Margery D. Lang, eds., Occasional Papers on Korea, No. 5. New York: Joint Committee on Korean Studies of the American Council of Learned Societies and the Social Science Research Council.

Kim, Jae-ŭn. 1974. Han'guk kajok ŭi simni: Kajok kwan'gye mit chiptan sŏnggyŏk. Ewha Womans University Press.

Kim, Kwang-iel. 1973. Shamanist Healing Ceremonies in Korea. Korea Journal 13 (4): 41–47.

Kim, Sŏng-bae. 1975. Hyangduga, sŏngjoga. Seoul: Chŏngŭmsa.

Kim, Taik-Kyoo. 1964. Tongjok purak ŭi saenghwal kujo yŏn'gu. Taegu: Ch'ŏnggu University Press.

———. 1968. The Life-Cultural Structure of a Yangban Village in Korea. In Proceedings, VIIIth International Congress of Anthropological and Ethnological Sciences, Vol. II. Tokyo: Science Council of Japan.

Kim, Tu-hŏn. 1949. Chosŏn kajok chedo yŏn'gu. Seoul: Ŭryu munhwasa.

Kim, Yong-sŏp. 1975. Han'guk kŭndae nongŏpsa yŏn'gu. Seoul: Ilchogak.

Kim, Yung-Chung (ed. and trans.). 1977. Women of Korea: A History from Ancient Times to 1945. Seoul: Ewha Womans University Press.

Knez, Eugene Irving. 1959. Sam Jong Dong: A South Korean Village. Ph.D. dissertation, Syracuse University.

Kopytoff, Igor. 1971. Ancestors as Elders in Africa. Africa 41: 129–42.

———. 1981. The Authority of Ancestors. Man (n.s.) 16: 135–37.

Korean Overseas Information Service. 1978. A Handbook of Korea. Seoul: Korean Overseas Information Service, Ministry of Culture and Information.

Kuhn, Thomas S. 1970. The Structure of Scientific Revolutions. Second Edition, Enlarged. Chicago: University of Chicago Press.

Kulp, Daniel Harrison, II. 1925. Country Life in South China: The Sociology of Familism. New York: Teachers College, Columbia University.

Kwon, Tai Hwan, et al. 1975. The Population of Korea. Seoul: Population and Development Studies Center, Seoul National University.

Lambert, William W., Leigh Minturn Triandis, and Margery Wolf. 1959. Some Correlates of Beliefs in the Malevolence and Benevolence of Supernatural Beings: A Cross-Societal Study. Journal of Abnormal and Social Psychology 58: 162–69.

Lebra, Takie Sugiyama. 1976. Ancestral Influence on the Suffering of Descendants in a Japanese Cult. In William H. Newell, ed., Ancestors. The Hague and Paris: Mouton.

———. 1979. The Dilemma and Strategies of Aging Among Contemporary Japanese Women. Ethnology 18: 337–53.

Lee, Hoon K. 1936. Land Utilization and Rural Economy in Korea. Chicago: University of Chicago Press.

Lee, Kwang-Kyu. 1975. Kinship System in Korea. 2 vols. HRAFlex Books, AA1-002, Ethnography Series. New Haven: Human Relations Area Files.

———. 1976. A Comparative Study of the Role of Descent in East Asia: China, Korea, and Japan. *Korea Journal* 16 (11): 12–22.

———. 1977a. Tongjok chiptan kwa chosang sungbae. *Munhwa illyuhak* 9: 1–24.

———. 1977b. Han'guk kajok ŭi sajŏk yŏn'gu. Seoul: Ilchisa.

Lee, Kwang-Kyu, and Youngsook Kim Harvey. 1973. Teknonymy and Geononymy in Korean Kinship Terminology. *Ethnology* 12: 31–46.

Lee, Man-Gap. 1960. Han'guk nongch'on ŭi sahoe kujo. Seoul: Han'guk yŏn'gu tosŏgwan.

———. 1970. Consanguineous Group and Its Function in the Korean Community. In Reuben Hill and René König, eds., Families in East and West: Socialization Process and Kinship Ties. Paris and The Hague: Mouton.

Lee, Man-Gap, and Herbert R. Barringer. 1978. Rural-Urban Migration and Social Mobility: Studies of Three South Korean Cities. Papers of the East-West Population Institute, No. 51. Honolulu: East-West Center.

Lee, Mun Woong. 1976. Rural North Korea Under Communism: A Study of Sociocultural Change. Houston: Rice University Press.

Legge, James (trans.). 1879. The Sacred Books of China. The Sacred Books of the East. Vol. 3. Oxford: Clarendon Press.

Li, Yih-yuan. 1976. Chinese Geomancy and Ancestor Worship: A Further Discussion. In William H. Newell, ed., Ancestors. The Hague and Paris: Mouton.

Lih, Jeong-duc. 1966. Home Is a Distant Heart. *Korea Journal* 6 (2): 23–31.

Lim, Yoon-taeck. 1979. Filial Piety: Answer to Parental Love. *The Korea Herald* (May 6).

Liu, Hui-chen Wang. 1959a. An Analysis of Chinese Clan Rules: Confucian Theories in Action. In David S. Nivison and Arthur F. Wright, eds., Confucianism in Action. Stanford: Stanford University Press.

———. 1959b. The Traditional Chinese Clan Rules. Locust Valley, New York: J. J. Augustin.

Lo, Hsiang-lin. 1972. The History and Arrangement of Chinese Genealogies. In Spencer J. Palmer, ed., Studies in Asian Genealogy. Provo, Ut.: Brigham Young University Press.

Madrigal, Moon Jee Yoo. 1979. The Role of Women in Korean Society with Special Emphasis on the Economic System. Palo Alto: R & E Research Associates, Inc.

Mansŏng Taedongbo, 1972, Seoul: Hangmun'gak (reprint ed.).
Martin, Samuel E. 1964. Speech Levels in Japan and Korea. In Dell H. Hymes, ed., Language in Culture and Society: A Reader in Linguistics and Anthropology. New York: Harper and Row.
McBrian, Charles D. 1979. Kinship, Communal, and Class Models of Social Structure in Rising Sun Village. In David R. McCann, John Middleton, and Edward J. Shultz, eds., Studies on Korea in Transition. Honolulu: Center for Korean Studies, University of Hawaii.
McKnight, J. D. 1967. Extra-Descent Group Ancestor Cults in African Societies. Africa 37: 1–21.
McMullen, I. J. 1975. Non-Agnatic Adoption: A Confucian Controversy in Seventeenth- and Eighteenth-Century Japan. Harvard Journal of Asiatic Studies 35: 133–89.
Michell, Tony. 1979–80. Fact and Hypothesis in Yi Dynasty Economic History: The Demographic Dimension. Korean Studies Forum, No. 6: 65–93.
Ministry of Agriculture and Fisheries, Republic of Korea. 1973. Yearbook of Agriculture and Forestry Statistics 1973. Seoul: Ministry of Agriculture and Fisheries.
———. 1977. Yearbook of Agriculture and Forestry Statistics 1977. Seoul: Ministry of Agriculture and Fisheries.
Moon, Hyun Sang, Han Seung Hyun, and Choi Soon. 1973. Fertility and Family Planning: An Interim Report on 1971 Fertility-Abortion Survey. Seoul: Korean Institute for Family Planning.
Moon, Seung Gyu. 1971. Child Training Practices in Rural Korea. Bulletin of the Korean Research Center: Journal of Social Sciences and Humanities, No. 35: 11–32.
———. 1974. Ancestor Worship in Korea: Tradition and Transition. Journal of Comparative Family Studies 5: 71–87.
Moose, J. Robert. 1911. Village Life in Korea. Nashville: Publishing House of the M. E. Church, South.
Nakane, Chie. 1967. Kinship and Economic Organization in Rural Japan. New York: Humanities Press.
———. 1970. Japanese Society. Berkeley and Los Angeles: University of California Press.
National Bureau of Statistics, Economic Planning Board, Republic of Korea. 1978. Korea Statistical Yearbook 1978, No. 25. Seoul: National Bureau of Statistics.
———. 1979. Korea Statistical Yearbook 1979, No. 26. Seoul: National Bureau of Statistics.
Newell, William H. 1976. Preface. In William H. Newell, ed., Ancestors. The Hague and Paris: Mouton.
Norbeck, Edward. 1978. Country to City: The Urbanization of a Japanese Hamlet. Salt Lake City: University of Utah Press.

Ŏm, Mun-ho. 1972. Saenghwarin ŭi tae kajŏng pogam. Seoul: Chŏngmun ch'ulp'ansa.

Ooms, Herman. 1976. A Structural Analysis of Japanese Ancestral Rites and Beliefs. In William H. Newell, ed., Ancestors. The Hague and Paris: Mouton.

Opler, M. E. 1936. An Interpretation of Ambivalence of Two American Indian Tribes. *Journal of Social Psychology* 7: 82–116.

Oring, Elliot. 1976. Three Functions of Folklore: Traditional Functionalism as Explanation in Folkloristics. *Journal of American Folklore* 89: 67–80.

Osgood, Cornelius. 1951. The Koreans and Their Culture. New York: Ronald.

———. 1963. Village Life in Old China: A Community Study of Koo Yao, Yünnan. New York: Ronald.

Otake, Emiko. 1980. Two Categories of Chinese Ancestors as Determined by Their Malevolence. *Asian Folklore Studies* 39 (1): 23–31.

Pak, Ki-hyuk. 1975. The Changing Korean Village. Seoul: Shin-hung.

Park, Sang-Yŏl. 1967. The Social Structure of a Korean Village Under the Control of Sanguinity. *Bulletin of the Korean Research Center: Journal of Social Sciences and Humanities,* No. 27: 70–98.

Peterson, Mark. 1974. Adoption in Korean Genealogies: Continuation of Lineage. *Korea Journal* 14 (1): 28–35, 45.

———. 1977. Some Korean Attitudes Toward Adoption. *Korea Journal* 17 (12): 28–31.

———. 1979. Hyangban and Merchant in Kaesŏng. *Korea Journal* 19 (10): 4–18.

Plath, David W. 1964. Where the Family of God is the Family: The Role of the Dead in Japanese Households. *American Anthropologist* 66: 300–317.

Pogŏn Sahoe-bu. 1973. Kajŏng ŭirye haesŏl. Seoul: Pogŏn sahoe-bu.

Potter, Jack M. 1968. Capitalism and the Chinese Peasant: Social and Economic Change in a Hong Kong Village. Berkeley and Los Angeles: University of California Press.

———. 1970a. Wind, Water, Bones and Souls: The Religious World of the Cantonese Peasant. *Journal of Oriental Studies* 8: 139–53.

———. 1970b. Land and Lineage in Traditional China. In Maurice Freedman, ed., Family and Kinship in Chinese Society. Stanford: Stanford University Press.

———. 1974. Cantonese Shamanism. In Arthur P. Wolf, ed., Religion and Ritual in Chinese Society. Stanford: Stanford University Press.

Pyun, Young Tai. 1926. My Attitude Toward Ancestor Worship. Seoul: Christian Literature Society of Korea.

Quinones, C. Kenneth. 1980. Military Officials of Yi Korea: 1864–1910. In Papers of the First International Conference on Korean Studies, 1979. Sŏngnam: The Academy of Korean Studies.

Radcliffe-Brown, A. R. 1952. Structure and Function in Primitive Society. New York: Free Press.

Rhi, Bou-yong. 1970. Psychological Aspects of Korean Shamanism. *Korea Journal* 10 (9): 15–21.

Ross, Rev. John. 1879. History of Corea: Ancient and Modern. Paisley: J. and R. Parlane.

Rutt, Richard. 1960. The Chinese Learning and Pleasures of a Country Scholar: An Account of Traditional Chinese Studies in Rural Korea. *Transactions of the Korea Branch of the Royal Asiatic Society* 36: 1–100.

———. 1964. Korean Works and Days. Rutland, Vermont: Charles E. Tuttle.

Sangree, Walter H. 1974. Youth as Elders and Infants as Ancestors: The Complementarity of Alternate Generations, Both Living and Dead, in Tiriki, Kenya, and Irigwe, Nigeria. *Africa* 44: 65–70.

Sarye ŭijŏl. n.d. Kyŏngsŏng [Seoul]: Sech'angsŏgwan.

Scarborough, Rev. W. 1964. A Collection of Chinese Proverbs. Second Edition. New York: Paragon Book Reprint Corp.

Seki, Keigo (ed.). 1963. Folktales of Japan. Chicago: University of Chicago Press.

Shima, Mutsuhiko. 1976. An Analysis of *Tang-nae*, or *Chib-an*, in Korean Kinship. *Minzokugaku-kenkyu* 41: 75–90.

———. 1978. Descent Group and Locality in Korea: A Tentative Proposal. *Minzokugaku-kenkyu* 43: 1–17.

———. 1979. Kinship and Economic Organization in a Korean Village. Ph.D. dissertation, University of Toronto.

Shin, Susan S. 1974. The Social Structure of Kŭmhwa County in the Late Seventeenth Century. In James B. Palais, ed., Occasional Papers on Korea, No. 1. New York: Joint Committee on Korean Studies of the American Council of Learned Societies and the Social Science Research Council (revised ed.).

———. 1978. Economic Development and Social Mobility in Pre-Modern Korea: 1600–1860. *Peasant Studies* 7: 187–97.

Smith, Arthur H. 1914. Proverbs and Common Sayings from the Chinese. New and Revised Edition. Shanghai: American Presbyterian Mission Press.

Smith, Robert J. 1956. Kurusu: A Japanese Agricultural Community. In John B. Cornell and Robert J. Smith, eds., Two Japanese Villages. Ann Arbor: University of Michigan, Center for Japanese Studies, Occasional Papers No. 5.

———. 1974a. Afterword. In Arthur P. Wolf, ed., Religion and Ritual in Chinese Society. Stanford: Stanford University Press.

———. 1974b. Ancestor Worship in Contemporary Japan. Stanford: Stanford University Press.

Smith, Thomas C. 1959. The Agrarian Origins of Modern Japan. Stanford: Stanford University Press.

Sofue, Takao. 1971. Some Questions about Hsu's Hypothesis: Seen Through Japanese Data. In Francis L. K. Hsu, ed., Kinship and Culture. Chicago: Aldine.

Somerville, John N. 1976–77. Stability in Eighteenth Century Ulsan. *Korean Studies Forum*, No. 1: 1–18.

Song, Chan-shik. 1976. Genealogical Records. In Chun Shin-Yong, gen. ed., Korean Society. Korean Culture Series 6. Seoul: International Cultural Foundation.

Song, Yo-in. 1976. The Meaning of Hwan'gap. *Korea Journal* 16 (12): 37.

Spiro, Melford E. 1967. Burmese Supernaturalism. Englewood Cliffs, N.J.: Prentice-Hall.

———. 1970. Buddhism and Society: A Great Tradition and Its Burmese Vicissitudes. New York: Harper & Row.

Takeda, Choshu. 1976. Recent Trends in Studies of Ancestor Worship in Japan. In William H. Newell, ed., Ancestors. The Hague and Paris: Mouton.

Tambiah, S. J. 1970. Buddhism and the Spirit Cults in North-East Thailand. Cambridge: Cambridge University Press.

Ting, Nai-Tung. 1978. A Type Index of Chinese Folktales in the Oral Tradition and Major Works of Non-religious Classical Literature. FF Communications, No. 223. Helsinki: Suomalainen Tiedeakatemia Academia Scientiarum Fennica.

Twitchett, Denis. 1959. The Fan Clan's Charitable Estate, 1050–1760. In David S. Nivison and Arthur F. Wright, eds., Confucianism in Action. Stanford: Stanford University Press.

Uchendu, Victor C. 1976. Ancestorcide! Are African Ancestors Dead? In William H. Newell, ed., Ancestors. The Hague and Paris: Mouton.

Van der Sprenkel, Sybille. 1962. Legal Institutions in Manchu China: A Sociological Analysis. London: Athlone.

Wagner, Edward W. 1972. The Korean Chokpo as a Historical Source. In Spencer J. Palmer, ed., Studies in Asian Genealogy. Provo, Ut.: Brigham Young University Press.

———. 1974. The Ladder of Success in Yi Dynasty Korea. In James B. Palais, ed., Occasional Papers on Korea, No. 1. New York: Joint Committee on Korean Studies of the American Council of Learned Societies and the Social Science Research Council (revised ed.).

Wang, Hahn-Sok. 1979. Sociolinguistic Rules of Korean Honorifics. *Il-lyuhak nonjip* 5: 91–118.

Wang, Sung-hsing. 1976. Ancestors Proper and Peripheral. In William H. Newell, ed., Ancestors. The Hague and Paris: Mouton.

Watson, James L. 1975a. Agnates and Outsiders: Adoption in a Chinese Lineage. *Man* (n.s.) 10: 293–306.

———. 1975b. Emigration and the Chinese Lineage: The Mans in Hong Kong and London. Berkeley and Los Angeles: University of California Press.

Weems, Clarence Norwood (ed.). 1962. Hulbert's History of Korea. New York: Hillary House.

Whiting, John W. M., and Irwin L. Child. 1953. Child Training and Personality: A Cross-Cultural Study. New Haven: Yale University Press.

Wolf, Arthur P. 1970. Chinese Kinship and Mourning Dress. In Maurice Freedman, ed., Family and Kinship in Chinese Society. Stanford: Stanford University Press.

————. 1974a. Introduction. In Arthur P. Wolf, ed., Religion and Ritual in Chinese Society. Stanford: Stanford University Press.

————. 1974b. Gods, Ghosts, and Ancestors. In Arthur P. Wolf, ed., Religion and Ritual in Chinese Society. Stanford: Stanford University Press.

————. 1976. Aspects of Ancestor Worship in Northern Taiwan. In William H. Newell, ed., Ancestors. The Hague and Paris: Mouton.

Wolf, Arthur P., and Huang Chieh-shan. 1980. Marriage and Adoption in China, 1845–1945. Stanford: Stanford University Press.

Wolf, Margery. 1968. The House of Lim: A Study of a Chinese Farm Family. New York: Appleton-Century-Crofts.

————. 1972. Women and the Family in Rural Taiwan. Stanford: Stanford University Press.

Wright, Arthur F. 1959. Buddhism in Chinese History. Stanford: Stanford University Press.

Yanagita, Kunio. 1946. Senzo no hanashi. Tokyo: Chikuma shobo. (1970. About Our Ancestors: The Japanese Family System. Fanny Hagin Mayer and Ishiwara Yasuyo, trans. Tokyo: Japan Society for the Promotion of Science.)

Yang, C. K. 1959. The Chinese Family in the Communist Revolution. Cambridge, Mass.: M.I.T. Press.

————. 1961. Religion in Chinese Society: A Study of Contemporary Social Functions of Religion and Some of Their Historical Factors. Berkeley and Los Angeles: University of California Press.

Yang, Key P., and Gregory Henderson. 1959. An Outline History of Korean Confucianism. Part II: The Schools of Yi Confucianism. Journal of Asian Studies 18: 259–76.

Yang, Martin C. 1945. A Chinese Village: Taitou, Shantung Province. New York: Columbia University Press.

Yi, Chong-su (ed.). 1962. Sarye chŏnghae. Seoul: Sinhwa munhwasa.

Yi, Hae-yong, and Han Woo-keun. 1976. Discussion: Korean Society. In Chun Shin-Yong, gen. ed., Korean Society. Korean Culture Series 6. Seoul: International Cultural Foundation.

Yi, Hŭi-dŏk. 1973. Développement de la notion de piété filiale en Corée. Revue de Corée 5 (2): 5–23.

Yi, Hŭi-sŭng. 1961. Kugŏ taesajŏn. Seoul: Minjung sŏgwan.

Yi, Ki-mun. 1962. Soktam sajŏn. Seoul: Minjung sŏgwan.

214   Bibliography

Yoder, Don. 1974. Toward a Definition of Folk Religion. *Western Folklore* 33: 2–15.

Yonemura, Shoji. 1976. *Dōzoku* and Ancestor Worship in Japan. In William H. Newell, ed., Ancestors. The Hague and Paris: Mouton.

Yoon, Hong-key. 1975. An Analysis of Korean Geomancy Tales. *Asian Folklore Studies* 34 (1): 21–34.

————. 1976. Geomantic Relations Between Culture and Nature in Korea. Asian Folklore and Social Life Monographs. Vol. 88. Taipei: The Chinese Association for Folklore.

Yoshida, Teigo. 1967. Mystical Retribution, Spirit Possession, and Social Structure in a Japanese Village. *Ethnology* 6: 237–62.

Yu, Hong-nyŏl (ed. supervisor). 1974. Kuksa paekkwa sajŏn. Seoul: Tonga munhwasa.

Zŏng, In-sŏb. 1952. Folk Tales from Korea. London: Routledge and Kegan Paul.

Character List

Agok
아곡 （衙谷）

an-bang
안방 （―房）

Andong
안동 （安東）

Andong Kwŏn
안동 권 （安東 權）

Andong Kwŏn-ssi sebo
안동 권씨 세보 （安東 權氏 世譜）

arem-maŭl
아랫 마을

butsudan (J)
佛壇

ch'ambong
참봉 （參奉）

chari-gŏji
자리거지

ch'arye
차례 （茶禮）

chesa
제사 （祭祀）

chigwŏn
직원 （直員）

chilgyŏngi
질경이

chison
지손 （支孫）

cho yul si i
조율시이 （需栗 柿梨）

chŏlmŭn saram
젊은 사람

ch'on
촌 （寸）

Chŏng To-jŏn
정 도전 （鄭 道傳）

chongjung
종중 （宗中）

ch'ongmu
총무 （總務）

chongson
종손 （宗孫）

ch'ŏngsong-hoe
청송회 （青松會）

Chŏnju Yi
전주 이 （全卅 李）

chosang
조상 （祖上）

chosang kut
조상（祖上）굿

chosang soni kasi sonida
조상（祖上）손이
가시손이다

chosang sungbae
조상 숭배 （祖上 崇拜）

chŏsŭng
저승

chugŏ poaya chŏsŭng alji
죽어 보아야 저승
알지

chugŭn sarami mŏgŭlkka?
죽은 사람이 먹을까?

Chuja karye
주자 가례 （朱子 家禮）

ch'ulga oein
출가 외인 （出家 外人）

chunggan-maŭl
중간（中間） 마을

chungsang chungbok
중상 중복 （重喪 重服）

Ch'usŏk
추석 （秋夕）

Chu-tzu Chia-li (C)
朱子 家禮

dōzoku (J)
同族

Hahoe Iltong
하회 일동 （河回 一洞）

Hahoe Yu
하회 유 （河回 柳）

han-ch'oni ch'ŏl-li rago
한 촌(寸)이 천리
（千里）라고

Hansik
한식 （寒食）

hoju
호주 （戶主）

hong tong paek sŏ
홍동백서 （紅東,
白西）

hŏnnap
헌납 （獻納）

Hsiao Ching (C)
孝經

hyanggyo
향교 （鄉校）

Hyo kyŏng
효경 （孝經）

ijang
이장 （里長）

im o
입오 （壬午）

insa
인사 （人事）

kaekkwi
객귀 （客鬼）

Kaesil
개실

Kagong-ni Hubuk
가곡리 후북 （佳
合里 後北）

Kagong-ni 4-ri
가곡리 사리 （佳
合里 四里）

Kaltam
갈담 （葛潭）

kama
가마

kananhan chip chesannal
torao tŭt
가난（家難）한 집
제삿（祭祀）날
돌아오듯

kap in
갑인 （甲寅）

kije
기제 （忌祭）

kijesa
기제사 （忌祭祀）

kŏnnŏp-pang
건넛방 （――房）

Koryŏ
고려 （高麗）

Koryŏjang
고려장 （高麗葬）

k'ŭn chip, chagŭn chip
큰집, 작은집

kŭngnak
극락 （極樂）

kut
굿

kut hago sip'ŏdo
manmyŏnŭri ch'um
ch'unŭn kkol pogi
silt'a

굿하고 싶어도
맏며느리 춤추는
꼴 보기싫다

kwisin
커신 （ 鬼神 ）

Kwŏn Chu
권 주 （ 權 鑄 ）

Kwŏn Haeng
권 행 （ 權 幸 ）

Kwŏn Kŭn
권 근 （ 權 近 ）

Kwŏn Po
권 보 （ 權 堢 ）

kyŏng o
경오 （ 庚午 ）

mach'an'gajida
마 찬 가 지 다

Mansŏng taedongbo
만성대동보 （ 萬
性大同譜 ）

minju-juŭi
민주주의 （ 民主主義 ）

misin
미신 （ 迷信 ）

mŏn sach'on poda kakkaun
iusi natta

먼 사촌 （皿寸） 보다
가까운 이웃이 낫다

mudang
무당 （ 巫堂 ）

Munhwa Yu
문화 유 （ 文化 柳）

musok
무속 （ 巫俗 ）

myo chari chot'a
묘 （墓） 자리 좋다

myo chari nappŭda
묘 （墓） 자리 나쁘다

Myŏngsa Simni
명사십리 （ 明沙
十里 ）

myŏnjang
면 장 （ 面長 ）

nae pogienŭn
내 보기에 는

nappŭn saram
나쁜 사람

noin
노인 （ 老人 ）

ŏgurhada
억울 （扣抑鬱） 하다

Ŏmma, naega wassŏ
엄마, 내가 왔어

p'a
파 (派)

Pangch'ukkol
방축골

panjang
반장 (班長)

pon
본 (本)

pŏrŭl chunda
벌(罰)을 준다

pulch'ŏnjiwi
불천지위 (不遷
之位)

pulgyo
불교 (佛敎)

Pungmangsan
북망산 (北邙山)

p'ungsu
풍수 (風水)

punyŏ-hoe
부녀회 (婦女會)

p'yŏng
평 (坪)

ri
리 (里)

sadon chip kwa twikkanŭn
mŏlsurok chot'a
사돈(查頓) 집과
뒷간은 멀수록 좋다

saenggi
생기 (生氣)

saja-bap
사자 (使者) 밥

san chesa
산 제사 (祭祀)

san nal
산 날

sangch'ŏng
상청 (喪廳)

sangju
상주 (喪主)

sangmin
상민 (常民)

sarang-bang
사랑방 (舍廊房)

Sarye p'yŏllam
사례편람 (四禮
便覽)

Sarye ŭijŏl
사례의절 (四禮
儀節)

sebae
세배 (歲拜)

Seoul saram
서울 사람

sigol saram
시골 사람

sihyang
시향 (時享)

sije
시제 (時祭)

sijip sari sik'inŭn kŏt ch'ŏrŏm
시 (媤)집 살이 시키는 것 처럼

so chongjung
소 종중 (小 宗中)

sŏdang
서당 (書堂)

sosang
소상 (小祥)

Sumi
수미 (須彌)

tae tonghoe
대동회 (大同會)

taesang
대상 (大祥)

talgong
달공

tangnae
당내 (堂內)

Tano
단오 (端午)

Tanyang U
단양 우 (丹陽 禹)

tongbang yeŭi chi kuk
동방예의지국 (東方禮儀之國)

t'ongjŏng
통정 (通政)

ttal chasigŭn todungnyŏn ida
딸 자식 (子息)은 도둑년이다

ttari sesimyŏn munŭl yŏrŏ nok'o chanda
딸이 셋이면 문 (門)을 열어놓고 잔다

T'ungch'eng Chang (C)
桐城 張

Twisŏngdwi
뒤성뒤

ŭijangso
의장소 (義庄所)

watta katta hanŭn saram
왔다 갔다 하는 사람

wim-maǔl

윗 마을

wǒn

원

wu (C)

巫

yangban

양반 (兩班)

yangjaga ssǔlte ǒpsǒ

양자(養子)가 쓸데 없어

yat'ǔn chosang

얕은 조상 (祖上)

yǒ

여 (女)

yǒm

염 (殮)

Yǒmna taewang

염라대왕 (閻羅大王)

yǒnbang-gye

연방계 (- - 契)

yǒn-sije

연시제 (年時祭)

Yu Sǒng-nyong

유 성룡 (柳 成龍)

yugyo

유교 (儒敎)

yusa

유사 (有司)

Index